FRAGMENTS *of* A WORLD

FRAGMENTS OF A WORLD

WILLIAM *of* AUVERGNE *and* HIS MEDIEVAL LIFE

LESLEY SMITH

The University of Chicago Press
Chicago and London

The University of Chicago Press, Chicago 60637
The University of Chicago Press, Ltd., London

Published 2023
Printed in the United States of America

32 31 30 29 28 27 26 25 24 23   1 2 3 4 5

ISBN-13: 978-0-226-82618-9 (cloth)
ISBN-13: 978-0-226-82619-6 (e-book)
DOI: https://doi.org/10.7208/chicago/9780226826196.001.0001

Library of Congress Cataloging-in-Publication Data

Names: Smith, Lesley (Lesley Janette), author.
Title: Fragments of a world : William of Auvergne and his medieval life / Lesley Smith.
Other titles: William of Auvergne and his medieval life
Description: Chicago ; London : The University of Chicago Press, 2023. | Includes bibliographical references and index.
Identifiers: LCCN 2022044587 | ISBN 9780226826189 (cloth) | ISBN 9780226826196 (e-book)
Subjects: LCSH: William, of Auvergne, Bishop of Paris, 1180–1249. | Catholic Church—France—Clergy—Biography. | Bishops—France—Paris—Biography. | Philosophers—France—Paris—Biography. | Theologians—France—Paris—Biography. | LCGFT: Biographies.
Classification: LCC B765.G84 S65 2023 | DDC 230/.2092 [B]—dc23/eng/20221121
LC record available at https://lccn.loc.gov/2022044587

♾ This paper meets the requirements of ANSI/NISO Z39.48-1992 (Permanence of Paper).

To Henrietta Leyser from the anchor-hold
Andrew Makower E. T. A.
and Christopher Tanfield *e latrina stultitiae extrahit*
For reading and friendship

CONTENTS

PREFACE AND ACKNOWLEDGMENTS

Historians always want to know about sources. Until recently, the major source for William of Auvergne was the 1674 edition by Hotot and Le Feron of his Complete Works (*Opera omnia*) in two hefty volumes and a supplement, usefully reprinted in 1963 by Minerva in Frankfurt. Although it is not in fact William's complete works, and the Latin of the printed texts is often incorrect, and the sermons it credits to William are in fact by William Peraldus, nevertheless it's so much better than nothing. The Jesuit scholar Roland J. Teske took the edition as the basis for his series of English translations of William's theology, which I have used extensively here. Everyone interested in William and in thirteenth-century thought owes Teske an enormous debt of gratitude, both for his translations and for a series of articles on William as a philosopher-theologian. Readers should be aware that historical theology is not the focus of this book, although it is as this type of scholar that William has, until now, mostly been studied. Since 2013, however, we have been able to put alongside this aspect of William's writing a comprehensive edition of his Latin sermons by Franco Morenzoni, to whom we also owe heartfelt thanks. Ignoring the advice of that modern colossus of sermon studies, Louis Bataillon, that he edit only a selection of the material, Morenzoni decided it all needed to see the light of day.

How right he was. Nearly 600 of William's sermons survive, most of them in the form of draft notes to himself (though the surviving copy is not in his own hand), so that reading them takes us right into his study or his pulpit. Unless noted, translations from these are my own. Whereas Teske's translations of the theological treatises are formal, I have tried to translate the sermons rather more freely, in line with how I imagine they might have been preached. Many of the same images or arguments reappear in more than one sermon, but in general I have given only one reference in the footnotes, which are meant as a starting point for further reading rather than as a comprehensive index. A third kind of source was presented by Noël Valois, whose engaging and comprehensive 1880 monograph on William's Life and Works unearthed mentions of William in the historical record—his actions as bishop, correspondence with the pope, references in the life of Louis IX, and so on. All these works will be found in the list of abbreviations at the back of this book. Some of William's writing is still available only in manuscript, particularly his biblical exegesis (for which there is an excellent study by Gilbert Dahan, listed in the bibliography) and the treatise on preaching, *The Faces of the World—De Faciebus mundi*—that suggested the title of this book.

What makes William such a treasure trove for a historian, however, is not so much the amount of available material as the singular voice that emerges from it. William spoke of the world as a book—one in which everything created by God could be read as a means for knowing the Creator. His working method, in the theological treatises as well as in the sermons, is to use everything around him as a series of analogies for explaining the complexities of the Christian faith. With endless creativity, ingenuity, and humor, William presents the most difficult concepts in ways he thinks anyone could understand. This isn't a way of talking down to his audience; it's a genuine belief that the whole point and purpose of the created world is to illuminate the nature of God. And for William, knowing about the nature of God is the point and purpose of human beings, since anyone who knows God will worship him. The teeming life that appears in his pages, with their references to birds and bees, angels and devils, wine, women, and song, is what makes this book possible. We have very little in the way of hard fact about William's life—not even a birth date; instead, we have a description of the world in his own remarkable language. In saying that, I don't mean to imply that what an individual writes is necessarily who they are; the link between literature and life is much more complex than that suggests. But for the vast majority of medieval scholars, almost all we have is their own writing, which is often highly formulaic, according to the conventions of the time. William sat rather loosely to those conventions, and his aim was always to adapt his arguments to his audiences; effective engagement with the reader or listener was always at the forefront of his mind. This book's attempt to imagine a life from William's writing is only possible because that gift for communication is still vividly evident, even after almost eight hundred years.

In addition to Roland Teske, Franco Morenzoni, and Noël Valois, I am deeply grateful to friends who have shared William with me along the way, and in particular to Henrietta Leyser, Christopher Tanfield, Sue Killoran (queen of librarians), and Bill Mander. The response of audiences of colleagues and students to William convinced me that Harpo might speak: thanks to them all for listening. Martin Kauffmann, Head of Early and Rare Collections at the Bodleian Library, Oxford, remains the *fons fontium*.

I am very pleased to acknowledge the work of Michael Athanson in producing the maps. The base map for France is © ALPAGE: Anne-Laure Bethe, Caroline Bourlet, Yoann Brault, Nicolas Faucherre, Davide Gherdevich, Hélène Noizet, Paul Rouet, and is used under Creative Commons licence (CC BY-SA).

Finally, my gratitude goes to two anonymous colleagues who read the manuscript for the University of Chicago Press. They embraced this attempt at a life with remarkably wholehearted and scholarly attention. The care they took to understand it, together with their penetrating and sympathetic comments, helped make it so much better.

The expertise of Sarah Patey of Le Mot Juste has helped make the final stages of production a pleasure. Lys Ann Weiss of Posthoc was an exemplary and encouraging copyeditor. I am grateful that Randolph M. Petilos fell under William's spell. His team at the University of Chicago Press, particularly Caterina MacLean, have done William proud.

—

Books were expensive and often hard to come by in the Middle Ages. Scholars relied far more on memory than we do now, so that authoritative texts were often given more in paraphrase than verbatim quotation and precise referencing was unusual. Readers will be relieved to know this isn't true of this book's text, but in a nod to medieval practice, I have left the epigraphs that begin each chapter without a specific source citation. In the age of search engines, finding out is so much easier than it was in the thirteenth century, but there's still a thrill in the chase.

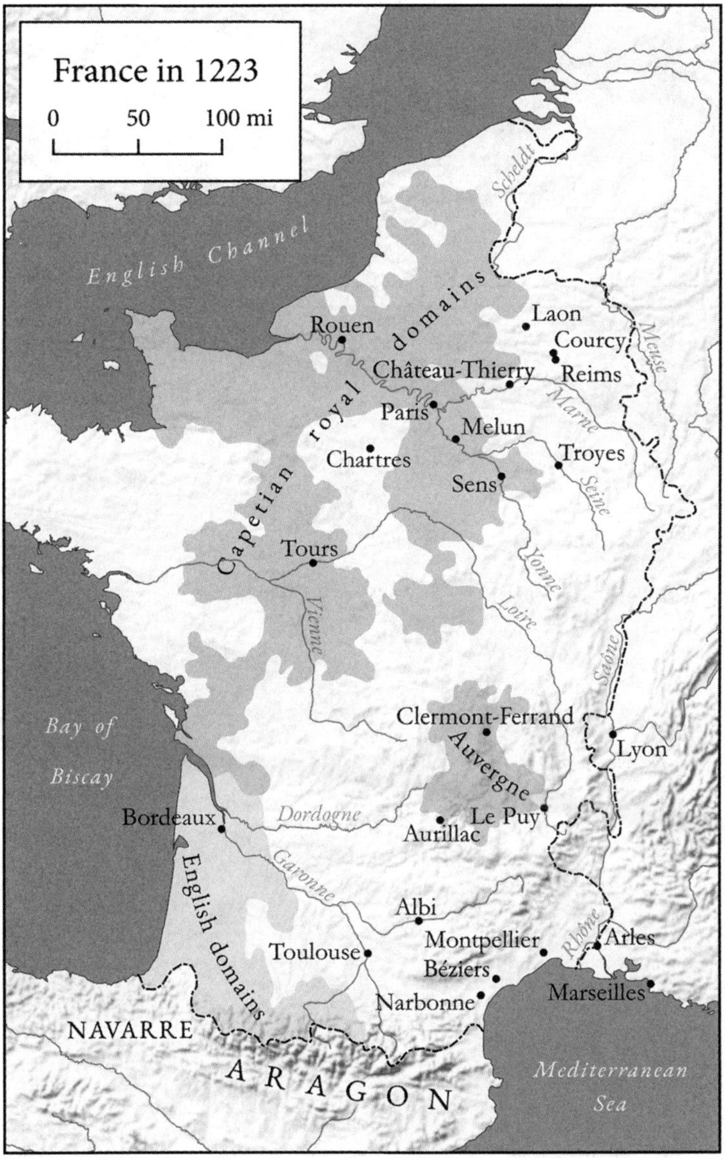

MAP 1 France (c. 1223)

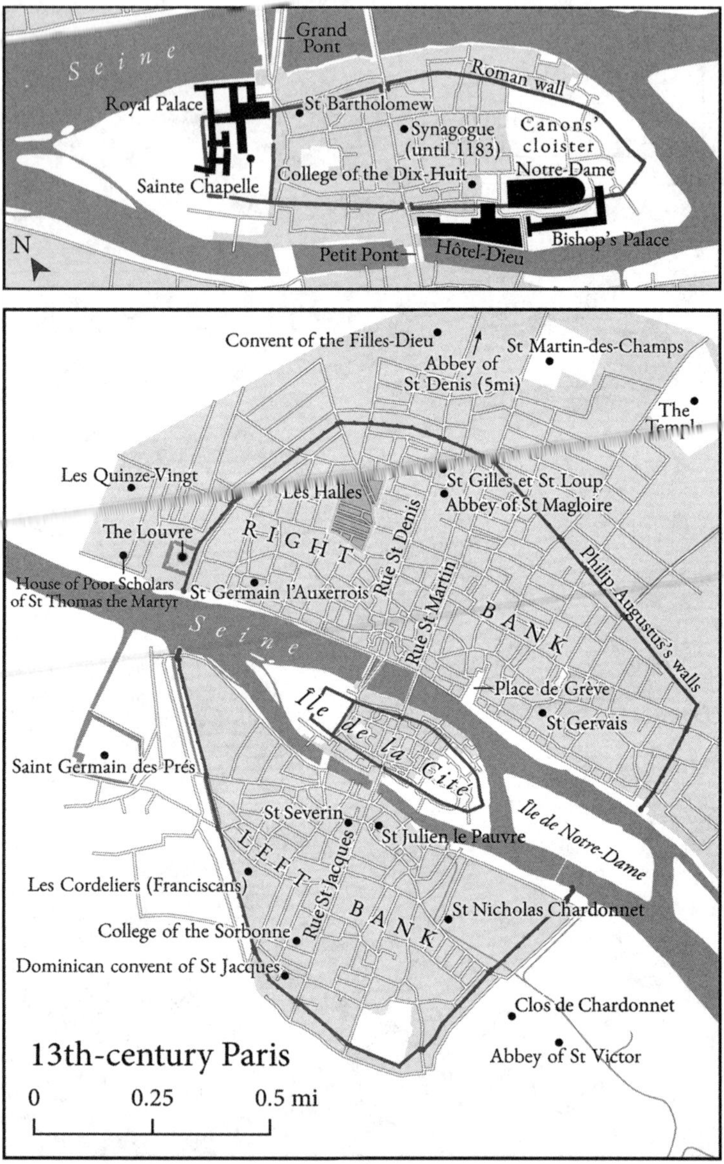

MAP 2 Paris (c. 1240)

FRAGMENTS *of* A WORLD

1

SEEING IN A SMOKY MIRROR

. . . a hill of beans

There is no more common form of ageism than thinking that the people of the past were somehow simpler and cheerier, less knotted and tangled, than we are ourselves. This book aims to persuade you otherwise. Its subject is a man called William who died in Paris in 1249. Born—when? we don't know—in the strange volcanic landscape of the distant Auvergne, he somehow made his way north to that bustling city, and forged a career as a professor in a university staking its claim to be the most important in Europe. Just when his scholarly life in Paris seemed settled, he found himself abruptly chosen to take the reins as its bishop: mixing with royalty, undertaking international diplomacy, becoming involved in interfaith disputes, all while doing the daily work of a pastoral leader. William's life coincided with a period of growth and expansion in Western Europe, and this was no less the case in his academic and ecclesiastical worlds than in Paris itself. Named as their capital city by the French Capetian monarchy, with policies and privileges designed to attract more people, more money, and more culture, Paris was to be a showcase for their own importance. The Capetians liked the idea of having learned men around, and with their encouragement the collection of small, often one-man schools dotted around town took on the institutional shape of a guild of teaching masters, nominally headquartered at the cathedral school at Notre-Dame and clustered in a hodgepodge of rooms on the left bank of the River Seine—the so-called Latin Quarter, named from the language of teaching. The cathedral itself was in the process of swapping its late Roman building for spanking new stone (for the most part, the same cathedral so recently saved from the flames), reflecting the renewal that the Church and the Christian religion itself was either joyfully undertaking or being dragged toward, depending on your point of view.

Against this background, the skeleton of William's life is quickly told.[1] He is said by his only previous biographer to have been born some time before 1180, in Aurillac in the Auvergne; but we have no firm dates, or even any evidence for his life until 1223, when he appears as a canon of Notre-Dame Cathedral in Paris, a position associated with his life as a theologian rather than an ecclesiastic, since he was not a priest. In 1223, he had just become a teaching master at the cathedral school, the proto-university of Paris, making him the equivalent of a professor, tenured for life. Yet in 1228, having traveled to Rome to speak to the pope, Gregory IX, about irregularities in the election of the new bishop of Paris, William was himself appointed to the role, and he spent the next twenty-one years at the center of a network of powerful and creative people. He died, still in harness, probably on Palm Sunday, 1249, and was buried in the scholarly Augustinian abbey of St. Victor, where his grave and memorial remained until their destruction in the French Revolution.

This book is an attempt to depict an individual who lived in an age when individuals are hard to find. I want to try to present a rounded person in an age when it's not at all clear that the very idea of individuality was much valued. The twelfth century has been touted as the age of the "discovery of the individual," a period of new self-consciousness and of individual self-definition, as opposed to corporate identity.[2] In our own era, when the focus on the individual can often appear all-consuming, this may be a difficult concept to grasp. The notion of the atomistic individual has taken center stage in liberal political and social thinking since the eighteenth century. Alternative conceptions that put the community before its members have often seemed troublesome, since the various large-scale experiments with communism in the twentieth century. But the importance of individuals and their place within the wider scheme of things is a concept with a dynamic history: the balance of importance between the one and the group has shifted back and forth over time. In the Christian Middle Ages this relationship was always seen as part of a wider picture—a whole universe created by a single sovereign God. Individuals had a place, but only within this greater scheme. So it isn't at all clear to me that William of Auvergne, unlike David Copperfield, would be entirely happy to find himself the hero of his own life.

William was born in the latter part of the twelfth century, at a time when anonymity was valued as a kind of modesty—a proper assessment of one's place in the world. I don't mean to assert that every medieval person was a shrinking violet who held open doors for others to pass through: certainly there was as much political and social self-aggrandizement in the Middle Ages as there is today. Nevertheless, it was much more usual for people to view themselves first and foremost as part of a group, as part of a common pursuit, rather than seeing themselves always as individuals. Even rulers were part of a dynastic cascade, with a limited supply of familial names that recurred in each generation. For an explanation of this perspective we can start—as we almost always can in medieval Europe—with religion. The Scriptures common to the Jewish and Christian faiths (the Hebrew Bible or Old Testament) begin with the book of Genesis, which tells of the creation of the world and everything in it, including time, the engine of history. Humans are part of this creation, albeit at the apex, and, in the more commonly told of the two creation stories, are all descended from a single ancestor, Adam, from whose side God draws a helpmate, Eve—who is to be mother to the human race. God places Adam and Eve in a paradise garden, Eden, where there is only one rule—not to eat the fruit of a certain tree. At the urging of Eve, who has been beguiled by the devil in the shape of a wily serpent, Adam eats the forbidden fruit, and the two are cast out by God, to make their own way in a hostile world, where the harmony of creation has become a babel of suspicion and suffering. The fault—which Christians call sin—of Adam and Eve's disobedience to God's rule is passed down through all generations of their offspring, no matter how their own lives are lived. Humans are united in a common heritage of "original sin" that marks out everyone equally.

But humans are also united in a common heritage that saves them from the consequences of this fate—a Messiah, who brings mercy to God's final judgment. Nobility, riches, intelligence—no human measure of status has valence in the scales in which the recording angel weighs the goodness of each soul and their devotion to God. Since no one deserves to get there, no one can work their own way into heaven; instead, everyone has to rely on the freely given help—the technical term is grace—of a loving God.

The Christian New Testament seemed to say that Judgment would come soon; certainly, Jesus's first followers believed they should live as though it were daily imminent. As time went on, this expectation was harder to sustain, though it remained an undercurrent in medieval thought, bubbling to the surface at certain times, such as the year 1000—the Millennium.[3] In William of Auvergne's lifetime, mystical millenarian thinkers such as Joachim of Fiore (d. 1202) argued that the world was entering its final age, and that the lives of holy men such as Francis of Assisi (d. 1226) were signs of the End Times.[4] In this reading, history and current affairs could—and should—be interpreted in the much wider context of the eternal divine plan. Seen in the light of eternity, the lives of individuals couldn't amount to a hill of beans.

And yet . . . the world had not come to an end, and life went on. Indeed, as the twelfth century progressed, it even seemed to get better. An accumulation of circumstances—a slight change in climate, which with technological developments in agriculture led to better harvests and provision of food; a period of relative political peace—offered more people the chance of life beyond mere existence, for the first time since the classical era. The extra time this provided for the pursuit of education, science, literature, music, art, and religion, among other things, was the foundation of the so-called "twelfth-century renaissance" in Western Europe, a flowering of human endeavor in all areas of life.[5] The theology that had seen humanity as an insignificant and unworthy element in the pattern of creation began to reimagine a narrative in which men (and, at least theoretically, women) had value as the image and likeness of God. We might all be in the gutter, but we could still look up at the stars.

God had not, after all, utterly condemned creation, nor—as the story of Noah and the Flood made clear—destroyed it out of hand.

And because they had been allowed to survive, humans had a duty to study the works of God and their place within them, in order to understand their Creator better. What was at one time derided as idle curiosity could in the twelfth century be justified as making the most of innate, God-given gifts for observation, experimentation, and reasoning. Even so, it was important for humankind not to get above itself. The well-known dictum that we are dwarves standing on giants' shoulders is a twelfth-century reminder that we need to know our place.[6] The giants are the wise men of the past, those closer to the beginning of the world. Like the modern theory of entropy, this view of history painted the expulsion from paradise as a kind of Big Bang, following from which things were getting progressively worse. Distanced from the point of creation, the present was not to be relied on; but the ideas and writings of our predecessors that had stood the test of time could bring us nearer to original wisdom than the questionable novelties of today. If we heed them, as the second part of the aphorism reminds us, although we remain dwarves in comparison to the greats of the past, we can, nevertheless, see farther than they did.

This meeting of dwarves and giants is an illustration of the paradoxical difficulty we have in reading the meaning of writers from the twelfth and thirteenth centuries. They work always with a canon of authoritative texts and authoritative writers, moving from the Bible downward. Their theory of learning was based on the study of and commentary on these fundamental materials. Learning was additive: to the recognized authorities one might add one's own dwarfish contribution, one more bean on top of a very old hill. Only these authorities were known and referred to by name; the "modern" (in Latin, *moderni*) writers of current and recent memory were simply anonymous—noted, if at all, merely as "others" (*alii*). Contemporary texts were unnamed, referred to only by their first few words; in the same way, medieval artists and craftsmen produced unsigned masterpieces of creative skill, which today are often known only by a sobriquet—the Master of the Leaping Figures, or the Master of the Apocrypha Drawings. Nevertheless, although they saw themselves as working in a long tradition of knowledge, medieval scholars did more than simply repeat what the past had provided. "Tradition" comes from a Latin word meaning "handing on," but the choice of what to accept and what to leave behind was far more carefully made, and often more individual, than medieval writers might have their readers believe. There could indeed be innovation and novelty in arguments made by reference to ancient authority; the skill of the reader lay in knowing how to spot it.

This reference to themselves as dwarves comes simultaneously with a twelfth-century explosion of new forms of knowledge and expressions of creativity in many walks of life. Like the Victorian age, this was an era of confidence and ambition. Reverence for the past sat alongside a belief in the present and the future, and in the potential for human beings to understand the world. This assurance, however, was not primarily the self-assurance of the individual but the collective assurance of the group: yes, *we* can. The lateral connections that made individuals part of families, towns, religious orders, craft guilds, or professions, and—it goes without saying—the Church, were a fundamental and essential part of every person's identity. To be yourself, you had also to be part of a greater whole.

This might then seem like an unpromising landscape in which to attempt to write about a single person. Hard to credit today, when everyone's fifteen minutes of fame becomes at least one volume of autobiography or a social media sensation, there are few medieval texts about individuals that are not just template hagiography—that's to say, standardized lives of saints, written to inspire the faithful to walk in the footsteps of Christ. Yet the extraordinary innovation of the twelfth and early thirteenth centuries does provide us with a small number of possible models, writings by and about particular people who stood out from the crowd. In William's world, the most famous, or notorious, of these is Peter Abelard (d. c. 1142), philosopher, theologian, and teacher, husband to Heloise and writer of the extraordinary "Story of My Adversities" (*Historia calamitatum*), extant in the form of a letter sent to Heloise, recounting his life and complaining about how he had been treated.[7] Abelard was intellectually brilliant—and knew it. His philosophical acumen was not matched by a deep self-knowledge; but his self-regard is what fuels his discussion of his own life, which is told with a remarkable lack of guile or self-awareness, giving us an almost unique insight into a medieval individual's view of himself. The only other place we come close to such a perspective is in the autobiography of a northern

French abbot, Guibert of Nogent (d. c. 1125), whose account of his life, and especially perhaps of the role of his mother in it, is as striking in its self-questioning as Abelard is in his self-confidence.[8] Bernard of Clairvaux (d. 1153), Guibert's fellow abbot and Abelard's intellectual *bête noire*, was one of the great personalities of the twelfth century. He would never have written specifically about himself, but in his many dozens of letters sent to correspondents across Europe he does reveal something of the state of his mind and, particularly, his health—his digestive system was a constant source of anxiety.[9] His remarkable life was eulogized by admirers after his death. This tiny flurry of materials, tempting though it has been to medieval historians, really serves to illustrate its own peculiarity. We just don't have writing by medieval people about themselves.

Slightly earlier than this trio, however, is a contemporary biography of a medieval superstar, the theologian, teacher, and archbishop, Anselm (d. 1109), written by his fellow monk Eadmer. Anselm's was an international career—not as unusual in the Middle Ages as we might imagine—being born at Aosta in northern Italy, living as a monk and scholar in Bec in Normandy, and finally, installed as archbishop of Canterbury in England. Anselm was an influential writer, the author of theological treatises, prayers, and letters, as well as his formal acts as archbishop; but what we gain from Eadmer's text is that rare prize for medievalists, a sense of Anselm's speech and conversation. Eadmer makes it clear that Anselm was valued as much for his talk and his personal presence as for his writing. His account of his illustrious brother monk has been mined by R. W. Southern in two separate attempts to write Anselm's life. But even as it reconstructs Anselm's personality and gifts, Southern's work makes it clear just how much we miss about most medieval people.[10] Anselm left a considerable body of writing, but in the twelfth century teaching was still thought of largely as an oral pursuit. Classrooms (not to mention pulpits, monastic meeting rooms, and the wide variety of other communal spaces) were places for talk, not for writing, and students came to hear and to learn how to speak.[11] This was still a culture in which the Roman virtue of oral argument was respected and taught from a young age; a man's way with words told you much about him. The habitual production of written documents was still in its infancy, often mistrusted, or seen only as part of the whole story, which could only be really told face to face.[12] In oral discussion, things could be said, arguments could be run, ideas could be stretched that could not or should not be written down.[13] Eadmer's Life of Anselm, in giving us a picture of the conversation of a man we would otherwise know only from his written words, serves to heighten our regret at the lack of similar evidence for most other medieval lives.

It's at this point, in fact, that the medievalist has to admit to occasional "early-modern envy": it's not that I'd *really* like to work on the Tudors, but it must be wonderful to have verifiable dating, caches of letters to and from correspondents, some even in identifiable autographs, a range of external cross-references, and even—holy of holies—a lifelike portrait. The human desire to make contact means we snatch at crumbs: the occasional note about a tone of voice or a capacity for friendship will make a medievalist's day. Sometimes I can't help but wish that William of Auvergne were Thomas Cranmer or Thomas Cromwell or Thomas More, sketched with his whole family by famous artists, or in portraits to be sent as keepsakes to friends. It's the people of the past, the individuals who made up the clouds of witness, who seize our imagination and make history so absorbing.

Earlier, I began to list the reasons why we might find William interesting. But where do I think we might begin to look for him, across the gap of more than eight hundred years? First of all, of course, there are his own writings. William wrote steadily across a career spanning almost three decades. Starting from his appointment as a teaching master at the university of Paris, in 1223, he continued to produce philosophical, theological, and pastoral works until his death in 1249. Even his installation as bishop of Paris didn't stem the tide; although he laments the demands on his time, somehow he found opportunities to write, and he wrote on an impressively broad canvas.[14] In an age that saw the development of the all-inclusive theological *summa*, William created his own, unique version in the form of a massive seven-part "Teaching on God in the Mode of Wisdom" (*Magisterium divinale et sapientiale*), which ranges from the nature of God to the particulars of how to live a virtuous life. He is interested in almost everything he can see or imagine, from the high concepts of Christian theology—such as the persons of the Trinity and the theory of forgiveness—to the details of everyday life, such as the behavior of dogs and spiders, or observations of small boys playing with bows and arrows.

Voluminous writings in themselves, however, aren't any guarantee that the underlying person will be revealed. Nancy Partner has rightly said that most studies of Thomas Aquinas are "an abstract theology with a man's name attached"; the problem is the lack of the *personal* writing that we can find in later periods, but which is almost entirely missing for ours.[15] So we are lucky that, to read alongside William's academic writings, we have the immense treasure trove of his almost six hundred surviving sermons. William took his appointment as bishop of Paris seriously, and in the twenty-one years he held the post, he was a regular preacher to all sorts and conditions of people who made up his flock. And, with astonishing luck, the form in which his sermons have come down to us is not as the common sort of edited "model" sermon, put together as a kind of template for other preachers to use, but in the shape of his own notes for himself (although surviving for us in a copy, not in his own hand) on what he wanted to say. This gives us a thrilling insight into his working methods, and the immediacy of the content of the sermons allows us to feel close to the working preacher and human being. His use of language is emblematic, and very much his own. In the sermons (written down in Latin, but sprinkled with words in the French vernacular, as reminders for what he would say when he spoke), "I" speaks to "you," in the singular form of verbs, signaling the directness with which William wanted to talk to his various congregations. Nothing is off limits in the sermons—the world is his oyster; or rather, as he says on many occasions, the world is a book, where on every page you can read something to teach you about the love of God.

An even bigger stroke of luck is the presence of humor. One of the hardest things to read across centuries is tone of voice, and in particular whether or not the writer means to be taken seriously—and that's before we consider the differences in humor across time and culture; just look at a book of nineteenth-century cartoons, if you don't know what I mean. But in William we have someone who was temperamentally playful, always looking for the funny side, and who sprinkles his writings with what are clearly jokes, some for an in-crowd—asides about clerics to other clerics—others at the level of slapstick ("latrines" are a favorite topic). What we don't know of course is: did his audience laugh?

Most academics are remembered only by their writings; but his unexpected commission as bishop of Paris gave William the chance to put his ideas about the Church and the world into action. He lived in an age of Church reform, when the popes of the twelfth and early thirteenth centuries were responding to the changing spiritual and religious circumstances that the "renaissance" had stirred up. We can see him working out the issues this provoked both in his episcopal legislation and activities, and in the material he produced for his diocesan clergy, such as the position he took on whether or not clerics could hold more than one paid position ("benefice") at once. We can also see his reaction to the unexpected events that living in the center of a thriving capital city regularly threw in his way. And because of his own central place in secular and ecclesiastical politics, we can even, on a few occasions, see William as others saw him, when he is spoken of directly by other actors at the time.

So we start out on this journey with a little more hope than we might have for many of the shadowy figures who inhabited the relatively less researched period that straddles the twelfth and thirteenth centuries. Nevertheless, for an individual about whom nothing—and I do mean nothing—is known until he was at least halfway through his life, it's clear that we won't be dealing with many of the certainties we generally think a biography should provide.[16] When I began working on William, too long ago now to think about, I imagined that something of that sort would be possible. I know better now. Instead, I've come to follow the example of the medievalist Beryl Smalley, who speaks of the protagonists of her *English Friars and Antiquity* as "ambushing" her, and making her write a different book from the one she'd planned.[17] I, too, have been ambushed by William, and have decided to take my cue from my subject. William wrote a treatise on preaching called *Faces of the World* (*De Faciebus mundi*) in which he explains his theory and practice of analogies (*similitudines*), images or impressions drawn from this world that function as a likeness or "similitude," a reflection of a deeper theological or spiritual reality; a worldly counterpart to a divine or eternal truth. The use of analogies is one of William's most characteristic and endearing features. It allows him to take his broad and careful observation of the world and exercise it in the service of his religion. Each of the myriad faces of the world can teach us, he says, something about the love of God.

This fragmentary method, collecting different facets of a life, is how I've chosen to approach William here. Rather than attempt to follow his story in a simply linear fashion, I've attempted to walk round him, looking at the variety of aspects that made up his life and personality, and considering them in a series of chapters rather shorter than is conventional in most academic history. Approaching our subject as a series of bits and pieces is reminiscent of Caroline Bynum's appreciation of "history in the comic mode"; and "biography in the comic mode" seems appropriate, given William's often playful character, and in the older meaning of comedy, given the success that the man from an unknown family in an out-of-the-way part of France made of his life.[10] Sometimes the material of the various chapters or fragments will link together, but sometimes the different facets are simply what they are—each one added to the hill of beans. The advantage of this fragmentary method, I want to argue, is an admission that a conventional account would neither properly represent the breadth of the available material, nor reflect its sketchy nature. Neither am I suggesting that the facets I'll present are the only ones I could have chosen or an exhaustive investigation—in fact, each short section could easily form the basis of a research article, or occasionally even a book, of its own. I've tried to choose the fragments that I think do justice to the material that William himself provides for us, and to build on that, but I'm aware that another historian could probably find an equal and opposite set of subjects and, perhaps, offer a different William. There's no single narrative here, but instead a hope of illuminating the reality of an individual medieval person in his variety, consistency, and contradictions. As someone once said about life and steak tartare, it's messy—but that's the point of the whole thing.

My intention, then, is to start by looking at William on his own terms and in his own time. That means I start with certain assumptions: that he had a sincere belief in the Christian God, and thought that this faith should percolate into all aspects of life. The Christian religion in the Middle Ages was exclusionist (only Christians could be eventually "saved" to live eternally in the presence of God) and missionizing (everyone should be given the chance to know this fact and to know Christ). This also means that he takes the existence of an invisible spiritual world for granted, and believes that it is more important, more real, even, than the earthly world in which he is living. I also assume that he was intelligent and educated, complex, and with his own rationality. Some of the things he says might strike a reader not used to the Middle Ages as credulous and gullible, but my experience is that medieval beliefs are often no more surprising than the background credulity of our own age—just different. Given the knowledge of the time, William is trying to approach the world scientifically and logically, and to live according to what he believes are its underlying rules. Because of his education and position, he was relatively powerful and well connected. He's also very interested in his various audiences and the question of how to communicate with them effectively and memorably; he's concerned to work out the psychology of the people he's speaking to, in order to make his presentation of the Christian faith more powerful and persuasive.

Some readers will see the gullibility in the biographer and not the subject. I admit to wanting to like William, but I have also worked long enough with medieval theologians to know that, for all the apparent similarities between their worldview and mine, there is always a gulf of startling difference. There may be occasions in the text when William's voice appears also to be my own: in attempting to convey the immediacy and presence of his thought, it may seem as if I share his convictions. This is not my intention. But reading William's words, I have found myself regularly drawn into conversation with him—sometimes agreeing, sometimes not; and if I have done my job well, I hope that every reader of this book might have the same experience of being enticed into an irresistible dialogue with the distant past. These men (and they were all men; women were not allowed in higher education) are, in our terms, religious zealots, and I'm sure they don't represent the majority opinion in the Middle Ages, those people for whom the importance of faith and organized religion would certainly have covered much more of a spectrum from sincerity to outright disbelief. Professional Christian theologians had more in common with their Jewish or Muslim counterparts than with most of the ordinary people around them, as William himself tacitly admits. Nonetheless, he had a deep and genuine sense of responsibility for the immortal souls of those in his care. What we shouldn't assume, just because of when he lived, is that he was unwashed, unkempt, unsophisticated in his tastes and appreciation of life, childish, or inherently less clever than we are. His life was as interesting and as real to him as ours is to us. We set off, then, to find more than a theology with a name attached; we set off to find a fellow human being.

2

HOME AND FAMILY

All that David Copperfield kind of crap . . .

Few children have no relations. This was probably even more the case in the Middle Ages than it might be today, since the notion of the nuclear family would not really have been understood. Even if your father and mother were absent, families were often large, so you would be likely to have other surviving blood relatives. If by mischance they were also missing, you could be part of a household, or a village, or an ecclesiastical community. Medieval commentaries on the Ten Commandments, considering what was meant by honoring your father and your mother, cast the net wide.[1]

William had parents; but we have no idea who they were. As far as I can see, he does not speak of his own family directly at all. This is frustrating, given how many other things he does talk about; and perhaps it is odd, given the personal tone of much of his writing. The "I" that speaks so often in William's work never says "my mother." Love, however, is a repeated topic, and love requires more than oneself. "All love is a relation," he says (following the lead of St. Augustine), "and looks to another," so really it makes no sense to say that you can love yourself.[2] And he knows how love feels: "love is like a hollow in the heart and a kind of hunger."[3] The metaphor of hunger—human love as a fore*taste* from the "mouth of the intellect . . . to the belly of love"—is a typically William-like use of the senses, and particularly those of smell and taste, to explain a deeper knowledge. This love is sensed as loss because humans at some level know that their love is merely a shadow of the true love of God, which is not a losing but a springing up: love, in God, is "like a fountain."[4] Love, too, is a like a weight, drawing lover to beloved, and when they rest in love together, the outcome is joy and delight.[5]

The vivid nature of these descriptions suggests that William grew up in a loving home, but exactly when and where that might have been seems to be beyond retrieval, given the surviving evidence. Current scholarly consensus puts the date of his birth somewhere between 1180 and 1190, but those numbers have only been reached by counting backward from the age of thirty-five, which was the generally accepted minimum age for becoming a professor at Paris. The more I've studied William and come to understand something of the scope of his knowledge and interests, the more I've thought those dates are too late; I agree with his nineteenth-century biographer Noël Valois that we are better thinking of William as having been born in the 1170s rather than the 1180s. Whichever decade is correct, it remains the case that our first attested date in William's life, 1223, when we know he was a master of theology and a canon of Notre-Dame, finds him at least halfway through his life.

Perhaps a more important question than when he was born is how wealthy his family were. Just as today, money was a key determinant of medieval life chances and options. Once again, we have no firm evidence, but there are at least one or two hints to piece together; unfortunately, they are contradictory. A 1635 text by a Carmelite friar from Aurillac, Fr. Dominique de Jésus, asserts that William had stated in a charter that he came from the family of the counts of Aurillac; to which a nineteenth-century compendium of local genealogy adds that he was a son of Durand of Montal and Dia de Corbonnières, and that he had at least three brothers, including one Géraud, archdeacon of La Marche. Unfortunately, the charter neither exists today nor is recorded in any other document, and the claim of nobility is made with no supporting evidence. The indefatigable Valois is skeptical; both perhaps were phantoms—useful for providing background color, but not real.[6] In comparison to these claims to status, Valois points to the fact that as bishop of Paris, William was known only as William "of Auvergne," rather than by a noble patronymic, as we see in some of his contemporaries; this, in his view, indicates much humbler origins.[7] Valois's case stands alongside an anecdote told by the thirteenth-century Dominican friar and collector of colorful tales, Stephen of Bourbon (d. 1261). Stephen (who may have known William in Paris) claims that, as a poor child begging for bread, William met a "woman of the people," who offered him alms on condition that he never became a bishop. Thus far the story is just about plausible, but the punchline—"A kind of presentiment made him refuse"—rather strains its credibility, as does the knowledge that the same scenario is attributed by others to Maurice of Sully, one of William's recent predecessors as bishop.[8] The only other material to bring to the question might be William's striking attitude to poverty, as evidenced particularly in his sermons. As we shall discover in a later chapter, poverty is one of the most regularly recurring themes in his writing, and is seen almost as a prerequisite or sign of God's favor. Nevertheless, William is never misty-eyed or unrealistic about what poverty actually feels like, or how difficult it is to experience. If he hadn't been poor himself, he certainly had known enough people who were.

A third possibility is that his family were neither particularly rich nor particularly poor, but came from what historians often call "the middling sort." This might point to an early education in a house of canons: clergy who lived together in a small community ministering to, and engaged with, the working people around them. Such a household would have given William a broad experience of the world and a greater sense of ease within it—just as we see in his writings.[9]

William's theology of children and families is very firmly grounded on the centrality of marriage, as we would expect. Marriage was a Christian sacrament—a place where God had promised to be present—and the influential writings of St. Augustine emphasized its importance both for the solidity of families and the mutual support of husband and wife. The basic medieval textbooks of theology and canon law, Peter Lombard's *Sentences*, and Gratian's *Decretum* (and its successors) laid out a structure of matrimony founded on the consent of the parties and the physical consummation of the promises they made to one another.[10] A crucial issue was the status of children. In his treatise on the sacrament of marriage, William sweepingly declares that children born out of wedlock cannot thrive; indeed, the offspring of sex outside marriage, or sex with prostitutes, or other forms of "nonstandard" sex, will perish, either completely or partially.[11] His meaning here is not naïvely literal—although he might argue that there is a literal aspect to his argument—but rather that only within a family can a child be "protected, nourished, properly brought up, educated and other necessary things": in other words, "it takes a village."

Children certainly need their families because they are born so helpless, especially in comparison to the young of some animals, who can walk, swim, or even fly to safety a very short time after birth; baby spiders (which, as we shall see in a later chapter, provide some of his favorite examples) can even spin a web and catch their own supper, but human babies need to be bathed as soon as they are born.[12] It's not that human babies don't have innate knowledge of how to survive, but that their fallen human bodies prevent their souls from using it.[13] "But who does not know the foolishness, in fact the darkness beyond every ignorance of a brute [animal], in which human beings are born and in which their souls exist until gradually through nurses or guardians or through the living of one's whole life, one makes progress somewhat towards learning?"[14] Often, babies don't even know their own mother's breasts, "not even after a while, until by frequently missing them . . . they learn."[15] In contrast, animals will suckle on any mother or eat any food they can find; whereas even when food is put into children's mouths, they cry and spit it out. As we'll see often in this book, William produces an image or an observation that brings us up short: human babies, he says, have lost the essential animal instinct to find the breast and suckle. This is one of many instances where his modern readers might wonder how William knew. How could this middle-aged, celibate, scholarly man describe the trials of breastfeeding or the behavior of toddlers? Was this book-knowledge, or did he have sisters, or did he talk to and observe women around him? However he knows, he uses his knowledge to make a theological point: that human children are all too liable to do themselves harm, in a way that a young animal never would, whether by refusing food or running toward fire, is proof of original sin; that's the only explanation for why human beings could be so far away from what is naturally good for them.

What do parents contribute to the child? Each has a part to play, but what they give to the child is only its body; the soul is infused by God.[16] This means that every child is its own person from the beginning, with a soul that endows it with individuality. Morally, this affirms that children can turn out very different from their parents, since the soul is the guiding force of every person, and not just a separate part of them.[17] This doesn't imply that parents have no role in setting a good example, "since children especially observe the conduct of their parents and imitate them most of all," but it does reflect what everyone knows: sometimes children follow their parents, and sometimes they do the very opposite.[18] What William terms an individual soul we would think of as innate personality—the nature that vies with parental nurture to make the finished human being.

Although husband and wife contribute equally to the production of the fetus, "children are said to be and are regarded more as children of their mothers than of their fathers": love comes from parenting, and there's no less parenting from mothers than from fathers.[19] But it's in the nature of fathers to want to give everything good they have to their children.[20] Still, in a well-ordered family, parents must be in control and show their children where the limits lie: "spare the rod and spoil the child" is a biblical proverb that had universal Christian approval. Woe to the children whose parents—whether mother or father—can't stand to see them spanked; it's the only way to teach them where danger lies, and make sure they avoid it.[21] It's hard work, William says in two sermons on the story of the Wedding at Cana, being married and bringing up kids.[22] His treatise on marriage doesn't sidestep the difficulties of supporting a pregnant wife and educating the children.[23] It's important, therefore, not to have more than you can support, even if you're the king:

> Even a powerful and wealthy prince could hardly provide for twelve children decently and competently in a way that was appropriate to his glory and magnificence. Undoubtedly he could provide clothing and food for them as though they were servants, and [do] this without burden or difficulty—but not for them as the king's children, as befits royal highness.[24]

William may have chosen the number twelve from biblical precedent (the patriarch Jacob had twelve children), but it was also diplomatically lucky, when the king he knew best, Louis IX, had a family of eleven.

And kids will be kids. They have nits but fight back against washing; they build snowmen; they're frightened by tales of bogeymen.[25] Boys play with bows and arrows; they think they can't be seen if they close their eyes; some throw stones at hanged men.[26] Generally, though, children are good children, and they tell the truth.[27] William's Bible told him that Jesus was born as a child to an ordinary family, an event that invested the relationship with a particular importance and power, and provided a new start after the disastrous example set by Adam and Eve, not to mention their fratricidal son Cain. On its own, this theological imperative would provide reason enough for him to use analogies taken from family life throughout his treatises and sermons, so we have no need to think these have anything to do with his own experience. But we can note his apparent flair for careful observation, and his sympathy for familial situations that, as a celibate scholar and cleric, were no longer his daily experience, or those of the similar men around him. It wouldn't be surprising, then, if he is drawing on his memories of his own home and childhood.

One thing we can be sure of is that William came from the South—the Midi. A thirteenth-century note in a manuscript of his *The Universe of Creatures* reads: "Master William of Auvergne, born in Aurillac," but whether this was accurate, we cannot tell.[28] Writing in Paris, he speaks of "the land of my birth," a recognition that he was not a local, but there is nothing more precise.[29] Even today, the Auvergne landscape of extinct volcanoes, mineral springs, and rich, rolling pasture is unique within France. In the twelfth century it was even more of a world apart, and a long way from the royal domain in the North: "no one thought that 'France' . . . included the lands lying south of the Loire, and especially not the lands south of the Massif Central."[30] Politically, it had a checkered history, as part of the Duchy of Aquitaine, and then annexed by France; political control swung back and forth, with much day-to-day rule in the hands of many individual local lords. But its relative isolation allowed it to be both independent and, in a sense, lucky—too far away to be seriously fought over, but sufficiently fertile not to starve; and left to its own devices for much of the time. The South in general was a land of its own where, in Joseph Strayer's reading, even apparent similarities with the rest of the country were superficial, covering up important political, legal, and cultural differences. In particular, the law of inheritance required an equal division of property between heirs, rather than everything going to the eldest son, which militated against the accumulation of large holdings of land and goods, in favor of a more equitable form of distribution.

The physical geography of the volcanic landscape meant that when they looked to the outside world, instead of turning north, the Auvergnois were much more likely to turn south, to the Mediterranean and Spain beyond the Pyrenees. In these directions there was long-distance communication, trade, and commerce. The economy of the South seems to have been much more rooted in money than in land, meaning that the feudal ties of the North, where wealth was based on service bound to landholding and landowners, did not exist in the same way. Much more was dependent on rent and cash payments, with smaller holdings and greater independence. Rather than building up great estates as seats of power, the nobility were more inclined to live in towns and work at professions or commerce. This was closer to the Italian model of urban living, with city consuls or councilors, and it may reflect a shared heritage of Roman culture and law; reminders of the Roman past are, even today, common in the southern landscape.

In comparison to other urban centers in the South, Clermont and Aurillac, the largest towns in the Auvergne, were not especially populous. Others, in Languedoc or Aquitaine, for example, were part of the expansion of towns that formed part of the twelfth-century renaissance. Montpellier (population perhaps 35,000) was a thriving, self-governing mercantile community with an important school of medicine and law, and a lively cultural scene.[31] Toulouse, slightly smaller, was one of the richest towns in France, trading as far afield as England and the Levant, exporting wine, grain, oil, leather, and metal ware. Politically, Toulouse was the property of its count, but mercantile success gave the wealthier citizens the confidence to speak out against him in their own interests. Bordeaux (population c. 20,000) was another flourishing community, with an economy based on wine. From the eleventh century, wine was a growth industry throughout the South and an important source of income. Marseilles, on the coast, was also a sizeable place, relying on the trade in shipping all sorts of goods, including people, both those who sought passage as pilgrims to the Holy Land, and those (mainly Arabs) who were sold as slaves.[32]

In the Auvergne, the sprawling nature of the area and its landscape was reflected in a lack of central political control, a vacuum of responsibility and order filled by the Church, which was at least a constant presence. The diocese of Clermont had an unbroken history from the early Middle Ages to the French Revolution, with a moment in the sun in 1095, when Pope Urban II preached the call to Crusade from its cathedral. The Church provided a stability that the shifting secular powers could not. The importance of these ecclesiastical institutions can be seen in the multiplicity of churches and other religious houses in the region, which developed its own brand of Romanesque architecture, paid for presumably by local subscription, and giving an idea of the region's wealth, even if it was not as affluent as some of its neighbors.[33] The plainness of the Romanesque style is coupled with an abundance of carvings on the capitals of columns, which supplement the usual biblical scenes with a profusion of "folk" art, depicting animals, devils, and mythical beasts. A notable and beautiful feature are the imposing carved and painted (and gilded) images of the Virgin Mary with the Christ Child on her lap: Mary calm and serious; Jesus portrayed as a miniature adult; both in robes influenced by the art of Byzantium. Local pilgrimage and local saints were popular, with Le Puy and Aurillac as pilgrim destinations.

Nevertheless, the lack of solid political organization anywhere in the region meant that, in comparison to their northern counterparts, southern bishops were poorer, less powerful, and less educated, even in towns like Toulouse. This had its good sides: clergy in the South appear to have been less corrupt than those in the North, but Strayer suggests this was simply a corollary of their all-round less energetic approach to life. Taken as a whole, the southern churchmen appear to have been of a lower caliber and less able to lead or set an example. Against ecclesiastical regulations that forbade relations with women, many priests lived with so-called concubines, and married in all but name. Pope Innocent III (1199–1216), a reformer for whom this state of affairs was not to be tolerated, suspended Berengar, the archbishop of Narbonne, and his fellow bishops of Toulouse, Béziers, and Viviers for neglecting their pastoral duties. They were rarely in their dioceses, he said; they were "blind men, dumb dogs who cannot bark . . . men who will do anything for money."[34] Despite this poor leadership, however, the attraction of the monastic life, especially for men, was strong, with important Benedictine foundations such as Grandmont, which at its height had 1,200 brothers.

The religious landscape of the South, however, went beyond Christian orthodoxy. The geography of the region, with its links to peoples around the Mediterranean, its proximity to Iberia, and its own patches of isolated mountain dwellers, supplied the ingredients for a rich soup, and there was a tolerance of those whose beliefs were not restricted to those taught by the authorized and orthodox form of Christianity. Both the most common twelfth- and thirteenth-century varieties of heretical religious practice were in evidence. There were, first, Waldensians, followers of one Valdes or Waldo, a formerly rich merchant or farmer who became known as "the poor man of Lyon." They preached poverty and the imitation of the life of Jesus and his followers in the Gospels. In terms of doctrine, they were not so far from orthodoxy, but their attitude to papal and ecclesiastical authority, especially in preaching without authorization, repeatedly led them into hot water. The second group were much more theologically dangerous. They professed a form of the dualist view of the universe, in which both good and evil forces were perpetually in combat with one another—a belief that neatly solved the orthodox Christian problem of why God allowed the existence of evil in the world; why bad things happened to good people. Dualists had a very long history. In the writings of St. Augustine (Augustine of Hippo, 354–430), himself once a dualist, they were known as Manicheans, supposedly after their founder, Mani. In William's day they were called Cathars, possibly from *catharos* (καθαρός) the Greek word for "pure," or Albigensians, after the southern French hilltop town of Albi, which was a center of their religion. William uses all three terms in his writing.[35]

In addition to this assortment of Christians, the South seems to have had relatively substantial numbers of Jews living especially in Toulouse, Narbonne, Montpellier, Arles, and Marseilles.[36] Jews were protected by Church (or "canon") law, and appear to have been able to live largely unmolested by their Christian neighbors. Their existing synagogues were allowed to function (although they could not build new ones), but in accordance with canon law they were required to wear distinctive clothing, and their relations with Christians were supposed to be restricted, particularly when it came to employing Christians as servants. How much these regulations were honored is not clear. Unusually, in the South Jews were allowed to hold property and so could become farmers and traders, rather than simply being confined to the despised professions in moneylending and credit. Moreover because of the commercial, money economy of the region, those in the South who worked in what we would now call financial services were valued more than their northern counterparts. We'll explore William's views on Judaism in a later chapter. One final group were the Muslims or Arabs (generally called Saracens in contemporary medieval texts). Their presence was not unusual (although, like Jews, they were supposed to wear distinctive dress), whether as traders or as slaves traded as human cargo. They also formed part of the intellectual culture of the southern schools, since their linguistic skills and heritage gave them access to the ancient Greek and Arabic texts that were debated and translated in the internationally learned communities of Spain, such as those in Toledo or Córdoba, and which Christian scholars—William most certainly included—began to seek out and devour from the twelfth century onward.[37]

There is always a difference between intolerance of "the other" on grounds of principle, and intolerance simply to make money. In the second half of the twelfth century, Saracens (both male and female) wishing to enter Montpellier had to pay a poll tax to access the city. But in general the majority Christian community of the South appears to have had a much more forbearing, if not broad-minded, attitude to these various minority groups than they might have expected to encounter elsewhere. In the opinion of Gavin Langmuir, in the South, the period up to the second half of the thirteenth century was one of good relations between Jews and Christians, and of real intellectual exchange, without the undercurrent of insult.[38] This may have been because the urban life of the region accustomed people to mixing with those who were different from themselves. It's possible, too, that the low standard of education of the local clergy carried through to their preaching and teaching, resulting in a kind of laissez-faire attitude in their parishioners, especially in regard to heterodox Christian believers, who were not simply tolerated but seen as a genuine alternative to orthodoxy; in support of this argument Strayer cites the regular election in Toulouse of known heretics to serve as consuls, running the city.[39]

For some Jews and Arabs there were more positive interactions with Christians in the learned communities of the South. At least from the mid-twelfth century there had been work on the translation of Arabic texts into Latin at the school in Toulouse, which had links both south to Toledo and north to an important group of scholars at Chartres. It was through earlier Arabic translations that many of the ancient texts of Aristotle and other famous classical scholars had survived—their Greek originals having been lost to time—allowing their (re-)discovery by Western Europe. Influential Jewish thinkers, such as Abraham Ibn Ezra (d. 1164) and Maimonides (d. 1204), were in direct or indirect contact with local scholars in the South. Jews in particular had a reputation as physicians, and seem to have been relatively common in the region: a persecution of Jews in Andalusia in 1145 caused a wave of emigration that may well have included skilled professionals. From about this time, the Christian schools of Montpellier became known as a center of medical excellence, and although it is not clear that there was cooperation between Christian and Jewish practitioners, in 1180 Count Guilhem VIII allowed any qualified person—which presumably included Jews and Arabs as well as Christians—to teach "physic." Certainly, Jewish and Arab medical texts were standard works for study and reference. John of Salisbury (d. 1180), a student and teacher in Paris and Chartres, claimed to deplore the standard of knowledge at both Montpellier and Salerno, and some Paris doctors also declared themselves horrified by what they knew of the teaching there.[40] Perhaps the theoretical approach of the northern physicians was at odds with a more practical and empirical method of the southern schools.

This relatively permissive cohabitation was broken not by internal disagreements but by outside agency, for example, by the preaching missions of a group of Augustinian canons from northern Spain led by Diego of Osma and Dominic Guzman, which paved the way for the formation of the Order of Preachers, or "Dominicans," and, eventually, the setting up of the process of Inquisition.[41] Serious violence was introduced with the Albigensian Crusade called by Innocent III after the murder in 1208 of his legate, Peter of Castelnau, whose tactics in trying to suppress the southern heretics had become increasingly harsh.[42] The actions and behavior of the Crusade's mostly northern French forces, led by Simon de Montfort, were deprecated by many in the South, and not merely by the Cathars or their sympathizers.

Nonetheless, it would be false to portray a simple black-and-white division between the tolerant South and the intolerant North, and we can perhaps see this most clearly in the literary production that became one of the region's greatest exports and strongest characteristics—the vernacular culture of the Occitan language. The political and geographical boundaries of the South were often blurred, but its peoples were held together by their distinctive language and the associations that came with it. The *langue d'oc* (*oc* being the southern word for "yes") was closer to the languages of northern Spain—Catalan and Castilian—and closer to its Latin roots than the *langue d'oïl* (*oïl* being in the northern word for "yes") spoken in the North. "A merchant from Narbonne would have been easily understood in Barcelona, but needed an interpreter in Paris."[43] Importantly, speakers of Occitan did not see their language as inferior, unlike the view of the English language held by the English aristocracy, who were members of an Anglo-Norman culture that came into existence after the Norman Conquest in 1066, and who still used the northern French language for courtly communication. Occitan was accepted as a vehicle for learning and culture; it had been a written language since the tenth century, and we have evidence for its use in early legal, scientific, and religious texts. In the twelfth and thirteenth centuries, Occitan was an important engine of creativity in poetry and music. Its love songs, composed and performed by celebrated troubadours (some of whom, such as Guilhem IX, count of Aquitaine, were also members of the nobility) found their way into all corners of Europe. But though the troubadour songs were popular, they did not reflect the live-and-let-live mentality observed in the commercial and educated culture elsewhere in the South: "[the troubadours] defined themselves principally in opposition to Saracens and Jews," who were painted in stereotypes and slanders.[44] It must be said, however, that they held much the same views of northerners, whom they viewed as drunken hooligans. The dislike was mutual: northerners thought the South was undisciplined, soft, and full of businessmen, lawyers, and Jews.

William, then, was not French. He was not even William—or rather, Guillaume. His first language would have been *auvergnat* (or *auverghat*), the local dialect variation of Occitan, and he was most likely Guilhem or Guillem—a very common name. But he would have been fluent in Occitan, too, and would have taken this bilingualism for granted, as did many medieval people.[45] In fact, since the language of higher education throughout Western Christendom was Latin, by the time William was living and working in Paris, in the *langue d'oïl* that he refers to as Gallic, he was functionally at least quadrilingual, using his different languages for different levels or registers of his daily business. And unlike most medieval scholars, who show little or no sign in their writings of stepping outside their Latin world of thought, William is often caught in between, mediating the ideas and experiences of one part of his life to the other. In a later chapter we'll explore William's fascination with language and expression; perhaps it was his early bilingual upbringing that set this spark alight.

He is certainly aware of mutual incomprehension and the need to learn languages young. In a sermon for the liturgical feast of the first Christian martyr, Stephen, William considers what it might mean to be "full of the Holy Spirit." The idiom of the Holy Spirit can't be understood, he says, by those brought up on a diet of this world, just as a Gaul can't understand a Teuton, or vice versa; and so if you tell him, in that unknown language, that he's been chosen to be emperor, he won't rejoice, because he won't understand. But for those brought up knowing God from childhood, it's easier to learn the language of heaven and retain it more firmly than it is for an old man; as they say, a young head's quick but an old one's wise.[46] Another homely analogy has God adapting his language to fit the world, so that human beings will be drawn to him, just as a nurse uses baby talk when children are young, but alters her speech as they grow up, so they learn to speak correctly.[47]

William's grown-up world in Paris, peopled with scholars and clerics who (at least in theory) were forbidden to marry or have sex, would have been overwhelmingly male. But much of the work that made life run—cooking, cleaning, laundry and other service professions—would have fallen to female servants. It's tempting to think that the references he makes to home and family are reminiscences of his own childhood and upbringing, although he never makes any such claim, and it's dangerous for a historian to assume any one-to-one mapping between the writing and the writer. What is striking about William's works, however, is his constant use of the everyday as a means of explaining God and faith, no matter how complex the theological point he is trying to make: God adapts his language to fit the world, so by reflecting on that world, William should be able to find God. This use of the everyday gives the impression of William as a keen observer, as someone very aware of the world and people around him. Did he know those anonymous female servants by name and take time to talk to them, or was his apparent engagement merely common knowledge, the sort of conventional wisdom that everyone knew, or that he'd picked up in books of fables and other tales that were so popular in the Middle Ages? That's not an easy question to answer; but what is particular to him is his choice to use these sorts of examples—by similitude or analogy—as his method of proceeding, whether in sermons, or in his philosophical theology. The same nurses who fit their talk to the children in their care have tricks for weaning them from the breast, smearing the tip of a nipple with something bitter, so that the baby begins to learn to spit it out.[48] Like the crafty nurse weaning her suckling, God, "the nurse or nurturer of the whole human race," teaches humanity to spit out the milk of childishness and turn to the solid food of the heavenly banquet. Worldly pleasures, although superficially enticing, are always laced by God with the bitterness of unfulfilled desire.

It's hard to believe that an upbringing in the South would not have left its mark, whether in the languages William spoke, the particular sorts of political community and economy he grew up knowing, or the variety and range of peoples inhabiting the region in some kind of tolerance and cohabitation. These are questions to keep in mind for later chapters. For now, however, we'll need to look at how William might have been educated, since to move on, he had to move out.

3

TEACHERS AND TEACHING

Learn everything; you'll find nothing is wasted.

One thing we can surely know about William's schooldays is that he was beaten. Beating children until they knew their lessons was a common trope at least from the Bible onward, and William refers to it in several places in his writing, sometimes literally ("chastisement is the truest judgment on and testimony to a teacher's solicitude"), sometimes allusively ("we ought to be taught to understand the evidence of our senses, and be flogged until we remember the lesson").[1] What we need to know, he adds, echoing the words of the beater to the beaten throughout the centuries, is that this hurts them more than it hurts us: their intention is not "to injure and harm," but "to heal and benefit."[2]

Some medieval scholars refer to their own masters, but William is not one of them. For a man who became a teacher himself, this may be surprising; but perhaps there were too many to single out one. Certainly, it seems to have been education, and his capacity to do well in it, that made the rest of his life possible: William spent his boyhood in the South, but his success came in the North; education was the key that allowed him to move from one world to the other.

We know so little about William's education, in fact, that the Valois biography ignores it altogether. This is clearly the wise approach, given such absence of fact; but schooling is so important, especially to a scholar, that to consider his life without at least some discussion of how and what he might have learned leaves too big a gap. In attempting to fill it, I shall marshal what we know about education at this time (which unfortunately is somewhat less than we know about the periods immediately before and after) to sketch in a few of the pieces of the puzzle.

What proportion of children at this time had any formal education, beyond what they learned at their mother's and father's knees, we simply don't know. It was probably not high: after all, beyond the basics of reading, writing, and arithmetic, this was true in much of Europe until at least the nineteenth century. In medieval households where children were taught to read, it seems not to have been uncommon for them to learn the skill from their mothers, using the Psalms as their textbook.[3] Outside the home, schooling might be provided at a local Benedictine abbey. Education was important to all Benedictine houses, since Benedict's Rule details the place of study in the life of every monk, and Benedictine libraries were famous for their collections of books of all sorts, whether or not they were Christian texts. Many Benedictine houses had boy oblates—children left there by their parents for schooling, with the expectation that they would eventually become monks—and some of these houses also opened their schools to the local population. If William was indeed born so poor that he had to beg for bread, it is difficult to see how education would have been an option, not merely because of the cost of schooling, but because of the loss of an income to his family while he was studying and not working. Yet, assuming that his remarkable intelligence and curiosity about the world was manifest from an early age, it's possible that a local cleric or lord singled out a likely lad and sponsored his education. If William's family were simply of "the middle sort," they could probably afford to send him for a little schooling.

If William was indeed born in Aurillac, he could have gone to the school at its most prominent church, the Benedictine abbey of St. Géraud, whose alumni included the future pope Sylvester II, Gerbert of Aurillac (d. 1003)—"the most distinguished scholar of his time"—and Peter the Venerable (d. 1156), the influential abbot of Cluny.[4] John of Salisbury, a man with outspoken ideas about teachers, declared the abbey school to be better than any other in France.[5] The abbey had been founded in 894 and was an important local center of pilgrimage, so its schoolboys (all the pupils at a male monastic school would have been boys) could have had the opportunity to see and even meet a wide variety of visitors. Aurillac, which is around 350 miles from Paris, was the capital of the more southerly, or "Haute," Auvergne, and although not as important as the northern (Basse Auvergne) capital, Clermont-Ferrand, it was still a place of some significance. In addition to these monastic schools, the Third Lateran Council of the Church, held in 1179, had decreed that every cathedral had to provide a schoolmaster, probably numbered among the canons, to teach the basics of education and religion:

> Since the church of God is bound to provide like a mother for those in want, with regard to both the things which concern the support of the body and those which lead to the progress of the soul, therefore, in order that the opportunity of learning to read and progress in study is not withdrawn from poor children who cannot be helped by the support of their parents, in every cathedral church a master is to be assigned some proper benefice so that he may teach the clerics of that church and the poor scholars. Thus the needs of the teacher are to be supplied and the way to knowledge opened for learners.[6]

This regulation would certainly have included the Auvergne churches at Clermont and Brionde. We should note, too, that as well as providing education for clergy and children, it also gives paid employment to teachers.

It was probably at such a school that William learned his first Latin. To be literate in the Middle Ages was to be "lettered" in Latin, the language of the Church and the Law, and of the all-important knowledge of the past. The curriculum was based on Greek and Roman ideas of what an educated person needed to know, grouped under the banner of the "seven liberal arts."[7] The syllabus had been revived and revised by Gerbert of Aurillac when he was master of the cathedral school at Reims, and it consisted of the study of language (the *trivium*) in the form of grammar, rhetoric, and dialectic, and the study of number (the *quadrivium*), in arithmetic, music, geometry, and astronomy. Teaching was heavily reliant on the textbooks produced by the northern Italian scholar, Boethius (d. c. 524), and his translations of various grammatical works of Aristotle. Boethius remained one of William's regularly quoted sources throughout his career.

For the majority of students, mastering the liberal arts would have been the limit of their formal education; they would simply never need anything else. But clearly, William was an exception. His next step would have been further schooling in the liberal arts, since achieving a bachelor's degree, or its equivalent, in arts was the prerequisite for further study in any of the four higher faculties of law (both civil and Church), medicine, arts, or theology. Qualifications, in the sense of a particular standard of achievement, were still somewhat haphazard, differing from place to place. There were no written examinations; instead, students were expected to be able to show their knowledge orally, and teachers attested to the adequacy of their skills. Since we know that William eventually became a master of theology in Paris, it's not unreasonable to imagine that this was where he now set his sights; but it was not his only option. For a southerner without much financial backing, the schools at Montpellier may have looked very attractive, especially toward the end of the twelfth century when the charismatic Paris master of liberal arts, Alan of Lille (d. 1202), came to teach there.[8] Montpellier was primarily known as a medical school, famous even by the early twelfth century, but its offerings in law and arts were also noteworthy, and Alan's presence would have been an additional draw. William does actually mention Alan by name, in a list of writers on natural history, and Alan's approach to his role as teacher, his certainty of the importance of arts and preaching (he wrote one of the earliest manuals for preachers), and his characterization of the world as a book in which God could be read all find their response in William's writings.[9] In addition, especially in the field of medicine, Montpellier was in contact with the Jewish schools in nearby Arles and Narbonne, which in turn were a conduit for Jewish and Arab texts from Spain and the important schools of Iberia. As we shall see, William was an early reader of Jewish and Arab/Muslim texts, and had an uncommon interest in non-Christian materials: if it was not the place where he first discovered these scholars, Montpellier could have alerted him to the idea that they were something to be reckoned with.

At some point, however, whether to continue in arts or to begin in theology, William found his way north, to the budding university at Paris, and to life in yet another language: while his education would have made him entirely comfortable studying through the medium of Latin, his daily vernacular was now Gallic, the *langue d'oïl*. As a southerner, he would have stood out. Paris attracted an international crowd, particularly from England, where the royal administration was an early employer of university graduates, but most of the French students came from the royal domain in the North.[10] He arrived at an interesting point in the institutional history of the Paris schools. This was the period in which the independent, one-man schools of the twelfth century were, with the practical encouragement of the Capetian monarchy, consolidating themselves into a guild of teaching masters, along the lines of the guilds of artisan craftsmen, forming the beginnings of a university. It's a period of transition we understand less well than those preceding or succeeding it.[11] It's not clear whether anyone could become a student, simply by turning up; in the earlier twelfth century, John of Salisbury describes just such a peripatetic course of study, shifting from master to master, and even place to place, as the fancy took him. We don't know whether William merely arrived in Paris and began to follow the lectures of one or more masters, or whether he would have needed—or in any case had—the personal recommendation of one of his former tutors: if he had indeed been taught by Alan in Montpellier, this could have provided an open sesame to his new university life.

The first charter of privileges for the masters and scholars of Paris was issued by King Philip Augustus in 1200, although the masters had been functioning as a more or less coherent group before that.[12] The main thrust of the charter was to free the university from the jurisdiction of the civil legal authorities, in favor of supervision by the bishop of Paris; whether the ultimate authority was the pope or the French crown was still to be decided. The 1200 charter, which came about in the aftermath of a drunken town-gown brawl (not an unusual occurrence, as we shall see later), came to be seen as the university's foundation document, but much about its organization still remained to be defined. The university was not a place, at this point, as much as a set of people; they were the university *at* Paris, not *of* it, so much so that, on more than one occasion, when disputes arose between the city and the scholars, they either threatened, or actually did, up sticks and go elsewhere.[13] We shouldn't think in terms of buildings and stability, as we might today. Teaching was carried on by a variety of masters in a series of rented halls and rooms, spreading out from the cathedral, south across the river to a warren of streets close to the Seine; larger meetings were held in churches. What distinguished the university from the earlier schools of individual masters gathered in these same places was a commitment to a shared curriculum, an integrated timetable, and a common set of standards of achievement. The masters were united in a common professional pursuit, from which idea they formed a *universitas*, a guild of craftsmen, which went beyond a place where students could pursue higher-level studies.

Not everyone was pleased with the transition from schools to university. In a sermon to his colleagues, Philip, university and cathedral chancellor from 1217 until his death in 1236, looked back with longing for the past:

> the old days, when each master taught for himself and the name of university was unknown, lectures and disputations were more frequent and there was more zeal for study. But now that you are united into a university, lectures and disputations are rare, things are hurried, and little is learned, the time taken from lectures being spent in meetings and discussions. In these assemblies, while the older heads are deliberating and legislating, the young spend their time hatching the most abominable schemes and planning their nocturnal raids.[14]

The Paris masters were not the first to organize in this way: the lawyers at Bologna were earlier out of the blocks, although their formal arrangements were different.[15] The Paris curriculum offered bachelor's and master's (that is, what we would call doctoral-level) study in all four of the higher faculties—arts, canon law, medicine, and theology—although it was for theology that Paris became internationally famous. The teaching of civil (Roman) law was forbidden at Paris by Pope Honorius III in 1219, since it drew too many students away from the less lucrative pursuit of theology.[16] Medieval universities tended to specialize, with Bologna as the apex of legal study, Montpellier and Salerno for medicine, and Paris for theology. Law and medicine were, of course, practical professions, and the inclusion of theology alongside them can give us a clue that it, too, was seen as a useful occupation. We'll look at William's view of the *point* of studying theology a little later.

Philip the Chancellor's lament confirms that there's nothing new under the sun. But his complaint nevertheless shows that the manner of teaching in the university, by lecture (*lectio*), disputation (*disputatio*), and preaching (*praedicatio*; his complaint is in the context of a sermon), was the same as in the earlier schools. Peter the Chanter (d. 1197), a famous master of the previous generation, had referred to this threesome as the foundations, walls, and roof of any study.[17] Our picture of exactly how students were taught is only partly clear, but broadly speaking, in the mornings, masters or higher-level students lectured (a term deriving from the Latin word for "reading") on set texts, which generally comprised one or more books of the Bible, and on parts of the compendium of theological questions (*Four Books of Sentences*) collected by Peter Lombard (d. 1160), a former head of the school at Notre-Dame and bishop of Paris.[18] The teacher went steadily through the text, explaining difficult words and phrases, pointing out contradictions or cross-readings from the Bible or other texts. They used the authoritative works of early Church Fathers, such as Augustine of Hippo, Jerome, Ambrose of Milan, or Gregory the Great, as well as some more "modern" scholars such as the Venerable Bede (d. 735) and Anselm of Canterbury (d. 1109), to provide answers, even if they did not always agree with one another. Points made by closer contemporaries could be referred to, but only anonymously and without commanding the same weight in argument. Then as now, the ability to closely read and question a text was seen as a valuable fundamental skill.[19]

Wider issues arising from lectures were dealt with in something more like a seminar—a *disputatio*—held in the afternoon. The class book for these exercises would have been one of the collections of opinions or "sentences" (*sententiae*) that set out series of problem topics, accompanied by the opinions of various authorities. Peter Lombard's *Sentences* was rapidly becoming the work of choice for this sort of teaching, but there were other twelfth-century collections in circulation, too.[20] Most disputations of this sort were probably confined to a master and his pupils, but there were also grander disputations (held on some Saturdays) in which a master was set a difficult problem and had to enumerate each of its aspects, consider the individual arguments, and then come to a conclusion—a "determination."[21] The lecture and disputation were the foundations and walls of the house of knowledge, but in the theology faculty there could be no roof without preaching, and the university chancellor and masters were all expected to take a turn, with sermons built around the exposition of the Bible, for which lectures were the first step.[22] Some masters were better preachers than others: the same chancellor, Philip, is known from about 700 surviving sermons, whereas Master William of Auxerre, a very highly regarded theologian and author of the influential *Summa aurea,* was clearly hopeless: "when he tried to preach, he did not know what to say . . . He had the gift for debating but not for preaching to people."[23]

The first extant statutes for the teaching of arts and theology in Paris were given in August 1215 by the pope's envoy or "legate," Robert Courson.[24] Robert had been a student of Peter the Chanter, whose approach to theology centered on the practical questions and moral conundrums that he saw as the Church's greatest challenge. Robert was a master of theology by 1200 and a teaching ("regent") master from 1203 to 1211, before being made a cardinal in 1212 and a legate for Pope Innocent III in 1213, set to working on the draft decrees or "canons" of Innocent's proposed General Council of the Church that was to be held at the Lateran church in Rome in November 1215. We'll encounter the influential legislation of Lateran IV, as it is known, in later chapters, but here we note that it included a restatement of the provision for the appointment of theologians to teach at cathedral and other schools, and mandated standards that all clergy should attain.[25] It can't be a coincidence that, as he was drafting the Lateran decrees, Robert Courson also formulated a set of statutes for the teaching at Paris. The document is comparatively short and unsystematic, but it set a minimum age for professors in arts (twenty-one) and theology (thirty-five) and for the length of the course—eight years for the higher level in theology. It specified books for the arts syllabus and forbade the use of Aristotle's works on metaphysics and natural philosophy, in response to a recent scandal. It gave masters jurisdiction over their students. It set a code of behavior and dress, both for students and for teachers. It considered the practical provision of rooms for teaching. It forbade receiving payment in exchange for qualifications. It forbade admission as a theology student to anyone who was not qualified or known to be of good character. Every theology student was to have a definite master—the days of John of Salisbury floating from school to school and master to master were over. Nevertheless, not all students stayed to the end of the course, unless they intended an academic career: credentials, as such, were less important than personal recommendation and connections.

By February 1223, William had graduated—the medieval term is "incepted"—as a master of theology and been given a coveted post as a canon of Notre-Dame.[26] (We'll look at what it meant to be a canon in a later chapter.) Courson's regulations would suggest that William had been a theology student since at least 1215, and must, therefore, have been under the supervision of a particular master. Most of the regent masters in the years when William must have been a student are men of whom little is known—with two main exceptions. William of Auxerre was teaching from 1219 to 1228, so William of Auvergne must have known him at least as a colleague. As we've already noted, he was an excellent theologian but poor at other aspects of the job. And Thomas Chobham (d. 1233/36) was teaching in Paris from 1212 to 1222.[27] Thomas had probably been a student of Peter the Chanter, who was keenly interested in the practical aspects of theology, and Thomas himself wrote an early and influential *summa* for confessors (*Summa confessorum*)—a manual for priests engaged in pastoral work. Thomas was active in the diocese of Salisbury in England, where he was part of the effort to reform and improve the quality of the clergy and their training for work with the laity—subjects close to William's own heart.

If the minimum age for incepting as a master of theology was thirty-five, and with both fees and living expenses to find, how did students make ends meet?[28] The figure of the poor student was already common in the Middle Ages:

> By far the largest element in the correspondence of mediaeval students consists of requests for money . . . Commonly the student announces that he is at such and such a centre of learning, well and happy but in desperate need of money for books and other necessary expenses.[29]

According to the studies of Baldwin and Dunbabin, very few masters would have come from the aristocracy—teaching was not a life likely to attract those with both private means and time on their hands; but at least half were from "the landed 'feudal' segment of society," with just about enough money to get by.[30] A few were fortunate enough to have ecclesiastical benefices—clerical positions that came with a salary, part of which could pay for a vicar to do the actual work while the holder was studying—but many relied on the support of patrons, often local ecclesiastical or commercial and professional men who were prepared to give others a chance.[31] All those studying for higher degrees had qualifications in arts, and could make a little money as tutors, but "the commonest form of patronage was the provision by a rich student of board and lodging for a poorer one, in return for some form of service," such as household work and general fetching and carrying.[32]

From the late twelfth century, a very few students at Paris might also be lucky enough to benefit from the foundation of two colleges for the poor.[33] In 1180, a rich merchant just back from a pilgrimage to Jerusalem, Jocius of London, bought space from the Hôtel-Dieu (the hospital/hostel attached to Notre-Dame) and endowed room and board for eighteen "scholar clerks."[34] The foundation thrived, and by 1231 had moved to other quarters with the name of the College of the Dix-Huit.[35] Slightly later, around 1186, Count Robert of Dreux, with the approval of King Philip Augustus and Pope Urban III, endowed a hostel of his own for poor clerks near the fortress at the Louvre. Whether or not this was initially intended for scholars is unclear, but by 1210 it was described as the House of the Poor Scholars of St. Thomas the Martyr at Paris.[36] At this early stage, these foundations were little more than halls of residence under a warden who enforced discipline and ensured daily prayer. Not all clerks, it seems, were always scholarly or pious. One of William's first responsibilities as bishop, in July 1228, was to step in to deal with the behavior of some of St. Thomas's residents:

> We have found that certain scholars who had long since lived off the goods of the same House, have been carried to such a pitch of insolence that they have attempted to break the doors of the House of the Brethren by night and violently to effect an entrance; others, as though secure of their victuals through having unduly long eaten the bread provided for students, making little progress and unwilling to study,

> burdensome to the real students, were molesting in various ways the quiet and studies of others.[37]

A familiar story. His solution was to restrict residence to one year only, unless a special committee recommended renewal; the miscreants, however, could be turfed out.

The most famous and successful collegiate foundation at Paris was that of the canon Robert of Sorbon, chaplain to Louis IX. Although the date of its foundation seems to be around 1257, after William's death, there is evidence that Robert had begun planning by 1245, and it is likely that William would have taken an interest in the enterprise. It was initially designed for sixteen students from all countries (soon expanded to thirty-six) who were already masters of arts and wished to undertake the long training in theology—a situation that increasingly seemed affordable only for members of the mendicant orders, who could support their fellow friars through the course; in the face of this competition, nonattached "secular" students (who were technically clerics, but ordained only into the lowest levels of the clerical hierarchy) were finding it harder to get by. Robert of Sorbon's regulations for his college resonate across the centuries.[38]

Robert's target students are much more like William's own trajectory as a student. These are men with a higher degree in arts who are embarking on a second BA in theology, to be followed by the doctorate that made them masters—more than a decade of study. They are serious scholars, not those at university simply for the career advantage it might give them, or the many who did not stay to complete the degree, but were content to leave after a period of study because the level they had attained and the connections they had made were sufficient to ease their way into a good job. When William incepted as a master in 1223 and was given his canonry at Notre-Dame, he began work as a professor. After so many years of study, he had reached the pinnacle of the academic profession. The number of teaching masters had been limited by Innocent III in 1207 to eight, which suggests that there were more candidates than posts.[39] We don't know how the choice for these coveted places was made, but references and reputation are the likely method. William was not a priest, so his canonry would not have had pastoral duties, but should be seen more as a research fellowship—necessary for making ends meet, since it was not clear that theologians could legally charge for sharing their knowledge of God.[40] The length of time masters stayed as teachers in Paris varied widely. Some moved swiftly to better paid and influential ecclesiastical posts, others continued as teachers, but whether by preference or because they couldn't do better for themselves, is unclear; the answer must vary across individuals. Although William taught only until 1228 when he was made a bishop, it's not clear that this was his original intention, given that he had not made the step of being ordained to the priesthood. It could well be that he saw teaching as his calling. The role of the master went beyond a commitment to teaching and research. The ideal master of theology was a man who balanced learning and virtue in equal measure. He had to be firm and command respect, but also compassionate with his students (even when they heckled). He behavior and actions had to show him as a man of sense, stability, and wisdom. Above all, he needed to be conscious that his subject bore on the salvation of both his students and himself.[41]

This image of the ideal master was one we can see William embrace and promote, especially in his writings as a bishop, since teaching was one of the gifts given by Christ: "some would be apostles, some prophets, some evangelists, some preachers and teachers."[42] The key was not which gift you were given, but how well you practiced it; it was the teacher's job to send out invitations to the heavenly banquet that God had prepared in heaven.[43] Not all were fit to do this: "false teachers, although wishing themselves to be made masters in the inner circle of the Lord, don't allow others to enter, because they set such a bad example. These and their like obstruct the route to the door to paradise, which would be open, if only a good lesson were on offer."[44]

In his treatise *On Vices* William works his way through a long list of biblical animals, considering what sort of human beings they represent. Having disposed, among others, of scorpions, lions, and crows, he reaches "deep sea fish, who are nourished in the salty depths of the sea and never leave it." Although they live in the saltwater, they take on none of its savor or tastiness ("alas!"), but by some devilish means—he doesn't know how—they refine away the saltiness, leaving only the unpleasant briny tang, along with tastelessness. These fish are like men who grow old in the study of theology or its schools: they swim in the "wholesome water of wisdom" (Ecclesiasticus 15:3), but nevertheless contrive to remain dull and boring.[45] It's not sufficient, he says, to know enough to teach theology; that knowledge has to flavor your whole life. In the words of Matthew's Gospel, "You are the salt of the earth," put there, like salt on the table, to give seasoning to everyone else. It's a topic he returns to: writing about the importance of zeal, William recounts the story of "a certain friend of ours" who fled from Paris because of the coldness of the lecturing and preaching in the schools.[46] "He feared that if he spent a longer time there, he would die of spiritual coldness," and "for this reason, he transferred to religious men burning with charity." Of course, zeal in itself is not enough: teachers also needed modesty and a capacity for judgment, which not all possessed. "Would that some similar insanities [he's talking of the fervent beliefs of heretics] were not found among the sacred professors of doctrine, that is, would that they zealously sought disciples not for themselves, but for Christ. Would that they removed this most evil intention from their midst of wanting to be called Rabbi [Matt. 23:7–8] by human beings and wanting Christian students to be known as a group, with their teacher's name . . . They do not care about the spiritual progress of their students, but about filling their own classrooms. And one very often hears no less shamefully than irreverently on the lips of such teachers: 'This is *my* clerk; this one attends *my* classes; this one is beginning under *me*.'"[47]

It's very typical of William that these opinions on teachers and teaching are expressed in analogies from the worlds of nature and cooking. In subsequent chapters we'll come back to William's love for both; but our final illustration is another reference to nature drawn from a long and interesting sermon for Palm Sunday, which he structures around the procession with palm branches that made up part of the liturgy for the day.[48] He begins by describing palm trees, which are botanically both male and female, and can only bear fruit if the "odor" of the male covers the receptive female. Woe to those teachers of sacred texts, and their students, he says, who despite being incessantly sprinkled with—indeed immersed in—the odor of Christ, despite grinding the leaves [a pun—referring both to the palm leaves and the leaves of books] by expounding and disputing texts, still bear no fruit. Anyone like that is not a palm tree, but like the oaks mentioned in the book of Isaiah (1:30) that drop their leaves. Oaks immersed in water become hard as rocks, and teachers have to beware lest, having been long immersed in the "wholesome water of wisdom," they, too, become hard and useless, or sharp and argumentative. Students of these teachers are in danger: a tutor should be the tree of knowledge of good and evil, but if all their knowledge bears no fruit in deeds, then instead of fruitful palms, the students will bear the fruitless branches of the oak. They won't be part of the Palm Sunday procession, where teachers and preachers who wash their hearers clean with their words are signified by the clerk sprinkling the congregation with blessed water, and where the active life of preaching and the contemplative life of teaching are represented by the lowest sort of cleric, the candle-bearers, who show the humility of those whose task is to spread light.

For William there was no question of teaching or learning for its own sake. This would be simple "curiosity"—the eagerness to know things that had no utility, and which was focused on the learner rather than the learning. He "rejects such persons," those "ridiculous apes of philosophers" who have missed the point of what they do. Learning is empty if it does not contain "the glory or the glorification of the Creator," for without this it cannot lead to eternal life; and without this ultimate end, all learning is deformed and curtailed: those who pursue it are fools rather than wise men, living and acting in contempt of God.[49] He hopes his own teaching is closer to this ideal:

> Doing, therefore, what we can, we have given some opportunity to the wise, and we have set forth for the exercises of mind not a dry arena of fruitless questions and disputations, but a highly useful and salutary gymnasium for conquering errors and for snatching the truth from their midst with noble triumphs.[50]

Teaching, then, was a noble profession; William may well have expected to pursue it for the rest of his life.

4

PARIS

How ya gonna keep 'em down on the farm,
after they've seen Paree?

After the fall of the Wall, in 1989, Berlin began to build. I remember visiting, half a dozen years later, when the cityscape was dominated by cranes. Scaffolding, wiring, giant pipes, enormous holes in the ground peopled by armies of workers; the night sky lit up by the sparks of oxyacetylene welding: everything was uncertain, in flux. But it was exciting.

Paris in 1200 was putting up walls, not pulling them down—but there was as much noise, motion, and energy as there was in 1990s Berlin.[1] The expansive "renaissance" of the twelfth century was manifest in a resurgence of life in towns, and in Paris we have an example writ large. The city had become the capital and main residence of the ruling Capetian dynasty, and the current monarch, the third Capetian king, Philip II, nicknamed "Augustus," both because he was born in that month (12 August 1165) and because of his great expansion of the lands in the royal domain, was determined to make it a city that lived up to his idea of his own and his family's importance.[2] If he could not, like his classical namesake, find his own Rome brick and leave it marble, he could at least find it wood and leave it limestone. Nevertheless, although Paris was a favorite location (who can resist an island?), the Capetians were still to some extent peripatetic rulers, until Philip IV, "the Fair" (1285–1314), settled down and made Paris the single royal residence.[3]

The city was not new. The island (Île) in the River Seine, or the land surrounding it, had been occupied by the Gauls and the Romans—who called it *Lutetia*, the "city of light"—and by most of their successors apart from the Carolingians (mid-eighth to later tenth century), who preferred to live farther east, closer to the River Rhine; but Hugh Capet and his successors reverted to the earlier site. The island position, of course, had its problems, especially with flooding. Major inundations occurred in 1197 and during the next decade, washing away the bridge that linked the Île de la Cité to the southern riverbank, and covering buildings up to the second floor; but the strategic, agricultural, and communications advantages outweighed the difficulties.[4] In addition, the Île was defensively attractive in an era when political boundaries were still very much fought over; it was surrounded by fertile land, which also gave room for expansion, and had deposits of limestone for building. And although the Seine was still a major river at this point, the intervening islands made it traversable; so bridges could link roads to the north and south, even as the river was broad enough for direct trade and traveling routes to the sea to the west and, via waterways, to the east and south.

The Capetians didn't have the island to themselves. For at least two centuries, the Île had been divided, with the bishop installed at the east end, presiding over a relatively modest Merovingian (eighth-century) basilica, and the king at the west end, in the expanded remains of the former Roman palace. The space between Church and State was thickly populated with houses, shops, churches, and even a synagogue, all of which spilled over the bridges to both north ("Right") and south ("Left") riverbanks. When Philip Augustus was crowned on 1 November 1179, aged fourteen, the royal palace towered over the island. His father and grandfather had added to the older buildings, so that they now boasted a Grand Tower (Grosse Tour) almost 12 meters (roughly 40 feet) in diameter and 30 meters (around 100 feet) high. Crossing the Grand Pont to the northern bank, the new king could take the rue Saint-Denis all the way (13 kilometers, or 8 miles) to the royal burial abbey of that name, now greatly enlarged and enhanced by Abbot Suger (d. 1151).[5] Just east of there, the older rue St-Martin went north to the shrine of the Tours saint. The settlement on the north bank was a thriving mercantile and commercial center, incorporating the "old market" site (*vetus forum*) on the quays of the Place de Grève along the Seine, handy for deliveries and onward distribution by barge and sail, and the "new market" (*novus forum*) at the fields of Champeaux to the northwest. Philip transformed the unprotected, outdoor stalls of Champeaux by providing lockable covered premises, which were given the name that survives today, Les Halles.

According to his chronicler, Rigord of St. Denis, the young king Philip was appalled by the state of his capital, which stank from the mud and detritus of the city. With financial support from the better-off citizens, he began work to pave the major roads and squares and to install street lighting, and he ordered the building of walls to enclose the entire city, expanding and renewing the previous fortifications. In the decade-long campaign, starting around 1189, the bourgeoisie were to finance the walls on the north bank of the river, while the king paid for those on the south. Archaeological remains suggest the northern walls ran for about 2.6 kilometers (1.6 miles), with thirty-nine towers and five gates; the gates could be closed at night and regulated traffic in and out. The walls south of the river covered 2.5 kilometers (1.55 miles), with thirty-eight towers and six gates.[6] The walls stood between 6 and 8 meters (20–26 feet) high, at a width of 2.6 meters (8.5 feet) at the base, with the towers and gates rising above them. Just outside the wall, Philip built the fortress that became known as the Louvre, the foundations of which can still be seen in the basement of the modern museum on the site. The walls were intended for defense, but it was perhaps not as important that every building was enclosed within them as that the surrounding inhabitants could reach their shelter if they needed to; and of course, the creation of an enclosed community meant that the king could levy tolls on those who wished to enter and do business within.

The 5.1 kilometer (3.2 mile) circumference of the walls gives some idea of how small the area covered by Philip Augustus's city was—roughly, 250 hectares or one square mile of land. The fortress of the Louvre and the major abbeys of Saint-Victor, St. Martin in the Fields, and Saint-Germain des Prés, as well as the church and complex of buildings belonging to the Knights Templar, were all outside the walls. Tiny by today's standards, Paris was by far the largest walled town in the kingdom of France, though it was easily outstripped by Ghent to the north (644 hectares) or Cologne to the east (401 hectares), both important trading cities with international reach.[7]

The royal family occupied the western end of the island, crossing to the north bank by the Grand Pont. At the eastern end of the island, the bishop crossed from his palace to the south bank of the river by the Petit Pont, the smaller structure bridging the river at a narrower point. Both bridges were lined with the shops and houses of artisans: those of the Grand Pont were gold- and silversmiths and money changers; the Petit Pont housed at least one teaching master, Adam. The Left Bank was much more open and less populated, covered by the gardens and vineyards that helped to feed the city. Its major features were three important religious houses: to the west, the Benedictines of Saint-Germain des Prés; to the south the Augustinian canons of Sainte-Geneviève, site of a flourishing arts school, and the only one of the three inside Philip's walls; and to the east, the Augustinian canons of Saint-Victor, which for most of the twelfth century had boasted a notable free school with famous teachers and an important library. From the Petit Pont, the rue Saint-Jacques ran south through the city, as the start of the pilgrimage route to the shrine of St. James at Compostela.

The ecclesiastical half of the Île was also in the throes of building works, since a new cathedral church was in the process of construction—an operation that continued for more than a century. Taking office as bishop in 1160, Maurice of Sully (d. 1196) compared his own, rather old-fashioned church to those being built or retooled in the new Gothic architecture, whether close to home, at Saint-Germain des Prés and Saint-Denis, or in surrounding cathedral cities such as Sens, Laon, or Noyon. With an impulse all too familiar from today's world, he resolved to replace the old basilica with an entirely new limestone church that pushed the limits of the modern style: longer, higher, and lighter. The vast building—in essence, the Cathedral of Notre-Dame still standing today, despite the recent fire—rose quickly, as the architect and builders solved the problems of marshy ground, the restrictions of the island site, and the crowded surroundings. Not only was it to be bigger and better than its ecclesiastical rivals, at 32.5 meters (more than 105 feet) high the choir vaults must have been designed to rival or even surpass the Grosse Tour of the king's palace to the west. To make his ambition even clearer, Maurice added a smart new episcopal palace and adjoining Hôtel-Dieu, housing a hospital and visitor center. Keeping services going during the building works must have been a challenge, although aided by the fact that the old cathedral was not demolished until the late 1190s. The new east end and choir were usable from 1182, although work on the rest of the church was still in full swing.

John Baldwin highlights a harangue "against superfluous builders" by Peter, the cathedral chanter in the 1180s and 1190s, who along with his duties as a teaching master in theology was responsible for the conduct of its worship. Protests against vanity projects had a long history going back to classical texts, but it is hard not to see a contemporary reference in Peter's disapproving tone. He reminds his hearers that Christ was humble, not grand. "Why do you want your houses so tall?" he asks. "Do you believe that the devil cannot scale them?"[8] Peter was presented with an even trickier problem by the cost of the works: what to do with donations given out of immoral earnings. The urban monetary economy of Paris needed its own financial services sector, which included the provision of credit, lending at interest, and the fixing of reasonable or "just" prices for goods. Money in itself was a difficult subject for the Church, but since it was clearly not going to go away, theologians such as Peter and Thomas of Chobham set themselves to decide how to make the best of the situation, which included advising on whether or not the cathedral authorities could benefit from the profits of moneylenders. Their rather hardline attitude (yes, but only after they had made restitution to their clients) might not have pleased ecclesiastical fundraisers. They were somewhat more sympathetic to another group of workers drawn to Paris by the availability of trade: prostitutes. One of Peter's former students, Jacques de Vitry (d. 1240), claimed:

> Casual sex was not judged to be a sin. Common prostitutes were everywhere in the squares and streets of the city, forcibly dragging passing clerics into brothels . . . In one and the same house there would be teaching rooms upstairs and prostitutes downstairs. The masters would be lecturing upstairs while the whores carried on their infa-

> mous trade below. The prostitutes would be arguing with each other and with their pimps in one part of the house, while the clerics argued and disputed in the other.[9]

These local women were eager to donate to the cathedral funds, and, perhaps surprisingly, Peter and Thomas saw them as workers who were entitled to the profits of their labor. Unless they were guilty of sharp practice toward their clients, by the use of makeup and other fraudulent deceptions, their money could be accepted.[10] We'll consider William of Auvergne's attitudes to money, merchants, and working women in subsequent chapters.

Estimates of the size of the Paris population during William's lifetime vary enormously, since there is no usable written evidence that might facilitate a calculation before the tax assessment rolls of 1292. Even then, the problem lies in assessing those who left no footprint as taxpayers: how many other people did any one taxpayer support? Conjectures have ranged from as few as 50,000 up to 210,000 inhabitants, with the current view veering toward the higher figure.[11] Of these, the numbers of those engaged in ecclesiastical or academic life is thought to have been never more than 6,000 to 7,000, with perhaps 3,000 to 4,000 in William's day, although clearly this would have been a variable total.[12] According to the royal historian, William le Breton, by the time Philip's walls were completed in 1211–12, population growth meant the Left Bank was filling with houses right up to the walls themselves, although this may have been a flattering reference to royal prescience in where to build and to the attractions of the king's capital.[13] Whatever the precise figure, it is clear that during Philip's lifetime there was a rapid growth in the numbers of town- and city-dwellers and a movement away from rural life, although the overall proportion of those who were urbanites would have remained small in comparison to today. Philip saw his city as the direct inheritor of the western progress of the baton of human civilization. What had begun in the Near East had made its way to Athens then Rome, and had now reached Paris. This progression of history is something William, too, notes: "God played in the clay [of the first created land] out of which great kingdoms took hold, throwing it now into the hand of the Indies, then to the hand of the Persians, then to the hand of the Babylonians, then to the hand of the Greeks, and most recently to the hands of the Romans" (the Holy Roman Emperor was still a vital political force in medieval Europe).[14] The rapid expansion and improvement in living conditions in the previous century had given the rulers of Western Europe the confidence to style their region as the rising center of the world; but those travelers who encountered the great, and long-inhabited, cities of the East, such as Baghdad and Cairo, each with a population estimated at around a quarter of a million, were reminded of the depth of urban culture to be found elsewhere.

As bishop, William found himself confronted with the effects of the increase in the Parisian population, especially as new areas of the city began to be settled. The Île itself was well provided with churches—thirteen, not counting the cathedral, the chapels within its cloister, or those within the royal palace—but coverage beyond the island was much patchier.[15] Growth in numbers of those living on the Right Bank, however, meant that the two very large old parishes of Saint-Germain l'Auxerrois—in itself covering almost half the area north of the river—and Saint-Gervais were inadequate for the expanding demands of their parishioners. In the late twelfth century, Saint-Germain was divided to deal with the rising numbers.[16] According to Henry of Suso (an archdeacon of William's who became archbishop of Embrun, a mountainous but thinly populated diocese in southeast France), "the parish church of St Germain l'Auxerrois [before it was divided], whose rector has the care of more than 40,000 souls, possibly had more than the archbishop of Embrun with all his suffragans."[17] When William became bishop, he further divided Saint-Germain, to provide better pastoral care for its inhabitants. But it is clear that in doing so he recognized a wider problem, for the reply to his application to the pope for permission to split Saint-Germain gives him a general authorization to break up larger parishes where he saw fit.[18] He had already created a new parish on the Left Bank. Here, the churches of Saint-Julien le Pauvre and Saint-Séverin had traditionally catered to the students and masters who lived there. William, however, was concerned about provision for those who were not part of the schools, but who had settled in the vicinity of the rue Saint-Victor, which ran southeast and out through the walls to the abbey. This area, called the Thistle Patch (Clos de Chardonnet), was being turned over to the cultivation of vines and much-needed housing space. It belonged to the Victorine canons, but they themselves seemed disinclined to take on pastoral work inside the city, so in 1230 William persuaded the abbey's prior to sell him a small piece of land where he could build a chapel and parish house.[19] The bother and organization would be William's alone, since the priest in charge would not be a member of Saint-Victor, but appointed by William. The chapel, dedicated to St. Bernard, was functioning by 1231, and by 1243 had become a parish church (now with the name Saint-Nicholas, Chardonnet) and was the subject of a dispute with the abbey. Once again, William did a deal with the prior: the abbey ceded more land in the same area, and the church was rebuilt, although keeping its former burial ground—a reminder that growing populations also require more space for the dead. Finally, in 1234 William built a chapel dedicated to St. Gilles and St. Loup (St. Leu), on the Right Bank, north of the abbey of Saint-Magloire and not far from the bustling market at Les Halles. Those living round the abbey were technically parishioners of the abbey's chapel of St. Bartholomew on the Île, opposite the royal palace, so although the new foundation was not a parish church in its own right, it nevertheless provided them with pastoral care much closer to home. Although William's Paris diocese was not the most senior of those in the royal domain, the problems raised by urban life made it perhaps the most demanding.

A notable feature of Paris in contrast to some other cities was its variety. Unlike the cloth-working cities of Flanders, for instance, it was not dependent on only one industry or trade. The presence of the king and his royal courts drew the aristocracy from their rural domains to grand townhouses near the palace. The bishop and cathedral had their own ecclesiastical constituencies, as well as maintaining close ties with the university and scholars. The ample road and river links were the engine of trade and commerce, which provided a source of wealth not reliant on the traditional ownership of landed estates. Those at the top of this triangle—who were not infrequently related to one another—were the city's powerful elite, wheeling and dealing, bartering favors and contacts in a way that would be wholly familiar to their modern counterparts. Cushioned by the comforts that money could provide, they nonetheless lived busy and stressful lives. In a sermon on the story of the child

Jesus teaching in the Temple (Luke 2:43), William sympathizes with those who find it difficult to find time for God: too many people, too many worldly troubles, too many anxious thoughts; it's not easy to remember the important in the face of the urgent, he says.[20] We'll see in a later chapter how well he knows these people—the women in their fashionable furs and the men with their commercial headaches: he sympathizes, but he doesn't excuse them.

Cascading down from the top came those who serviced their needs: the clerks and administrators; the doctors and lawyers; the chefs, vintners, and dealers in foodstuffs; the tailors, dressmakers, shoemakers, and milliners; the ostlers, farriers, boatmen, and providers of transport and haulage; the musicians and entertainers; the makers and decorators of books; the builders and repairers, architects and masons; hairdressers and beauticians—those who made and those who served.[21] These, too, had their suppliers and their servants, who in turn looked down to others: Paris was a delectable cake of many layers. Of course, it attracted thieves: William describes the canny villain who knocks gently on a door or window to see if there's anyone awake; if there's no answer, he's safe to break in, but a loud shout of "Who's there?" will send him running.[22] The gap between the fortunate at the top and the desperate at the bottom was wide, reflecting an age in which any form of organized welfare provision was minimal, but possibly no different from modern-day America or India. In some ways, indeed, the rich and poor (and the masses in between) were more "in it together" than their counterparts today. Everyone was subject to natural disasters. The floods of the 1200s, for instance, must have been devastating for those whose houses were drenched up to the second floor; but they equally forced both the king and the bishop to evacuate their residences, at least temporarily. Fire was a perennial occurrence where wooden houses were jammed together in narrow streets, and was always a cause for anxiety when heating and cooking were reliant on open hearths, no matter how large the household. This isn't to say, of course, that the wreckage caused by fire and flood were felt equally by the haves and the have-nots, but no one was entirely immune to their effects. The same is true for the effects of disease and illness. Before the widespread availability of penicillin in the twentieth century, the greatest number of female deaths occurred in the period surrounding pregnancy and childbirth, and this was true for rich and poor alike. Many other people would have been born with disabilities or would have become disfigured or maimed—sometimes by judicial process, as William notes, or from the pillories and gibbets set up around town; beyond simple prosthetics, such as wooden legs and feet, iron hooks for hands, or wheeled chairs and carts, not much could be done for them.[23] Unable to work, many had little choice but to beg. The citizens of medieval Paris would have been less shocked by such sights than we are today.

Some more everyday experiences would have been common to all. Smelly and messy trades, such as butchery and the concomitant work of tanners and parchment makers, were situated on or close to the quays, as street names suggest. Even for the better off, the odors of medieval Paris would have been stronger than anything we're used to today. Living on a river was useful as a ready means of waste disposal, and everything must have eventually made its way down to the water. But the elaborate Roman systems of human waste disposal had not survived to the Middle Ages, and the gutters of many roads would have been little more than open sewers. William compares the cleansing properties of the sacrament of confession with the "gate of filth" by which all sorts of rubbish leaves the city. One of his favorite sermon images is "the latrine of luxury" or lechery, which it's all too easy to fall into—and much too difficult to get out of. The image is a classic example of William's approach to teaching the Christian life—using a familiar situation to arouse a sensual memory, evoked in vivid language; all aspects of his world we'll explore in later chapters.

The smells were not only human. Medieval Parisians lived far closer to animals, even in the city, and depended on them much more than we do now. Horses were ubiquitous among the better-off classes, and in more than one sermon William details the various types and grades of horse that his hearers would have known and understood as having different uses and symbolizing different status. Mules and oxen were common beasts of burden and draft. Although their dung littered the streets, some people knew how to make money from it.[24] Domesticated animals, such as cows, pigs, and hens, would have been common in parts of the city, as well as in the markets; they, too, make their appearances in his writing, along with all sorts of fish, which were essential for keeping the regular Friday meatless fast that all Christians were supposed to observe. But not all animals were for eating. Bears in chains were part of the entertainment industry.[25] And dogs of all shapes and sizes make appearances in hundreds of medieval manuscript illustrations as both helpers and companions. William writes about dogs with genuine affection and knows that friendships can stand or fall on your attitude to my best friend: "love me, love my dog," he says; will you put up with an annoying pooch for my sake?[26]

The city's population was not only composed of those who had been born there. The university recognized the heterogeneity of its younger (arts) students, and organized discipline according to four "nations"—French, Norman, Picard, and English—which were loose enough to cover those hailing from Spain to Finland, from Hungary and the Slavic lands to Ireland.[27] As well as Christians like William, who had come from other parts of France or Western Europe, Paris was home to a sizeable and learned community of Jews. According to King Philip's chronicler, Rigord, they had come to Paris long ago from all over the world and had "laid claim to" almost half the city.[28] They were especially concentrated on the Île, where the current estimate of the population just before Philip became king suggests that, of the c. 6,000 dwellers on the island itself, around 1,000 (17 percent) were Jews, although this dropped to around 3–5 percent of the numbers in the rest of the city.[29] Although Jews had protected status in the Christian religion, this did not stop them being on the receiving end of discrimination and animosity, partly because of their role as moneylenders. In 1180 Philip expelled them from the royal domain—only to readmit them in 1198, because they were too useful to live without. There was also a smaller group of Muslims, or at least Muslim converts, though numbers are hard to come by; we do know that in 1248 ten such men were studying Near Eastern languages at the university, in order to work as missionaries.[30] As we'll see, William was very aware of both religious groups.

Philip Augustus died in 1223, the year William became a canon of the cathedral. His son, Louis VIII, reigned for only three years, dying when his own son, Louis IX, was still a child, so that his wife,

Queen Blanche of Castile, took over as regent, a role that in many ways she never quite relinquished. Louis IX was an ascetic and deeply religious man (he was canonized as a saint in 1297), but also an able administrator; his dual sense of duty, to God and to France, made for criticism, even during his lifetime. In 1238 Louis acquired a remarkable religious relic—the crown of thorns from Christ's crucifixion—that had been pawned to the Venetians by the emperor of Constantinople, Baldwin of Courtenay, who was desperate for money.[31] It arrived in Paris the next year, and William took part in the elaborate ceremonial around its reception, which included the king and his brother, barefoot, carrying the relic to Notre-Dame, and then to the royal palace chapel.[32] A thirteenth-century source claims that William took the opportunity to suggest to Louis that he institute a general annual holiday in celebration on 11 August.[33] Louis determined to build a chapel at the royal palace to house it and his other relics, including parts of the True Cross, also newly obtained from Baldwin. We can surely catch William speaking of the relics in a sermon on the honor due to saints. Kings and princes, he says, are glorified when they possess any sort of holy relic, when they adore them and kiss the traces the saints have left behind. The Cross comes to the brow of emperors from the execution of thieves. Saints recognize the world for what it is and ridicule it, just as the Jews ridiculed the Lord Jesus with the crown of thorns, for the world's praise is an illusion. The clamor of the crowd, and the cross on which Christ ascended and assumed the imperial purple—of an emperor and a martyr—are the voices of the friends of God.[34] Louis's Sainte-Chapelle, still one of the wonders of Paris, was consecrated in April 1248, just a year before William died.

Which was better, town or country? Christianity had a somewhat complicated relationship to city life: the Bible begins in a garden, but it ends in the heavenly city of Jerusalem, the vision of peace. Along the way, however, the Hebrew Bible tells the stories of the Tower of Babel, with its multiplicity of languages that hindered rather than helped communication, and the twin cities of Sodom and Gomorrah, so wicked that they were entirely destroyed; and at the Apocalypse, Jerusalem is contrasted with Babylon, a byword for depravity. Medieval theologians took their lead from Augustine of Hippo, whose work, *The City of God*, divided human beings into inhabitants either of the City of God or of the earthly city. These were not physical places but attitudes of mind and heart: were your thoughts and desires fixed on the eternal, or were you content with the pleasures of the here and now? No one could be sure of their citizenship, but God kept a tally for all—and distressingly few would eventually find themselves among the chosen.

William knew Augustine's writings well, and his influence is plain. "I ask you not to look at *me*," a sermon begins, "even though I'm here in Paris, but to turn your eyes to him from whom all good comes."[35] But William was also a man of the urban South and a long-time Parisian. In his work on the Christian sacraments, William states his belief in the innate sociability of human beings (echoing Aristotle, whose works he had known since the arts course), and embarks on his own long metaphor, which contrasts the city as it could be, built by God and of perfect beauty, with cities as they are, where humanity lives like trees in a wood, or rough stones in a quarry, as yet unshaped to their higher purpose.[36] There are bad sides to city living, of course: the desolation of loneliness, the lack of spiritual people, and the crush of humanity, with its disordered priorities and desires.[37] Yet, to become the society they can be, to become the community of God, humans must leave the countryside and rustic life, abandon crude dwellings and boorish manners, and move to the city to become proper citizens with civilized manners and urban courtesy. No matter how good country life outside the city might be, it is nothing in comparison to excellence attained by those who freely come together to live as citizens of God.

William is employing an urban metaphor for an urban audience, so it's perhaps unsurprising that he prefers to stress the perfectibility—and preferability—of city life over a return to rural roots. He must have known that the rustic alternative wouldn't wash. "Town air makes you free," went the saying, recognizing the legal emancipation of those owing feudal service to a lord, if they could live as town dwellers for a year and a day. Though the city might be crowded, busy, and impersonal, it had opportunities and entertainments that the countryside could never offer. The same anonymity that allowed beggars to starve on the streets gave the possibility of self-reinvention for those constrained by the limitations of rural society, gave chances that just weren't available elsewhere. "Paris—it's paradise," said those who came to its twelfth-century schools.[38] William knew too much of the darker side of city life to think it was quite that simple, but that didn't stop him squeezing all the tumbling variety of urban life into his own literary world.

5

BISHOP

The care for souls is the art of arts.

We've moved straight from William the teacher to William the bishop, without stopping at William the priest, because that was his journey, too. When Gregory IX made William bishop of Paris in 1228, he had first to ordain him priest.[1] All university students and teachers had to be "clerks in holy orders," but in practice this could mean simply joining the lowest level of tonsured clerics, so that you came under the jurisdiction of the Church rather than of the secular authorities. When William was made a canon of the cathedral in 1223, it seems he hadn't bothered to progress beyond this stage. Notre-Dame maintained a "chapter" of fifty-one canons, which included eight "dignitaries," or those holding specific posts within the cathedral, including the dean, the chancellor, the chanter, and three archdeacons, each representing part of the diocese, who acted as the bishop's eyes and ears.[2] The canons had to be male, of legitimate birth, freeborn, and not in servitude; but only some official positions, such as the dean and the canon penitentiary, who was in charge of hearing confessions, had to be priests. All received salaries ("prebends"), from income derived from land and property holdings separate from those of the bishop; some were paid more than others, partly depending on whether or not they had responsibilities elsewhere and could not be available for cathedral duties as they were supposed to be. In 1230, as bishop, William levied a penalty on the absentees, who were henceforth to reside mainly in Paris and to say the liturgical offices and celebrate mass in the cathedral (or provide a qualified substitute, if they were not priests) every day. In a sermon, he compares clergy who don't carry out their duties to eunuchs who want to be married but don't have the wherewithal to carry it through; or adulterous nephews who don't sleep with their wives and yet won't give them a healthy divorce. This isn't genuine chastity, he says, it's the infernal continence of the devil. Such men don't want the love of a woman, they want a servant—and money.[3]

Rather more than half the canons were lucky enough to live in one of the thirty-six houses in the cloister to the north of the cathedral, which were owned communally by the chapter, but rented out to individuals for life. The cloister formed a "tiny clerical city," with three chapels, a chapter house for meetings, a jail, and a refectory, although this latter was not in regular use.[4] It was exempt from all secular jurisdiction, including royal taxation. Cloister life came with strict regulation, particularly with regard to women: none could stay overnight except your mother, sisters or other close relatives, and especially no women servants, other than a nurse. The aim was to create an atmosphere of quiet contemplation, although the 1245 ruling forbidding all animals except working animals, and which specifically mentioned bears, apes, noisy caged birds, and other animals kept only for amusement, suggests that this might not always have been achieved. Indeed, the regulations of 1325 go as far as to detail suitable clothing and restrictions on beards and long hair, and to forbid gambling, except at Christmas.[5]

William's canonry was probably associated with his teaching role, providing him with a kind of fellowship to support his academic work.[6] The question of how to pay theologians had been debated since at least Peter the Chanter in the later twelfth century: it was surely wrong to take money for educating people about God, but even teachers had to eat.[7] In theory, the cathedral school was situated in the canons' cloister, and at one time the students had lodged in the canons' houses; but as early as 1127, this was judged too disruptive, and the school moved to an area on the bishop's (south) side of the cathedral. Some canons, however, rented rooms to singers in the cathedral choir. In his twenty-one years as bishop, William was able to shape the character and personnel of the cathedral canons by his appointments, and by chance a surviving statute from two months before his death in 1249, concerning the taxation of those housed in the cloister, allows us to see how many of them were. William, it seems, turned away from the customary practice of appointing members of the local aristocracy, in favor of choosing talented and conscientious newcomers. The Paris chapter, "more than many others in the West," formed a cultural and religious elite, with an emphasis on university-trained men, "at the forefront of clerical meritocracy."[8]

In 1227, William had been a canon for four years when Bishop Bartholomew died. The canons elected one of their own, Nicholas the Chanter, as his successor. But the election was not unanimous, and William was unhappy with the process, which he thought had violated the rules laid down in the decrees of the Fourth Lateran Council of 1215. Nicholas stood aside, claiming that he had never wanted to be bishop, and a second election was held. This gave the post to the cathedral dean, Philip. Again, William argued that the process had been illegitimate, and this time his objection triggered the intervention of the pope, Gregory IX, who instituted a local inquiry that upheld William's concerns. It was a privilege of the cathedral canons that they could appeal directly to the papacy, so William traveled to Rome, where Gregory took matters into his own hands and made William bishop.[9] "A man of eminent learning, without a stain on his character," was the pope's judgment—one that he was soon to regret and retract, when William didn't do as he was told.[10]

Was William surprised to find himself made bishop, or had he gone to Rome with this precise intention? Perhaps he himself didn't know. In 1228, William was a serious scholar with no obvious ambition for a well-paying ecclesiastical post elsewhere—a route other graduates and masters looked to pursue.[11] Roland Teske, tireless translator of much of William's theological and philosophical work, describes him as "very pushy," as someone who managed to "convince" Gregory IX to appoint him bishop of Paris.[12] I wouldn't characterize William in quite this way. He's certainly confident in his own interpretation of the Lateran decrees, and seems to feel responsible for following their intention. But he appears not to have wanted even to be ordained a priest, never mind a bishop. Still, being a priest and being a bishop—being in charge—are two very different things. We might even speculate that it was only when William recognized who the other candidates might be that he decided to try for it himself.[13] I do think that William was never interested in being a bishop merely for the status, the money, or the power for its own sake. From the start, his focus was on betterment of his clergy and laity. If the reforming decrees of Lateran IV provided the motive force behind his efforts at improvement, his appointment as bishop gave him the means and opportunity for carrying them out.

The bishop was not part of the canons' chapter; his jurisdiction ran in the diocese, not in the cathedral. He lived in the relatively new episcopal palace built by Maurice of Sully, situated to the south of the cathedral alongside the Seine, with its own chapel and musicians, as well as a staff to aid him in his work as chief pastor and administrator, leading his flock. Although the bishop of Paris was subordinate to the archbishop of Sens, Walter of Cornut, the importance of Paris as a place gave its bishop influence. The diocese comprised the whole city, as well as some of the smaller surrounding towns and villages, and the bishop had secular as well as spiritual power over the local lords and lands, which provided the funding for the palace and his entourage. When William returned from Rome, he was installed as bishop during a day of celebration that started at the abbey of Sainte-Geneviève and culminated in him being carried to Notre-Dame in his chair (*cathedra*) on the shoulders of these same lords—an experience he recalled in a later sermon.[14] There, according to tradition, the cathedral canons to whom he no longer belonged refused him entry unless he first swore to uphold their rights. So began a busy and peripatetic leadership, on foot and horseback around the churches, communities, and parishes that were his responsibility, preaching to all sorts and conditions of congregations. From the ordinary "people of Paris" to monks and nuns, clergy, and scholars, on special occasions and ordinary Sundays, William preached his way around his diocese year after year. Judging by the almost 600 surviving sermons, he was brilliant at it; but more importantly, he simply persevered, doing his duty by his fellow Christians and leading by example.

We can see William's own distillation of the role of bishop in his treatise against the accumulation of ecclesiastical benefices—the practice of clergy holding more than one paying position, known as pluralism, and which we'll return to later.[15] It's typical of him that he begins the discussion of a specific problem with a broad consideration of context. The danger of pluralism is that it casts shadows on the Church—the shadows of greed, ambition, sex, and corruption, where the devil lurks. To dispel the darkness, the bishop needs to be sure of himself and of those he appoints to help him. William sets out the roles a bishop must fulfill to prove the purity of his vocation. First, he must be the spouse of his Church, a role signified by his episcopal ring, and he must be its father, begetting children—that is, appointing clergy—who are born of Christ, not demons. A bishop with the wrong priests is a cuckoo, throwing the mother bird's true eggs out of the nest so as to substitute its own. A bishop must also be an architect, like Solomon, building the house of God. This house must be built not from scraps, like a bird's nest, but from the solid knowledge of truth; so to substitute your own nephews or sons for properly trained builders would be ruinous. God's house must have interior as well as exterior decoration—with sculptures that are bishops, pictures that are teachers and defenders of the Church, and bas-reliefs that are priests and minor clergy: this is the mystical body of Christ. The bishop must be a leader who can choose the right men and bring them together to fight the devil and his army. Once again he says there's no point in gathering a flock of nephews or other children with no knowledge of battle; those on the payroll must be strong and learned. Next, the bishop must be not only a pastor himself, but a leader of pastors. His strong shepherds must want to feed their sheep, not only take their wool and milk, and must be equipped with a crook, a whistle, a stout stick, and a dog—that is, with learning, the ability to captivate, the sense of when to admonish, and the power to protect when wolves circle. More prosaically, the bishop must be an able administrator, who knows how to choose the right people. He must be a steward of all the officials in his diocese. Finally, he must be a plowman or carter, leading from the front, and ensuring that the right animals are yoked to the right machines: it's because God's wagon today is drawn by fat bulls—rich clergy and bishops—that it has overturned and is lying in the mud. Most of all, the bishop must have the right intention in everything he does: honoring God must come before all other considerations of money, position, friendship, or family.

But a bishop could not do everything on his own. As we've seen, Paris was growing fast, and William was running to catch up—acquiring papal agreement to redraw parish lines, seeding new churches and chapels, and refurbishing others. The parish system was creaking in a city with an immigrant population and a lack of tradition. In a university town, and with a cathedral full of canons, there should have been no shortage of helpers, but as we've seen in the case of William of Auxerre, academic brilliance did not always translate into practical pastoral ability. New problems required new solutions, and accordingly, William turned to a new international force of men, who traveled without parish affiliation, who were answerable to the pope, and who specialized in the preaching and penitential ministry that Lateran IV had envisaged. He turned to the mendicants.

The two new orders of mendicant friars ("begging brothers") were strongly associated with their founding figures: the northern Spanish canon, Dominic Guzman (d. 1221), for the Order of Friars Preacher (Preachers, or Dominicans), and the Umbrian merchant's son, Francis of Assisi (d. 1226), for the Order of Friars Minor (Franciscans).[16] Although often spoken of together, they were in many ways unlike, and in fact, it's not at all clear that Francis meant to found any sort of "order" at all. Both were lucky to have slipped through the net of Lateran IV, where anxiety about the proliferation of untried forms of religious life had forbidden any new religious orders.[17] But in the case of both Dominic and Francis, the papacy recognized something that could be useful.

Dominic's vision for his new brothers was of an educated and mobile band trained to preach and hear confessions. Conceived in Toulouse, down near William's part of the world, the Friars Preacher were a response to the heterodox beliefs and diverse population to be found there. Needing skilled men, Dominic quickly set up houses in Bologna, home of Europe's principal law school, and Paris, home to the theologians. He was certainly in Paris for a general chapter in 1220, and it is not impossible that William heard him speak: Dominic is always lauded for his practicality, but he was also a person of immense charisma. Francis's ideal community, in contrast, was a less organized affair. Francis himself was suspicious of excessive study, but if his Friars Minor were to take Christ to the world, then at least some of the brothers believed that must involve higher learning. What the two groups had in common was a commitment to the *vita apostolica*—the life shared by Jesus and his disciples, as depicted in the New Testament. This was not a new ideal: Christians, from the Desert Fathers to the "father of monasticism," St. Benedict of Nursia, had tried to live the Gospel life; they differed, however, in which parts of the Gospel they regarded as most important. By the beginning of the thirteenth century, influenced by the growth and increasing importance of the monetary economy and the mercantile classes, the key characteristics of the apostolic life were increasingly seen as being centered on the renunciation of money, property, and goods. Whereas traditional monastic orders, such as the Benedictines and Cistercians, had forbidden their members from owning anything as individuals, while continuing to hold property in common, the mendicant orders renounced even common ownership. They were to live from day to day, owning nothing and reliant on God to provide.

This conception of a life with Christ was not exclusive to Francis and Dominic. An emphasis on poverty and preaching was a feature of other groups as well, such as the Waldensians and Humiliati, which the papacy regarded with more or less suspicion, often dependent on their willingness to obey Church authority and their attitude to the prevalent social order rather than on their particular theology. Intent on remaining inside the fold, Francis and Dominic convinced the pope that they could fulfill a need, not only by offering a new form of religious life that appealed especially to the commercial middle classes who wanted to step away from the rat race, but also as trained men living under a rule (unlike parish priests) who could be sent anywhere they were needed to plug the gap in the Church's ministry to the urban laity.

Dominic sent a first group of seven friars to Paris in 1217, to study, to preach, and to found a priory.[18] As student and canon, William would surely have watched as, followed by the Franciscans, they worked to establish themselves in the city. For both orders, the decade of the 1220s must have been filled equally with exhilaration and trepidation, fighting to be accepted within the Church, while weathering the death of their magnetic founders, whose loss might easily have spelled the end of their experimental way of life—certainly for the Franciscans, and perhaps even for the more structured Dominicans. It was crucial to the success of both that they be accepted within individual dioceses; Francis makes it plain in his rule that his brothers should not preach except with the agreement of the local ecclesiastical authority. The attitude of the bishop of Paris was a make-or-break issue. It was the city of serious students in theology and the Bible, but it was also a city of teachers; both orders were as keen to poach as they were to learn.

It was not obvious that the mendicants would be welcomed into either the diocese or the university; both had much to lose. A letter of August 1231 from Gregory IX to William, to the archbishop of Tours, and to the archbishop of Rouen details the bad treatment the friars were receiving in France.[19] The brothers were not permitted to reserve the sacrament in their chapels; they could not celebrate mass every day; they could not have a church or bell tower; they could not have a sanctified cemetery within their convent walls; they had to attend local parish processions, say their first mass in the parish church, and be buried there. Their candles, lamps, and church ornaments were all taxed by the surrounding secular clergy, who demanded a proportion ("tithe") of their kitchen garden produce and levied duty on the construction of their houses. They were obliged to come to the diocesan general meeting or synod, and their ministers and guardians had to take an oath of fidelity to the local bishop, if he had not appointed them himself. Those who refused were driven out of the area.

The pope had been a supporter of Francis and his followers (including the women followers led by Clare of Assisi) when he was still simply Ugolino, cardinal bishop of Ostia. He appointed William and the two archbishops as his agents in making sure this harassment stopped. "The Franciscans," he writes, "would from now on turn to them whenever they sensed a cloud on the horizon in any diocese, relying on them for support, help and consolation." Two years later, Gregory wrote to the three men again: "Your care in the matter has been praiseworthy. Zealous of the interests of the faith, you have fulfilled our expectations in completing the mission we gave you. You have defended the Order of Friars Minor, beloved of God, from attack and insult."[20] In 1231, Paris was alive with antimendicant feeling, but William had already proved himself sympathetic to the friars; Gregory must have felt he could rely on him for support.

It's ironic, therefore, that William's attitude to the friars had been demonstrated by deliberately ignoring Gregory's orders. In 1228, announcing his choice of William as bishop, Gregory had sent his glowing reference to the cathedral canons; only a year later he wrote: "we regret having made this man."[21] The falling out came with the strike of university masters and their dispersal from Paris in 1229.[22] During the annual pre-Lenten Carnival, a drunken student attack on a publican and his neighbors was quelled by riot police sent in by Blanche, the queen regent, who it was claimed had been acting on the advice of Bishop William and the papal legate, Romano, cardinal of Sant'Angelo. The uproar had taken place on land belonging to the abbey of Saint-Marcel, and the prior had appealed to William and the legate to restore order; rather than acting on his own, William turned to the queen. The university masters protested the proportionality of the response, which had ended in the death of several students, and, since students were at least nominally clerks in holy orders, they questioned the interference of the state in matters where jurisdiction belonged to the Church. Given that he had so recently been one of their own, the masters must have expected William to take their side, and they were clearly surprised when their protests were ignored. In an attempt to bring matters to a head, the masters (not for the first time) suspended their lectures; but when by Easter their strike had proved less than effective, the majority of masters upped and left, some going to Oxford and Cambridge, some to other French schools, including Toulouse.

Pope Gregory and Louis IX (no longer legally a child, and so able to act as king) sided with the masters, but William and the legate held their ground and refused to mediate, much to the pope's annoyance. He even called William and Philip, the cathedral chancellor, to the papal court; William did not go.[23] It was not until April 1231, more than two years after the initial brawl, that the situation was resolved, when Gregory issued the bull *Parens scientiarum*, confirming and extending the scholars' privileges, which were to be overseen by the chancellor, and laying out the areas of jurisdiction for each of the parties.[24] In practice, this was not to prove as simple as it seemed, and on at least one other occasion the masters complained to the pope that William was acting beyond his jurisdiction. William responded, as he had in 1229, that it was the masters who were ignoring the rules and behaving in ways mainly designed to line their own pockets.

The undoubted winners from all this were the mendicants. The friars were not inclined to side with the university party and go out on strike: Dominican students in Paris were taught in-house by their own master, Roland of Cremona. They stayed on in Paris, under royal protection, with teaching as usual, infuriating the university masters, who saw them as strikebreakers. It may have been as a pragmatic interim solution that William, who as bishop had a duty to provide teaching in his diocese, in 1229 granted Roland the general licence to teach—making Roland of Cremona the first Dominican licensed as a master in the Paris schools, and conversely giving the Paris schools their first Dominican professor. In response to his licence, Roland opened up the Dominican school to nonmendicants, offering the city's students an alternative to their missing masters. The following year, Roland's own teacher, master John of St. Giles, took the Dominican habit midway through preaching a sermon, and was also allowed by William to keep his teaching chair.[25] Shortly afterward, Master Alexander of Hales took the same route to the Franciscans, and William again allowed him to keep his teaching post in theology. By 1231, when the striking masters returned, the mendicants held three of the twelve Paris professorships in theology. This was the beginning of a trend that by 1254 would lead to mendicants dominating theological teaching in Paris, occupying twelve of the fifteen chairs. The masters of this period—the Dominicans Thomas Aquinas and Albert the Great, and the Franciscan Bonaventure, in particular—were among the most eminent scholars of the Middle Ages. We know from remarks by Bonaventure and Roger Bacon that they were present when William took part in theological debates in their school.[26] William's response to the coming of the friars to Paris made their careers possible.

Pope and masters alike were disconcerted by William's failure to support the university against the civil powers. Here was a master who was also a cleric; this was a case of privileged jurisdiction that he himself could claim. But they had misjudged their man. William refused to allow student status to be an excuse for bad behavior. Soon after becoming bishop, in July 1228, he had personally visited the college of Saint-Thomas at the Louvre, where out-of-control students had broken down the canons' door. He ordered that, from now on, scholarships would be held for one year only, with a possibility of renewal only for those vouched to be of good conduct and making progress in their studies.[27] He was particularly awake to the perils of alcohol (another Lateran IV decree). And his sermons repeatedly speak of the need for those under the Church's jurisdiction to set a good example: "Just as king Solomon kept apes, so the Church has layfolk who ape or model themselves on the behavior of clergy. Clerics must, then, beware lest a lay person is caught up in their bad example, trying to walk in bigger shoes."[28] In the mendicants, William thought he had found men after his own heart: educated and serious, as we'll see later, they shared his focus on preaching and poverty.

Lateran IV had also forbidden clergy to hold more than one paid position in the Church.[29] The accumulation of such posts or "benefices," a practice known as pluralism, had been condemned long before 1215, but papal dispensations meant that the condemnation had often been observed in the breach. William was determined to root pluralism out of his diocese, calling a meeting of the Paris theology masters in 1235 and again in 1238 to discuss the issue. He could not himself make rules for the wider Church, but if he could get the massed ranks of the theologians to agree to what constituted pluralism and to support his campaign, he would have powerful support. The first meeting was not unanimous, but by 1238 he had won: the masters agreed that no cleric could hold a second benefice if his first was worth more than fifteen Parisian pounds.[30]

William's first attempt had been frustrated by two dissenters, one a Master Arnald, and the other his longstanding colleague, Philip, the cathedral chancellor, who held at least one other post elsewhere. Although William's arguments persuaded neither man, both were out of the picture by the end of 1236, Arnald leaving to become bishop of Amiens, and Philip dying just before Christmas. Philip's opposition to William on the issue was ferocious. His role as chancellor involved oversight of the texts used at cathedral services, and as well as being a prolific preacher he was the author of more than eighty poetic works, almost all of which were set to music. At least two of these, *The Hypocrites, the Bogus Bishops* (*Ypocrite, pseudo-pontificos*) and *In Truth I Have Discovered That the Entire Clergy Is Given Over to Wickedness* (*In veritate comperi*) seem to have been directed against William personally, given lines like this: "They scrutinize every single purse and hiding place before their eyes." The antagonism may have dated back to William's appointment as bishop, since one of the candidates whose election William had overturned was Philip's own nephew.[31]

According to a contemporary source, the Dominican Thomas of Cantimpré, William was present as Philip was dying. He urged him, for the good of his immortal soul, to resign his additional posts and pay back the money from his own wealth. Philip refused, offering instead an experiment: he would die in possession of the benefices, and then they would see whether a pluralist really was damned. Thomas then recounts an early-morning scene in William's private chapel: the lamp dims, and a ghostly figure appears. "Are you from God?" William asks. "No; although he made me, I am cut off from him." It is, of course, Philip, condemned to eternal punishment—because his personal conduct was a scandal and a stumbling block to the faithful; because he did not give away his excess wealth; and because, against better judgment, he had retained his many benefices.[32] If we read him right, it was a fate William himself barely escaped. He recalls a time when "a friend of ours" was charged by a bishop to find "a good man" to fill a vacant position, and offered it to William.[33] A worried William reminded his friend that the bishop could not act beyond his authority, which was to offer the job to "a good man," which put William out of the frame. By the grace of God, says Thomas, he avoided the fate of a pluralist.

The decrees of Lateran IV were the "to do" list for William's episcopacy, with the sole exception, perhaps, of the desire for Crusade and the recovery of the Holy Land, which was attached to the main document as a long, final codicil.[34] He seems to have had little taste for military expeditions; indeed, according to Valois, although he was frequently called upon as an informal arbitrator for ecclesiastical disagreements, in his own diocese William delegated to others those judgments which could not be decided amicably.[35]

In 1231 the pope employed William and Walter of Cornut, archbishop of Sens, as his representatives in the peace negotiations between France and England.[36] Asked by Gregory IX in 1229 to bring men to support the the pope against Emperor Frederick II, William instead sent only money.[37] In 1225–26 William had watched from Paris the suffering of both sides in the so-called Albigensian Crusade, organized by Louis VIII to rid William's southern homeland of its infestation of heretics. This dismal episode ended in deaths on both sides, including that of the king himself, whose reign had hardly begun. William is known to have been an advisor and friend to Louis's widow, Blanche of Castile, but he may even have known the queen much earlier, since Blanche cultivated a circle of her fellow Spaniards and those who enjoyed the culture of the southern Mediterranean.[38] The queen's intense grief at Louis's death may have cemented William's preference for peaceful resolutions. Even when dealing with a king as eager for Crusade as Blanche's son, Louis IX, William was not to be convinced. In 1244, he was at Louis's bedside as the king regained consciousness from a fever that had taken him to death's door. Louis asked William to receive his vow that, should he recover, he would go on Crusade. After initial refusals, William gave in, so as to quell Louis's agitation, telling him (according to a contemporary source) that when he was properly well again, he would think back on the request, take advice, and change his mind. Louis, however, was not to be moved, to the extent that, in 1247, William—supported by Blanche and Louis's brothers—told the king that he must have lost the use of his senses when he made the vow; to leave for the East would turn his kingdom upside down. Unwilling to listen, Louis threatened a hunger strike if he couldn't have his own way.[39]

"All good people," William says, "are either penitents, or monastics, or peacemakers."[40] In a sermon to priests he is equally clear. God expects three things from his clergy: the fruits of their hands in consecrating the Eucharist and anointing the sick with the oil of unction; the fruits of their mouth, by making more Christians when they preach his word. But primarily, God requires the fruit of their lips, which should always be speaking of peace and reconciliation. "The lips of priests should be peacemakers, for they should secure peace among the people—I speak of the peace of reconciliation from enmity."[41] In Philip—and doubtless, others—William made enemies; his quick tongue and sometimes intemperate language, the impatience with "fools" that often leaps off the page, can't have made him universally liked. As bishop, however, he believed his job was to make peace.

6

LANGUAGE

Caught in the web of words . . .

William's language is what makes reading him unlike reading any other medieval scholar. He has an extraordinary way with words. They spill out from his pages and gather in corners, chattering; they open a window that looks back through centuries to a city stuffed with life. Do they really allow us to know him, or does the language construct a world that he wanted to project, but which never really existed? In this chapter we'll look at William's own remarkable, tangy use of language, his views on the importance of preaching, his belief in language as a way to God, and his idiosyncratic humor.

The most vivid encounters with language are to be had in William's preaching. Almost 600 of his sermons survive, according to their tireless modern editor, Franco Morenzoni, and they are a marvelous resource, preserved in a form unlike other medieval homiletic collections.[1] Medieval sermons have generally come down to us as edited collections, either from a single author, or as multi-author gatherings sorted by subject, by scriptural text or time of the Church year, or even by audience.[2] They were generally intended for use as models: less-gifted preachers could learn from, or even simply copy, the work of skillful practitioners. Like Cicero's letters or speeches, what remains to us now is a deliberate confection that others could imitate or utilize for their own needs. That's not what we have with William; instead, the vast majority appear to be a copy of William's working notes for his own use. This gives us a delicious opportunity to catch the sound of William's preaching voice and to get a sense of his working method. With texts or ideas he knows very well, he doesn't write things out in full; he just reminds himself what to do next. At the start of a sermon on the Good Samaritan, for instance, he writes, "Tell the tale" (*Narra historiam*). One such rubric is particularly ambitious: "Tell the whole story of the Gospel." As he moves through a sermon, William uses similar "notes to self," such as "go through this point by point," or "continue along these lines." Thus, some parts of a sermon are written out in detail, while others are just bullet points.[3] This accounts in part for the varying length of the sermons—the longest being around twenty pages, while the shortest are barely half a page—with an average sermon four or five pages long in the modern edition. The length also depends on the complexity of the argument; for bits of the Bible he can expound on autopilot, he hardly needs a note; for others with longer biblical passages, or where he is led from text to text, he is more careful to note the path of his thinking and write out his "script" in full.

The language of the sermons is utterly distinctive, as is his employment of similitudes or analogies to draw spiritual lessons from everyday life. Many medieval sermons use "exempla"—little moralizing stories that could be inserted as needed or appropriate; this is not William's way. His method is to bring the complexities of Christian theology down to the realities of daily life—*which kind* of daily life was dependent on his audience. He might describe the devil as an innkeeper, or portray God leading a limping donkey, or recall a bird drinking from a holy water stoup in a church, to show his hearers that everything they knew and saw around them was part of a life of faith. In all his writings, William's language is immediate, vivid, and down to earth. It finds the mystery of faith in the everyday:

> The concrete, equally, may become a vehicle of mystery, beauty and depth, a path into the emotions, the imagination, the spirit . . . The concrete is readily imbued with feeling and meaning—more readily, perhaps, than any abstract conception. It readily moves into the aesthetic, the dramatic, the comic, the symbolic, the whole wide deep world of art and spirit.[4]

These words of the twentieth-century neurologist, Oliver Sacks, could easily have been written by William. They sum up his view of God's creation, and of the language he can use to explore it.

The sermons are written in Latin, but most would have been preached in the vernacular, to suit the audience. William regularly includes Gallic words or phrases in the text, often introduced by something like "as is commonly said" (*ut vulgo dicitur*) or simply "*gallice*." Elsewhere he turns a French word into Latin, declining or conjugating accordingly. Sometimes these gallicisms are a translation of what he is trying to say—reminding himself how he will express the Latin word when he comes to preach it—and sometimes they are things that he perhaps never had to say in his Latin life—types of horse or cooking pot, or the word for women's makeup. As we've already seen, William must have been at least quadrilingual—at home in his native Auvergnat dialect, in Occitan, in the Gallic French of Paris, and in Latin; and this multilingualism is reflected in his constant interest in the power of language as a gift of God. An example from *The Universe of Creatures* is drawn from "the vernacular Spanish," and involves multiple meanings for the same word: William's southern upbringing may have given him a smattering of Spanish, or he may have picked up some knowledge in Paris, since Queen Blanche of Castile liked to surround herself with compatriots.[5] And he's aware of the difficulties of translating ideas from one language to another: although he shows no sign of knowing Greek, he suggests at one point that Aristotle's meaning might be clearer in the original and "is other than our Latin usage expresses."[6]

Much is about tone. William often employs common proverbs and sayings—more than a hundred, according to Morenzoni—some still in use today: "pearls before swine," "castles in Spain," "a pig in a poke," "the cat that got the cream," "what the eye doesn't see, the heart doesn't grieve for," and a favorite, "love me, love my dog."[7] These are generally quoted in Latin, but surely all had vernacular equivalents. His spontaneous shifting between languages is one of the things that makes the sermons striking, because of the strong impression it gives of his desire to communicate. William wants to make contact with his hearers, and he'll use every trick he can to do that. It's a way, as Morenzoni rightly notes, of establishing a kind of cultural complicity with his hearers—of breaching the "fourth wall" between the pulpit and the pew. Was he successful—or did he come across as modern vicars often do when they try to sound "in touch" or "down with the kids"? Alas, we cannot know—no accounts of William preaching survive—but it's certainly a far cry from the complaint of his Dominican contemporary, Hugh of St. Cher, about clergy who insist on preaching in Latin to show off their knowledge, when few in the congregation would understand or, vice versa, about congregations who wanted Latin sermons, whether or not they understood them, because it made them feel clever.[8]

No matter how many were in the audience, William addresses them in the singular form of "you" (*tu*). Just as the biblical Ten Commandments are framed in that singular form of the verb, so William uses the *tu* form to make it clear that the words he speaks, and the lessons of Christianity, are aimed at every single person who's listening. When he addresses the audience as a type—"Oh, sinner," "Oh, brother," "Oh, Christian"—this too is in the singular form, the only common exception being his closing perorations to "brothers" (*fratres*), when preaching to fellow clergy, monks, or perhaps even university scholars.

As bishop, William encouraged the activities of the mendicant Franciscan and Dominican Orders, known for their new form of pastoral preaching, in his diocese. Morenzoni has suggested that it was William's own preaching style that influenced the Paris mendicants and set the course for their own well-documented use of proverbs, stories, and colorful language.[9] We know from contemporary sources that Francis of Assisi had his own unorthodox preaching style, whether it be the circle of ash he silently drew for the sisters at San Damiano, or his dancing in the open air proclaiming the love of God. This was preaching in a new way; so judging what influence William might have had on the Paris brothers is not so simple. What's clearly true is the weight both he and they laid on the activity of preaching, along with the importance of responding to a particular audience and speaking to them in terms they would understand.

In many sermons to preachers William emphasizes the solemnity of their calling. Over and over again, William speaks of the preacher as the mouth of God. For the mouth to speak well, it must be filled by God, which requires humility and learning. To be filled by God is to be filled with love; and the nature of the human heart is that its size is only restricted by the amount of love it contains. Without love and compassion, the preacher becomes the mouth of the devil. But it is impossible for the love of God to be without joy.[10] Michèle Mulchahey memorably employed Hugh of St. Cher's phrase, "first the bow is bent in study and then the arrow is loosed in preaching," as the title of her book on Dominican education.[11] The bow and arrow (taken from the story of Esau the hunter, in Genesis 27) make regular appearances in William's sermons, although with a slightly different exegesis, or interpretation. For William, the preacher is the bow and doctrine is the arrow. No matter how true in itself, the arrow cannot fly straight unless the bow is sound. "You [*Tu*] expend many arrows in preaching," he says. "How many wild beasts have you brought back to the Father?" A preacher needs to have washed his lips in confession; to have the fear of God; and to be serious and mature, so he won't be laughed at. He must be free from the poison of gossip and speaking ill of others. And when he has these personal qualities, the preacher must be trained, for some men wish to shoot without a bow—a reference to heretical sects in which the laity could preach? The figure of the bow is itself then taken apart: the bow is the preacher's intention, his heart, made up of the wood of rectitude and the string of compassion. Without these, the bow will fire the arrow backward toward the archer, because preaching will simply be vanity. But when all is ready, then the preacher burns with fire, shooting shining sparks, for the Holy Spirit is given in tongues of fire.

The bow and arrow metaphor is reworked in several ways: God's bow is the preacher's heart, which must go regularly and willingly to God for renewal. Without this renewal, in confession, the arrows will be like the toy arrows children shoot, unable to do any damage to the old enemy, who will seize the bow for his own use. But in the hands of God, a proper preacher will terrorize the evil one and put him to flight. More generally, William frequently distinguishes between the curved and the straight. As the properly loosed arrow flies in a straight line, not a curve, so too your will, your beliefs, your loves, your intention, or your focus on God can all hold to a straight line or be bent out of shape: "he's bent, the man who does good works only for his own good, careless of the glory of God or the good of his neighbor."[12]

Gossip, backbiting, and detraction: these sins of the tongue go directly against the purpose for which God created language. Talk was central to medieval religion: it had brought the whole of creation into being. "God said . . . and there was . . ." is how Genesis describes the making of the known universe, from the creation of time to the creation of human beings; when all is done, God has Adam give names—words—to everything he has made. For Christians, this centrality was even clearer. God had sent his only Son in the form of a human being, but his true name according to John's Gospel was the Word (*Logos*, in the original Greek). God had sent his Word so that all who heard it might live. To the early Church this knowledge was in the nature of a command; it was their duty to make sure that the Word was heard. Belief in God was no longer something you were largely born to, which came as part of belonging to a tribe or a people. The "chosen people" was a group you could join, when you had heard the Word of God. Just as Jesus had traveled the roads of Israel, talking about God to anyone who would listen, so from the beginning Christianity became a missionizing religion, preaching the Good News of the Messiah who had come to give life to everyone who would follow, wherever they had started out. For William, entry to that life was effected through the words of baptism; it was supported by the words that turned the bread and wine of the Eucharist into the body and blood of Christ; and it was completed at death, when the priest spoke the commendation of a soul to God. It meant that language was divine, and the use of language was a gift that should be used with care.

It was a gift that entailed an indissoluble link between language and truth, a question discussed at length by Augustine of Hippo. Augustine argued that hand in hand with the power of speech came a responsibility to speak the truth—or rather, the Truth—for God's whole purpose in creating language was that humans should use it to praise him. What exactly constituted truth was a complicated question, and Augustine addressed it at least in part by two treatises on the nature of lying.[13] His definition of lying, his classification of lies into eight types, and his discussion of intention and deception were highly influential for subsequent medieval conceptions of language.[14] Not-lying was in itself not enough; words should be used for good, a sentiment William echoes in a sermon: "Woe to those lawyers and their like who misuse their knowledge of letters and speaking, all of which they have from God, by attacking poor people and encouraging unjust litigation and suchlike."[15]

Language was a gift given only to human beings. Its importance is such that William claims we can tell that crows and ravens have more perfect and noble souls than other animals, because of their ability to learn to speak: "For their souls come very close to rational [human] souls, as is shown by the human speech that they acquire as a result of long association with human beings and by a cleverness in borrowing and lending and certain other things."[16] The intelligence of the avian corvids, which modern research affirms, is demonstrated for William by their capacity for linguistic mimicry. "Notice that it is natural for an intellect, as is obvious in us, to speak and generate words. It is not content with its own proper interior speech, but also speaks in external and exterior words through the body . . . [I]t is the mark of the most intelligent to speak the most and of the most perfectly intelligent to speak the most perfectly . . . Make sense, if you can, of an intellectual power in act and in silence. With us this is surely impossible."[17]

Human language is itself only a mimicry of the perfect language of God. Creation is the exterior word given shape and existence by the interior word in the mind of God. As an image of that interior word, it conveys an image of the Creator.[18] It's for this reason that, in one of William's favorite images, the world is a book, in whose words we can read the image of God, as long as we realize that the words are not the speaker himself. Creation begins, from necessity and from eternity, with the single generative word by which God the Father gives birth to God the Son, the exemplification of God's creative intellect and the exemplar of what will be created exteriorly by both.[19] This Son who is God's Word is

> an utterance living in the ultimate degree of life and vitality . . . an outpouring and overflowing in the ultimate degree of outpouring and overflow . . . For an utterance of another sort could not be the first utterance, that is, of the first speaker.[20]

God creates the whole universe through a single act of speaking, such is the potency of his utterance. Although "the utterance of the

Creator is one in the ultimate degree of oneness," that word contains the multiplicity of all that is and all that is not, without confusion or mixture.[21] William's analogy is to an army trumpeter sounding an order to the troops:

> Though that sound is but one or single, so many and so manifold and varied ranks in the army go forth as a result of this sound. At the single sound of the trumpet some run to erect machines; some run to weapons of defense; others to weapons of attack. Some hasten or prepare to dig under walls; others to fill trenches; some to positions of fighting or crafts. Thus, by one sign given to the soldiers by the leader such diverse activity is found in the soldiers and other warriors. In the same way, when the Creator speaks once and emits, as it were, the single ineffable spiritual sound of his speech, the universe of natural products goes forth in the world, as if the universe of creatures heard his word. For if, by the one will or intention of the one king or prince who intends to take or storm some castle or city, so great a multitude of effects and instruments goes forth in the army or in the siege of that castle, or if this happens by one word by which he commands his army to storm that castle, why is it surprising if by the word of the omnipotent Creator, though it is one in every way, the countless variety of effects goes forth in the world?[22]

The aptness of the analogy illuminates his argument about creation, and the richness of the description sheds light on warfare and command. William's use of language for analysis and explanation is typical of his idiosyncratic and imaginative approach to teaching about God.

He's acutely aware, however, of the inadequacy of trying to use a human understanding of grammar to talk about God, even though he frequently resorts to the rules of grammar and the knowledge of grammarians as "a key to the structure of being."[23] For instance, although it's traditional, he says, to refer to the Trinity in the neuter gender as "it," but to the first and second persons of the Trinity in the masculine gender as Father and Son, and with the pronoun "he," these terms are attempts to represent our understanding of the relationships and modes of being: "they are not vacuous or empty words or modes of speaking, as some have said in their folly"—which is probably a reference to the group of twelfth-century scholars known as Nominalists—"but the truest signs of the truest of things, provided we hold fast to the fact that it is not as yet certain how it can be truthfully and faithfully said that there are both one and many things in God."[24] The entirety of God is not only incommunicable to any created thing, but has an essential incommunicability—a careful linguistic distinction, made by taking part of a verb or adjective (here, "incommunicable") and turning it into a substantive noun ("incommunicability"), that is characteristic of William's manipulation of language.[25] We can see the problem again when he explains that God is not merely omnipotent but is essentially and substantively omnipotent, an idea conveyed by a quotation from Exodus: "Omnipotent is his name."[26] The paradoxical structure of the Christian Trinity was a struggle for all theologians, and it was made more difficult by the binding grammatical rules of the inflected Latin language, where adjectives, nouns, and adjectival verb forms all have to "agree" in gender, number, and case.[27] If the word "omnipotent" here is simply an adjective, it would have to agree with its subject (the three persons of the Trinity) and be written in the masculine plural form; but although comprised of three persons, the Trinity itself is singular and neuter (an "it")—a formulation William takes from the creed that begins the canons of the Fourth Lateran Council.[28] And since an adjective cannot rightly *name* a word, but only describe it, "omnipotent" cannot be a name of God. The easiest way to get round this linguistic problem would be for William to create a new word, the substantive noun, "omnipotentness," from the adjective "omnipotent." Despite his verbal creativity elsewhere, however, he is unwilling to do it here:

> This sort of use as a substantive is neither necessary for us, nor should we accept it, for we should avoid every bad appearance and avoid not only being disproved but also seeming to be disproved. When the words we use are sufficient for us to express our intentions, it is quite pointless to assert and make up new words. No expression is so clearly and obviously false that no true signification can be given it; nonetheless, we who were commanded by the Apostle "Keep free from profane novelties in speech" [1 Tim. 6:20], should not [make up new words].[29]

Instead, William proposes to use "omnipotent three," so he can stay within the bounds of both language and orthodoxy. Although in other places he is happy to engineer new words from old ones when they suit him, here he shies away, perhaps because he wants to prove the truth of the Trinity in common terms, without having to resort to neologisms.[30] It matters to him that language as it is ordinarily and widely understood can correctly express God.

The problem of finding words for God takes on even more significance in the light of William's interest in the works of Aristotle, especially as mediated through the Arab scholar, Avicenna. Roland Teske has convincingly argued that William's definition of God, in the sense of how God should properly be named, changes with his reading of Avicenna's *Liber de philosophia prima*.[31] Rather than employ the expression that God taught Moses, *Ego sum qui sum* ("I am he who is," or "I am who I am"), which was common to Judeo-Christian theology, William states that:

> Aristotle and all his followers . . . correctly named [the first principle] "being necessary through itself" [*necesse esse per se*] . . . Being necessary through itself is its proper nomination.[32]

This phrasing doesn't occur in William's early writings from the 1220s, such as *The Trinity*; but ten or fifteen years later, when he is finishing *The Universe of Creatures*, it has become his common usage, and despite his reference to Aristotle, it comes directly from Avicenna. He lines up further with Avicenna when he commonly refers to God simply as *Primus*, "The First," a stripped-back appellation that reflects his attempt to find the simplest correct way of speaking about God. Both usages fit in with his method in these treatises, which is to argue as far as possible from reason alone, without the use of Scripture or other knowledge revealed to believers by God.

In addition to these particular borrowings, the philosopher Étienne Gilson argued that William adopted Avicenna's style of argument—a continuous building up of material, rather than the scholastic question-and-answer form, directed very personally to the reader, and with frequent digressions, carefully signposted, from the main argument.[33] It's certainly true that these are all features of William's writing, and are part of what makes him so distinctive among thirteenth-century scholars. Peter Biller accurately characterizes the effect: "It is difficult to convey to anyone who has not read both William of Auvergne and contemporaries, such as William of Auxerre, writing within strict and constricting forms, the extraordinary air of freedom which blows through William of Auvergne's prose."[34] His theological treatises, such as *The Trinity,* aim at philosophical rigor, but maintain a personal quality. He is very present in the language, often referring to himself as the proponent of the text: "I say, therefore"; "You have heard from me"; "I reply to this"; "I told you before." And as noted at the beginning of this chapter, he speaks to his reader as "you" in singular forms of the Latin: "you ought to consider" (*considerandum est* tibi); "my soul and yours" (*animam meam et* tuam); "for you, however, to know the face" (*faciam tamen* te *scire*).[35] This technique lends a striking immediacy even to the complexities of Trinitarian theology or the problems of the soul. He may have taken it from Avicenna, but as we saw earlier, he could also have learned it from the Bible.

William's place in the history of scholasticism situates him just before the overwhelming triumph of the *summa* form, in which topics were dealt with by raising and solving problems in linked series of questions. This way of working was taken up by scholars such as his contemporary, William of Auxerre, in his *Golden Summa* (*Summa aurea*), and *summae* became the signature works of the thirteenth century.[36] The title *Golden Summa* gives a sense of how popular and influential William of Auxerre's achievement was; but though we can admire his comprehensive organization and knowledge of sources, reading this William, as Biller noted, is a much more distant and constrained experience than reading "our William." William of Auvergne chooses not to proceed according to this dialectical method. Instead, he prefers a narrative style, with argument piled upon argument, often linked simply by the word *amplius* (literally, "more"). Once again, he may have taken his lead from Avicenna, but the narrative exposition of theological ideas dated back to the early Church Fathers. What he certainly has in common with Avicenna, however, is his delight in digression, and his noting of the return to the main argument. This allows him space to expand on some subjects, while keeping the main aim in sight. After pausing to visit a beauty spot off the beaten track, he returns to the main road of the argument, alerting his reader that he is taking up again where he left off: "Meanwhile, I shall return to the point from which

I digressed at the occasion of this question"; "After this I shall return to the point where I was."[37] And unlike many medieval writers, William generally does keep faith with his overall structure, knows a digression when he sees it, and remembers to return to the highway.[38]

All written language is an encoding of speech. In some circumstances this renders writing a poor relation to oral communication, when inflection, pitch, and other nonverbal cues are lost. Nowhere is this more the case than with humor, and it is with trepidation that I end this chapter trying to persuade you that William is funny. Few things are harder than spotting a joke from another age; changed sensibilities mean that genuine laughs from the past—without having to be explained—are few and far between. A few things, often pictorial, are universal—a bored face sketched in the margin of a manuscript, or a giant snail chasing a knight in armor—but literary humor is much less easy to be sure of. Worse still is trying to find humor in the writings of clergy, since jokes from the pulpit are almost never funny, no matter what the date; most come with an invisible giant arrow reading, "laugh here."

But for all his belief in eternal damnation, William knows that "a smile transforms your face."[39] Asked how he remembered so many quips, he said he never heard one without writing it down or committing it to memory.[40] Sometimes this is clear in his slapstick humor and wordplay; more generally it's just an underlying tendency to see life from the funny side. He uses humor as a way of making contact with his hearers or readers, of linking to a shared human condition, and as a means of fixing what he says in the memory. Leaving a dinner, a certain nobleman (is he drunk?) leans over too far, loses his balance, and falls into a latrine—perhaps just a ditch at the side of the road.[41] Utterly ashamed at being covered in filth, he determines not to try to get out—he'll just give up and die there. His friends, "many noble men," are horrified; to save him, they all jump in, too. United in squalor, they can persuade him to climb out with them.[42] The story is an allegory of the penitent sinner: if you've fallen into sin, don't just stay there, don't be too ashamed to ask for help: we're all in this together. And don't, he adds, despise those who get down into the gutter to help out those already there.

It's the way he tells 'em, of course, rather than the words on paper. Painting a picture, using his voice, comic timing, the pause, the nod, the wink . . . then turning a joke into a lesson, without seeming to be too heavy, losing the atmosphere and the moment. The story also illustrates one of William's characteristics, in that it doesn't demonize one group at the expense of another. The poor folks in the congregation can laugh at the fate of the toff, but nobles come out of this well, too; and don't make fun of those trying to help, either. We start out laughing at the proud man in the latrine, but we end up ruefully smiling at ourselves. In several sermons, William's protagonist is a cleric who should know better—he's making fun of himself, or people just like him.[43] In his treatise *On the Virtues*, he appears to pun on the similarity in Latin between the name for the underworld or hell, "Avernus," and his own Auvergne, "Alvernus" or "Arvenus": "the descent to Avernus is easy," he warns.[44] His love of wordplay is clear even in the story where he's bested by a man to whom he's given ten pounds to marry a prostitute—a *Fille Dieu*, or Daughter of God—to save her from sin. Instead, abandoning the woman at the cathedral, the scoundrel goes off to splash the cash. Meeting William later, he tells him not to worry about her: she's at her grandmother's house—Notre-Dame![45]

Don't give your heart to your stomach, or you'll leave your worldly goods in the latrine.[46] The latrine of luxury, or lechery, is one of William's favorite images, tied in with the colorful language of the senses. In a sermon to nuns, William ends with one of his favorite themes: bad habits will turn human beings into beasts. If you're greedy, you can all too soon become a pig; if you're angry, a dog; lazy, a donkey, and so on. The Lord doesn't cheerfully hear the croaking of frogs, the grunting of pigs, the braying of donkeys, the roaring of lions, the hiss of snakes.[47] Standing in front of the sisters, in full episcopal rig, William ends his sermon making animal noises. Could they believe their ears? Did they dare to laugh out loud? Whatever their reaction, for the nuns, as for the modern reader, the occasion—and the message—must have been unforgettable.

7

KNOWING

I respect faith, but doubt is what gets you an education.

The default state of human beings is joy. Humanity should be joyful because its ultimate end is a life of eternal blessedness in the presence of God: "the state of natural rest of our souls is blessedness," for "the usefulness of every usefulness and the fruit of all fruits is eternal happiness."[1] This is God's intention for all creation, and that knowledge puts in the shade any of this life's transitory pain and suffering, and gives perspective to worldly desires and values. "This joy is an almost continuous serenity of the heart from the presence of God who dwells in it, which even adversity does not cloud or obscure . . . and you will find it in many holy men whose countenances are always happy and joyful."[2] Bear in mind, however, that joy is not always easy to recognize. "For this joy is something serious that does not turn into laughter": in line with a long philosophical and theological tradition, William distinguishes easy laughter, which springs from superficial pleasures—or, worse, the misfortunes of others—from the grave depths of joy.[3] Confusingly, joy can arise from the recognition that you are a sinner: "and you will generally find in holy men that their countenance never glows with a more pleasant splendor than when the grace of compunction embitters their hearts and floods their faces with tears."[4]

Since for Christians this joy entailed knowledge of Christ, how could William be sure that it was equally available to everyone? How could those who had died before Christ was born, or who inhabited lands not yet reached by the Gospel message, respond to the Word of God? William is convinced that God would never ask the impossible, and he agrees with Augustine that God had therefore provided a variety of ways of recognizing the right path, even for those with no knowledge of Scripture, including the direct revelation of truth to any individual.[5] That was not an unusual view; an all-merciful God must surely give the whole of creation the opportunity to recognize and worship their Creator, "because it is not possible to come to eternal happiness by walking, flying, swimming, or by any other action than by the services of the most sacred worship . . . nor by any other path than by his pure and most immaculate religion."[6] Where William is in a minority, however, is his belief in the importance of explaining the fundamentals of the Christian God and creation in ways that might satisfy nonbelievers, or those who were skeptical of the Bible as an unchallengeable textbook of truth.[7] Of course, he most often preached to the converted—literally, in the case of his hundreds of surviving sermons—but they weren't his only audience, at least in his own mind.

We can see his sense of a dual audience in the massive seven-part work that sits at the center of his academic achievement, the *Magisterium divinale et sapientiale*.[8] The title is difficult to translate with the nuance of the Latin, but Teske's "Teaching on God in the Mode of Wisdom" rightly conveys the sense that William is as interested in *how* this teaching is done ("in the mode of wisdom") as in what is taught ("on God"). The *Magisterium* is William's version of a *summa theologiae*—those works of summary and summation that became the archetypal product of thirteenth-century learning. William's university career was just too early to catch the wave of this sort of writing: he stands at a sort of hinge point between the expository treatises of the twelfth century and the fully question-and-answer practices of the thirteenth.[9] So baldly stated, this is too broad-brush a distinction between the products of the twelfth-century schools and those of the thirteenth-century university, since some earlier scholars—notably the three Peters, Peter Abelard, Peter Lombard, and Peter of Poitiers—had addressed theological material by collating authoritative opinions (in Latin, *sententiae*) on an ordered series of questions; and they in turn were following the lead of the school of Anselm of Laon which taught not only by lecture-commentary on the Bible, but also by seminar-type considerations of specific individual issues. And for their part, the thirteenth-century scholars still continued to write commentaries on Scripture. But the needs and demands of Parisian students of the 1250s were different from those of the 1150s—and that change is reflected in the characteristic output of each era. William was a highly respected thinker in his time, but his scholarly reputation did not really survive his death. For all the originality, philosophical skill, theological sensitivity, and sheer verve of his writing, the fact that it did not fit easily into a single mold, particularly the thirteenth-century preference for a dialectical, question-and-answer method of proceeding, is surely an important reason for his subsequent obscurity in succeeding generations; his questions were harder to shoehorn into the template that the increasingly professionalized academy had constructed.

William's work falls into no single camp; he blazes his own trail. The *Magisterium* was written over the whole course of his career, from around 1223 to the early 1240s; we know from internal references that the individual sections were not written in the final order, and that he went back and revised at some points. Like the liberal arts that made up his early education, the *Magisterium* is made up of seven substantial treatises, although we can't be sure whether this had always been his plan, or whether the design evolved as he completed each of the separate treatises. He had an idea of at least a "first teaching" (or "part") of the whole thing, though he doesn't say how many other parts there were in total. We can puzzle it out by looking at his working method for each of the treatises—at how he intends to make his arguments and impart knowledge to his readers. This gives us a first section consisting of *The Trinity*, *The Universe of Creatures*, and *The Soul*, followed by a second section comprising the short treatise *Why God Became Man* (which included its attendant work, *On Grace*), and finishing with a third section, once again of three parts, *On Faith and the Laws*, *On the Sacraments*, and *On Virtues and Vices*. The first section, then, deals with God and images of God in creation and in the soul, which is the image of God in nature—the theological underpinning of faith. The third section recounts the laws, support, and norms of behavior that God offers to those whose aim is to join him in heaven. In between, looking back to belief and forward to praxis, is the keystone of the Christian religion, the incarnation, addressed through that most difficult question, *Why God Became Man*. Medieval texts were not structured to build to a final climax, but instead often placed the most important points at the center of things, which is the design that we have here: a single work made of seven parts, divided as three, one, three. Seven, three, and one, all prime numbers, were thought in the Middle Ages to signify an inner power. For medieval scholars, this was not a matter of magic or superstition, but rather a recognition that God had made number as well as words, and indeed that, whereas the meaning of words could be slippery, number was stable and easier to grasp. The Bible brims with significant numbers, and in one, three, and seven we have the unity and trinity of God, the three visitors to Abraham, the three days between crucifixion and resurrection, the three denials of Peter, and the wholeness and completion represented by the seven days of creation, seven last words of Christ on the Cross, and seven gifts of the Holy Spirit, among many other possible examples.[10] Considerations of number as well as words were hardwired into an educated medieval view of the world, beginning with the liberal arts *quadrivium* of arithmetic, geometry, music, and astronomy. By structuring his masterwork as a pattern of 3–1–3, William ties it to the strongest numerical powers.

The purpose of this gigantic text is principally to impart knowledge of God, not for the sake of knowledge by itself, but so that God "may be exalted and acknowledged to be God and Lord of the ages and that human souls may be persuaded or rather convinced to honor and worship him," and in addition that "errors by which one is turned from the ways of truth or paths of rectitude, through which one comes to this end" of worshipping God, shall be destroyed.[11] But how can the necessary knowledge be attained? In the prologue to *The Trinity*, which seems to function as an introduction to the whole *Magisterium*, William lists three separate ways.[12] The first is by prophecy or revelation, by which he means not that you must be a prophet or mystic yourself, but that you believe those who were, in most cases through the medium of the Scriptures. This is the most common means to knowledge, and useful for both the learned and unlearned. The second way to knowledge is by obedience to the dictates of religion, acting purely from faith that this will please God.

This sort of knowing is a greater aid to salvation than the first, because it requires a sincere subjugation of your own will to God's law. Both these first two types come as a divine gift. The third way of knowing is via proofs and inquiry. This is the way of those who philosophize, and is the least preferable of the three, because it appeals only to the learned, who can use it to discover their errors, and it leaves the unlearned in the dark.

It might seem surprising, then, that William declares that his mode of procedure in the *Magisterium* will be predominantly this third way, the way of proofs and inquiries, even though he has made it clear he thinks little of those who require this sort of argument and certainty. It's not because of any inherent superiority of method or result that he undertakes to argue in this way—indeed, "belief of this sort, that is, belief persuaded and incited by proofs, has no merit or favor before God"—but it is the only method that will satisfy those whose usual way to understand the world is to philosophize, and "in going along with their customary procedure, we shall try to satisfy them."[13] In fact, he's contemptuous toward those who need this kind of definite knowledge, rather than relying on their own understanding, like a lover whose love is dependent on the changeable characteristics of his beloved rather than on the virtue of his own steadfast commitment.[14] This sort of understanding, which believes because of persuasive arguments or proofs, walks like someone bent over or limping, needing these proofs for support, rather than his own faith, "like an unbelieving merchant who only believes a buyer if he gives him a pledge, guarantee, or security . . . But you know that the exaction of a pledge or other guarantee is only because of the smallness or feebleness of belief or because of the lack of it."[15] Those who "intend to approach God by the path of proofs and signs alone, even if they somehow make progress philosophically in this sort of knowledge, rightly give God an insult by such a belief of theirs, fall away and are repelled further from religion, and are deprived of the loftier kind of knowledge. For one knows in a loftier, nobler, and absolutely more certain way by virtue than by art": the mode of wisdom is greater than the mode of proofs. William isn't condemning philosophers as such here, only those who have no idea that philosophy has a purpose other than knowledge and argument for its own sake. They learn, not in order to glorify their Creator or for the reward of eternal happiness, but simply in order to know: "I reject such persons," he declares, as "not genuine philosophers, but most ridiculous apes of philosophers, which is what they really are."[16]

Nevertheless, the *Magisterium* will have failed if it cannot address these philosophers on their own terms; he has to play them at their own game and win. "Understand, then, that in all these particular treatises, I do not use the testimony of any law, nor is it my intention to build on received wisdom, either generally known or believed by people through testimonies [of faith], but [to argue] through unbreakable proofs."[17] In the first part of the *Magisterium*, therefore, which presents the three treatises that deal with the theological fundamentals of the faith, describing and analyzing the nature of God, of creation, and of the soul in terms of complex, abstract ideas, William sticks firmly to the path of proofs, ignoring Scripture and arguing by reasoned propositions. A precise understanding of knowledge of this sort, of the metaphysical nature of the relationship between the persons of the Trinity, for example, is not necessary for salvation. It doesn't have to be clear to the unlearned; but for those who do wish to understand it, the only acceptable form of explanation is via the path of proofs and investigation—"the mode of those who philosophize." In the second and third sections, however, which deal with belief in the incarnate Christ, God's laws and precepts, the sacraments, and the life of virtue, he lays out knowledge both by proof and inquiry *and* by means of revealed and prophetic wisdom. These were the practicalities of salvation for all who wished to be saved, and William thought it his duty to make knowledge of them accessible to all, with biblical quotations, narratives of exemplary lives and miracles, and a general tone that is less about persuasion than explanation. "We need not proceed in it by the paths of proofs, but will rather write by the path of narratives that are by themselves evident to anyone who reads or hears them."[18] He was entirely aware of this variation in approach and his changes in method. Beginning the treatise on *Virtues*, he says:

> we will with the help of God begin to examine these in the mode of wisdom and by the paths of proofs, until their being, which involves some question and contradiction, is established, so that you may acquire certitude on the questions and opinions that have previously

> existed (and also still exist) about them. After this, however, we will speak about these things in other ways, in order that the knowledge of them may not only be clear in many ways, but also pleasing and productive of the desire by which the perfection of our souls is helped, by which they are aroused and also armed for wars against the vices and sins, and by which virtues and morals are made desirable to our souls, not only because of the hope of rewards, but also because of their perfection, grace, sweetness, and healthiness, and the multitude and beauty of their marvels.[19]

This is knowledge by more than philosophy and for a greater end. But this is not to say that William is not well read in philosophical materials. We've noted already that he was an avid consumer of the newly translated philosophical works of Aristotle and his Arab commentator Avicenna; his engagement with their ideas and arguments, even while the use of Aristotle was prohibited for arts students, facilitated the acceptance by the university of these challenging newcomers as partners to think with. William's attitude to them is, as ever, nuanced and individual. He neither wholly accepts nor wholly rejects their propositions, but takes each contribution on its own merits, judged by its usefulness for his overarching project of advancing knowledge for "the perfection of our souls."

All cutting-edge research in some sense builds on the past, even if it is just to reject the accepted paradigms of the day. The theologians of medieval Paris were working at the coal face of their discipline, looking for new materials while remaining faithful to the methods of their predecessors. This involved no little sleight-of-hand. Christianity believed that things had gone wrong almost from the beginning, with the disobedience in the garden of Eden, so for a theologian, to discover how things ought to be involved looking backward toward creation, rather like the current Big Bang theory of astrophysics, where matter is constantly growing increasingly distant from the original position. To be new was to be suspect, if there were no roots in the revealed, tried-and-tested knowledge of the past.[20] And yet, the sort of stagnation that attitude implies is belied by the creativity and innovation of the theologians of the twelfth and thirteenth centuries, who transformed the scope, presentation, teaching, and distribution of their discipline, and made the faculty at Paris a hub of expertise for government and papacy, as well as the Church at large. Reliable knowing began with a consideration of what the Bible said on any particular issue, with the New Testament valued over the Old, and with an elaborate system of interpretation to aid in deciphering the meaning of such an ancient set of texts, few of which provided an unequivocal message that wasn't contradicted or refined in another part of Scripture. Guides to understanding were provided by the commentaries of "patristic" texts, the works of early Christian "fathers" of the Latin Church, in particular, Augustine of Hippo (d. 430), Jerome (d. 420), Gregory the Great (d. 604), and Ambrose of Milan (d. 397), along with translations of some of the early Greek interpreters, such as Origen (d. c. 254). By William's day, these patristic materials had been read, collated, and reinterpreted by some trusted later scholars, such as Bede (d. 735), Hrabanus Maurus (d. 856), and Paschasius Radbertus (d. c. 860), and in the twelfth century biblical commentary was distilled into the great compilation of authoritative exposition that became known as the *Ordinary Gloss*.[21] In addition to such textual commentary, the opinions of these authorities were brought to bear on specific theological problems, such as the number and meaning of sacraments, or the nature of the incarnation of Christ. This working method brought together the revelation of Scripture with the certainty of tradition presented according to the dictates of reason. While adhering to this mode of proceeding, the scholars of the twelfth and thirteenth centuries nevertheless expanded their field of vision by admitting a somewhat wider range of authorities to those who could be adduced in any argument. Since Aristotle and other "pagan" classical texts were already known in the arts curriculum, when more of his works or those of his commentators became available, they were pounced on by the expanding community of university scholars, even though some parts had been forbidden by the pope.[22]

William drank in the new translations of Aristotle and the Arabs with an eager thirst, but they were not the only grist in his mill. The number of authorities he uses in his works, as recognized by Valois, runs to more than sixty, not counting Scripture, and embraces a remarkably wide range of material.[23] But in the *Magisterium* he makes it clear that authorities are to be worked *with* and not simply accepted without question:

> let it not enter your mind that I want to use the words of Aristotle as authoritative for proving for what I am going to say. I know that authority can only amount to a dialectical argument and can only produce belief, while my aim both in this treatise and everywhere I can is to provide demonstrative certitude, after which you are left with no trace of doubt.[24]

By a dialectical argument he means one that pits opinions against one another, before judging which seems the more convincing, though none might pass the test of the searching application of reason—of "demonstrative certitude"—for those for whom reason is the only measure. Using this scale, even Scripture is not enough to convince:

> we have not brought forth these testimonies [from the New Testament] in order that we may rely on them and use them like roots for the good, since we are not dealing with those who believe the testimonies of the Scriptures, but in order that we may show that the truth of the faith that we are seeking is found in them.[25]

He will use reason to prove the truth of Scripture, rather than Scripture to prove the truth of "demonstrative proofs." It's interesting to speculate on the audience that William had in mind for these treatises. He seemingly cannot believe that anyone would be foolish enough, as the Psalmist says, to hold that there is no God: how can such an abundance of creation not witness to the actions of a Creator?[26] It's surely for this reason that, in the early treatises of the *Magisterium*, he prefers to use the term "Creator" or, remarkably, Avicenna's simple "First," instead of "God." "God" comes laden with the baggage of belief, but the idea that there was a "First" might be understood and even conceded by all.

Working out exactly what the whole tangled web of Scripture might possibly teach, and how it did so, had preoccupied theologians and exegetes (biblical interpreters) from St. Paul onward. "Learn to respect Scripture," William advises; "though it is written in a simple and humble way, profound, difficult and hidden truths are contained in it."[27] One established method when a literal understanding of the text seemed impossible, or simply to expand the available range of meaning, was to shift to "spiritual" senses of interpretation, whereby the plain words were read as referring to an allegorical or moral or eschatological subject. A text on blindness, for example, could easily be taken as a reference to those who were blind to the faith. For Christians, the actors and actions of the Old Testament were frequently read as prefigurations of the New, so that David, king and savior of the Jews, could be seen as a "type" of the Christ who was to come, and in that way was meant as a lesson to Jews in how to recognize the Messiah. For William, how far such spiritual readings could be stretched, especially when divorced from any roots in their literal meaning, was a matter of concern. He reports criticism of commentators who don't *ex*pose the meaning of the text so much as *im*pose their own reading on it.[28] As an example, he uses the exegesis of the story of David committing adultery with Bathsheba and causing her husband, Uriah, to be killed.[29] David, here seen to be a traitor, an adulterer, and a murderer, was nonetheless said to signify Christ, while the innocent Uriah signifies the devil. Reading the text in this way gives rise to outrage in many who hear it, he says, and harms or even destroys their faith. True to form, William acts on his beliefs. In the rest of the work *On the Laws*, where this criticism is made, instead of reading the 613 laws given to the Jews by Moses as holding only spiritual meaning or else being superseded completely, he defends their literal meaning: "The whole Law contains nothing which lacks a rational cause for commanding, forbidding or narrating. There is nothing absurd or irrational in it, and this appears clearly in many items which have obvious worth and usefulness."[30] In his subsequent use of Scripture, he avoids the exaggerations of spiritual exegesis and concentrates instead on *similitudes*, or analogies and comparisons "drawn from the book of nature and art," as long as they are easily explicable.[31]

The "book of nature and art" is one of William's favorite topics. The image of the heavens rolled together like a scroll for reading is biblical.[32] We can find it in the writings of Augustine, but it was the early twelfth century that really saw a renewed interest in nature as a path to God, especially from scholars influenced by Plato's *Timaeus*.[33] In Paris, the Augustinian canon Hugh (d. 1142), master of the important school at the abbey of St. Victor, and Alan of Lille (d. 1202), who may have studied at St. Victor, both expanded on the theme: "this whole sensible world is like a kind of book written by the finger of God . . . and each creature is like a kind of letter."[34] Hugh was long dead by the time William reached Paris, but his influence lived on, and it's also likely that William used the well-established library at St. Victor, which would have held all of Hugh's works. Although in William's lifetime the commercial book trade in Paris, based on the piazza outside the cathedral, was flourishing, access to books was still not easy, when each had to be made by hand and supply relied on the availability of accurate exemplars for copying.[35] A good private library might hold only a dozen or so items. The cathedral would have had its own scholarly library, aside from the books used in the liturgy, but links between Notre-Dame and St. Victor were close—many canons and bishops were buried there—and the abbey library would still have been a draw.[36]

In one of several sermons, William brings together two of Hugh's characteristic themes—the world as a book, and the three attributes of God: power, wisdom, and goodness:

> The book of nature is the universe of created things in which we read the power, wisdom, and goodness of God. For the power of God is read in the multiplicity of created things; his wisdom is read in their beauty and ordering; his goodness in their usefulness and sweetness. All created things enlighten us, and yet we are in darkness. All teach us, and we are unlearned. All warn us, and we do not fear. All promise us, and we do not hope. All invite us, and we do not come. All goad and lash us, and we do not hasten to our refuge.[37]

We read this book by our senses; but beware—they can play you false. In the Eucharist, for example, your eyes and tongue sense only bread, and your nose only wine. When this happens, you must rely on faith, which has a greater light than any of the senses can impart.[38] Nevertheless, they are "ministers and runners who go out hither and yon and report back [to the soul] whatever external events they learned."[39]

William's writing is awash with sensual language. At home in the complex abstractions of speculative theology, he yet delights in expressing them in the down-to-earth physicality of the senses. Sight: the world is beautiful to look at, even if it is a shadow—"an unlikeness of incomparable distance"—of the beauty of the Creator.[40] Smell: sin stinks; "woe to those wretched people who wallow in lust like a beast of burden that rots in its own dung and sleeps in the reeking stench of the latrine . . . from which all heavenly creatures avert their eyes and noses."[41] Touch: Christ heals the sick with a touch; children scratch itchy heads.[42] Taste: no food has taste without salt; God gives three good saltings to creation.[43] "Christ himself makes a holy wafer from dry, stale bread by the wound in his side . . . The salt of the passion can make anything soft and delicious."[44] Nothing is too high or low for his notice: angels have noses, and drunken young men fall into open sewers; his world encompasses both extremes and everything in between.[45] When it comes to hearing, William talks about music—it's everywhere in his texts. On the grand scale, it is part of Plato's harmonic universe; for the individual, it can cure depression and melancholy.[46] Music is often his example of deep knowledge, knowledge known so habitually and interiorly by the body that it can almost not be forgotten. Humans may sin, but that doesn't mean they have lost their fundamental knowledge of the good. You may play a wrong note or sing badly, but that doesn't mean that your inner musicality has gone; and some good practice will put things right.[47]

William doesn't agree with Plato that harmony is what gives the universe its being, but he recognizes that Plato's theory was born from the "force and power of harmonious proportions which are so powerful in our souls that our whole souls seem to be placed in their power."[48] At the whim of the expert musician, the listener is moved in seconds from sorrow to joy, from turbulence to tranquility, from fear to hope, from weakness to magnificence. Music resonates so deeply that humans make instruments, and the soul desires to make "the heavens resound with harmonious melodies"; "each and every thing cries out, in fact sings; that is, it sounds forth the praises and glory of the creator beyond all musical sweetness."[49] God himself is a musician whose instrument is Christ, for the universe is "like a most beautiful canticle, because he himself plays the harmonies on his lyre, which is the only-begotten Son of God and . . . the individual ages or generations are individual odes or melodies of this canticle, and the individual creatures are like individual words or syllables in these songs."[50] The closer a soul is to God, the higher and clearer is its voice:

> the most lofty and most noble creatures sing like the highest and clear voices, but the sensible and inanimate creatures sing lower like heaviest and lowest voices, while the rest of creatures, sounding forth in accord with their variety, some lower, others higher and sharper, bringing together the extremes in a marvelous harmony, produce a melody of wondrous delight, a melody not audible by bodily ear but delightful for spiritual ears with its ineffable sweetness.[51]

But as ever, the good can be turned to bad. The devil, too, has tunes, and they are sung in taverns, brothels, theaters and everywhere we find sin.

So was he musical? Reading William, it's easy to recognize that interior resonance of music that he describes so well; his discussion of what constitutes an acceptable physical response to music as an expression of joy reads like the words of a man who can't help tapping his foot.[52] Hours in Church would have been accompanied by music, and Notre Dame at this period was a site of particular creativity in the development of polyphony.[53] But we must remember that the medieval study of music began as one of the subjects in the numerical branch of the liberal arts, a highly theoretical discussion of proportion and ratio, and it's another sign of the strength of William's training in arts that he understands this theory well.[54] Nevertheless, his reflections on music do appear to go beyond the abstract. Reading only his sermons, we might be forgiven for thinking that he despised music and musicians, because he is so scathing about their doleful effects on the easily led, whether in pubs, theaters or all the other places where the devil plies his trade. Yet his comments on the skill of performance and his belief in the power of music to heal and console tell a different story. Once again, music was one of God's gifts than humanity could use for good or ill, and the trick was in knowing which was which. It was the very potency of cheap music, and the ready response of his senses to these dangerous tunes, that taught William that knowing was always a slippery business.

8

JEWS

Am I not a man and a brother?

The only place in current historical debate where William can be guaranteed a presence is in writing about the Paris Jews, and specifically in discussions of the so-called Talmud Trial of 1240 and the subsequent burning of Jewish books in 1242.[1] The Jewish Talmud ("Teaching") comprised two ancient collections of opinions on difficult biblical legal and theological subjects; and although it had long been part of the armory of biblical interpretation, these events around 1240 saw it taken out of the context of scholarship and thrust into an unwanted limelight. William found himself with a central role in these episodes and the events that led up to them, in which Louis IX destroyed cartloads of Jewish learning. Burning books is always controversial, and burning Jewish books especially so, in light of the Nazi bonfires of books in Berlin's Bebelplatz in 1933, so the whole shameful business and those who took part in it—which included Pope Gregory IX, Louis IX, Blanche of Castile, and Walter of Cornut, the senior archbishop of France—have come under detailed historical scrutiny and often condemnation. In this chapter, we'll try to put William's part in the trial alongside references to Jews in his writings, and his use of Jewish sources, in the hope of achieving a bigger, if not simpler, picture.

By the thirteenth century, Jews in Northern France walked on eggshells. For Christians, Jews had always held a unique theological position. The two faiths shared Scriptures and history, if not an interpretation of what they meant; most importantly, they shared the worship of a single, incorporeal God—all knowing, all powerful, and all good. They shared a belief in an initial creation, which had gone wrong when the first humans disobeyed orders, pitching themselves into lives of pain and suffering instead of the intended joy. But both also believed that God would give them a second chance, sending a Messiah to redeem the world from its own ignorance, and to fulfill God's designs. For Jews, this Messiah was still to come; for Christians, he had already appeared in the person of Jesus of Nazareth, who had been put to death by Jews too blind to realize his true identity. Only a few perceptive Jews and Gentiles (non-Jews) had recognized him for what he was, and recorded the story in the Gospels and Letters of the New Testament. At this point, the new religion might have chosen to condemn all Jews who did not elect to follow the Christ, as he was known in the Greek language of their new Church, and to ignore the Hebrew Scriptures or declare them to have been superseded by their own sacred books. But the links with Judaism were too strong for such a simple response. Jesus himself was a Jew, and his reported teachings made it clear that he had come "not to abolish the Law but to fulfil it."[2] Christians were, in a sense, Jews, but more so. Moreover, surrounded as they were by believers in very different types of deity, what Jews and Christians had in common, especially their monotheism, was much more important than their differences. Christians chose to retain both the Hebrew Scriptures (as the "Old" Testament) and a recognition of Jews as the original people of God. God had promised them much, and those promises still stood; they had lost sight of the true path, but God could put that right in the end. In the meantime, therefore, Jews were to be tolerated, lived with, and even protected.

Gilbert Dahan divides the history of medieval Judaism in Europe into three parts. His portrayal up to the First Crusade in 1096 is one of integration, with Jews involved in agriculture and craftsmanship, as well as mercantile commerce—which did not necessarily involve moneylending. This is not to say that there weren't problems and expulsions, especially in Spain, nor that the policy of the Church wasn't to pursue missionary evangelism with the "Christ-killers"; but under the rule of Charlemagne and Louis VII, "the Pious," in particular, they could live in relative security.[3] The next period, between 1096 and the persecutions that began in the late thirteenth century, was one of a steady deterioration in the treatment of Jews by the majority group. "Admittedly, they still retained their place in society, they were neither marginalized nor considered foreigners, but disturbing signs were multiplying."[4] The worst of these were allegations of Jews killing Christian children and stealing Christian eucharistic wafers, in order to desecrate them.[5] Whether or not they believed these accusations, some rulers used them as an opportunity to expel Jews, to whom they were often in considerable debt, from their lands. When the Jews left, these debts could no longer be collected.

During this second period, covering the twelfth and thirteenth centuries, Judaism, like Christianity, was changing—not in its fundamental beliefs, but in the way these might be defined and codified, how they could and should be studied, and how faith should be observed and practiced. For the scholars of both religions, this involved some changes in the books at the heart of their studies, with the "plain" Bible giving ground to commentaries and theological questions. As Anselm of Laon (d. 1117) is a leading name in the consolidation of Christian Bible commentary and theological questions at this time, so the rabbi known as Rashi (d. 1105; his name is an acronym for *Ra*bbi *Sh*elomoh *Yi*tshaqi, or Solomon, son of Isaac), who ran a school in Troyes, about 150 kilometers, or 90 miles, from Laon, was the preeminent Jewish biblical and talmudic commentator of the day. His work, like Anselm's, was fundamental in setting the direction of scholarship for the next two centuries. As Christian exegesis had its developed system of literal and spiritual interpretation, so Rashi emphasized the "plain meaning" (*peshat*) of the text, rather like the Christian literal sense, in contrast to *derash*, which "sought for" a meaning that fitted a passage of Scripture or Talmud to contemporary life. Rashi's work was carried on by his learned grandchildren, especially Rabbi Shemuel ben Meir (d. 1160; known as Rashbam), and through *Tosafot* ("additions"), commentaries on the Talmud that took Rashi's interpretation as their starting point. Similarly, on the Christian side, commentary on the *Four Books of Sentences* by Peter Lombard (d. 1160), which took questions arising from the Bible and arranged and discussed them in a theological order, by topic, became the standard scholarly approach. Traditionalists, such as the monks Bernard of Clairvaux or Rupert of Deutz, deprecated this form of working: they thought the foundations of the faith shouldn't be haggled over like the price of fish. Classroom arguments might certainly range far from anything that could and should be preached from the pulpit. Like debates on Christian theological questions, discussions of Talmud had been part of Judaism for centuries; but what was understood as a hermeneutical technique by a scholarly elite could look scandalous to those outside the academy.

Most Jews in France lived in the South.[6] Nevertheless, when Philip Augustus was crowned in 1179, ruling alongside his father, Louis the Pious, there were perhaps 1,000 Jews in central Paris on the Île de la Cité, with more on the Right and Left Banks and in the surrounding towns of the kingdom—perhaps 5,000 in all.[7] Unlike his father, Philip took a hard line against "his" Jews, who should have been able to expect his protection. His 1180–81 seizure of their goods (to be returned for a ransom) was the first example of such action by a French king; in 1182 he expelled the Jews themselves and turned their synagogue on the Île into a church, although he allowed them to return in 1198, when he realized that their presence elsewhere only enriched his neighbors; in 1192 he burned eighty Jews in retaliation for the death of one of his men. Those Jews who did return after 1198 no longer lived on the Île but in a new district on the Right Bank, the Marais.[8]

Church policy toward Jews was contradictory. In his bull *Sicut Iudeis* of 598, Pope Gregory I directed that they should be able to practice their religion, not be subject to forced baptism, and have security in their lives and property.[9] While this was not overturned, policy such as Innocent III's 1215 decree from the Fourth Lateran Council, that Jews had to wear clothing that would mark them out—often, a yellow star of David, as hideously reused in the twentieth century—increased their isolation; Innocent was determined to reduce contact between the two communities.[10] Gregory IX, the pope who chose William to be bishop of Paris, reiterated the Lateran prohibitions of Jews holding public office and the enforcement of distinctive clothing, but he also wrote in 1233 to the archbishop and bishops of France, decrying the treatment of Jews by some of the French regional rulers, and ordering them to speak out:

> We order . . . that you make every effort carefully, in our name, to warn all the faithful Christians in your dioceses and to induce them not to harm the Jews in their persons, nor to dare rob them of their property, nor, for the sake of plunder, to drive them from their lands, without some reasonable cause or clear guilt on their part, but rather to permit them to live in pursuance of their laws and their former status, as long as they do not presume to insult the Christian faith . . . Such kindliness must be shown to Jews by Christians, as we hope might be shown to Christians who live in pagan lands.[11]

It is with Gregory that the dispute over the Talmud in Paris begins. The trial—or inquisition or disputation or hearing: the nature of the event has had different interpretations—seems to have begun with lobbying by a Parisian Jewish convert, Donin, who took the Christian name Nicholas.[12] Sometime between 1235 and 1239, he put together thirty-five articles in which he claimed that the Talmud was full of error, and he petitioned Gregory IX to do something about it.[13] Donin had turned against his former faith: he seems to have been one of those who promoted the idea of the "blood libel," which falsely asserted that Jews killed Christian children.[14] His central allegation was that the Talmud (and its rabbinical interpreters) had become more important than the Bible, an accusation surely familiar to the pope since the balance between the words of the biblical text and their theological exposition was one that Christians also found difficult to strike. Still, faced with claims that the Talmud promoted the killing of Christians or the idea that God sinned and cursed himself, Gregory could not ignore them entirely. Pressed by Nicholas Donin, he wrote letters to the crowned heads of Europe (and their archbishops) ordering them to seize the Jews' books on the first Sunday of Lent 1240, and take them to the local Dominican or Franciscan convent for investigation. Should they be found to contain errors, they were to be burned.

But Gregory didn't send these letters directly. Instead he sent them, via Nicholas, to William, with a note, dated 9 June 1239, asking

William to send them on, "as soon as you think it expedient."[15] Why did Gregory use William as his postal service, rather than sending the letters himself, and why was the date for the seizures set so far in advance? The first Sunday of Lent 1240 was nine months away. One modern scholar argues that Gregory knew William to be a Jew-hating southerner, who could organize the book-destruction for him—and, if it all fell to pieces, William could take the blame.[16] If that was his thinking, Gregory's plan seems to have gone awry, for the only letter that seems to have arrived was that sent to Louis IX in Paris, whose hardline attitude to the Jews was well known—and he had Nicholas Donin on his shoulder. Only in Paris were the books rounded up as specified, and taken to the Dominican convent, where they sat for two years, until they were finally burned in 1242.

Louis appointed his mother, Blanche of Castile, to chair the hearings into the charges, supported by Walter Cornut, archbishop of Sens and the senior bishop of France; Adam of Chambly, bishop of Senlis; Odo of Châteauroux, the chancellor of Paris; and William, together with several of the regent masters of the university, including Louis's chaplain, Geoffrey of Belleville. Walter of Cornut was known to be sympathetic to Jews. He employed a Jewish father-and-son team, Nathan and Joseph, surnamed "Official" in the Christian records, as part of his episcopal administration, and it was Joseph who wrote up the statements of the "defending" rabbis.[17] Odo, in contrast, took a much harder line.[18] The case against the Talmud was made by Nicholas Donin, with Rabbi Yehiel ben Joseph, head of the Tosafist school in Paris and teacher of Joseph ben Nathan "Official," as the primary Jewish spokesman, supported by at least three other distinguished Jewish scholars: Judah ben David from Melun, Samuel ben Solomon from Chateau Thierry, and Moses ben Jacob of Courcy.[19] The Jewish account (as written up by Joseph) is scathing toward the Christian clerics, including Walter, but paints Blanche as a fearless and sympathetic chair. She dispensed Yehiel from swearing an oath on the Gospel that he was telling the truth, as long as he would state that he was doing so on his honor, and she assured him that the crown would let no harm come to his community: "it is our intention to protect you and all that is yours. All who do harm to you incur sin and iniquity. Thus we find in our books and from the pope."[20] Despite the complexity (and occasional obscenity) of the debate, Blanche was "engaged by the arguments, equal to the exegesis and unfazed by the obscenities."[21] Yehiel's account suggests he thought he had won the day. Certainly, no action was taken while Walter of Cornut was still alive, and the Dominican friar Thomas of Cantimpré records that the Jews asked for the return of their books, and with Walter's support (given as the result of a bribe, according to Thomas), some were given back; but in 1242, some twenty cartloads were burned in the Place de Grève. Walter died in the spring of 1241, and it may have been he who had saved them thus far, but Gregory IX also died in August of that year, and his successor, Innocent IV was, at least to begin with, less sympathetic.

Burning had also been the fate of some unorthodox Christian books, such as those by David of Dinant in Paris in 1210, and it has been argued that the inquiry regarded the Talmud as similarly misleading the Jews from a proper understanding of their Scriptures. It seems to have been the masters of Paris, led by chancellor Odo, who kept the question alive, rather than the clergy. The masters were increasingly anxious about the correctness of all theological statements and a perhaps increasing propensity to unorthodoxy, as we can see from the condemnation of Christian theological positions by the university in 1241 and 1244.[22] By 1247 Pope Innocent was himself in exile in Lyon, and had been approached by a delegation of Jewish scholars asking to be allowed to have their copies of the Talmud returned, as they were essential for their scholarship. The pope wrote to Louis in support of this restoration, as long as the books were inspected and passed fit for study. However, since the judge in this case was Odo, no longer chancellor but papal representative in France, the inspection was failed.[23] But it was Innocent's contention that, as God's vicar on earth, he had oversight not only of Christians with regard to the Gospel, but also of pagans who contravened the law of nature, and of Jews who "invented heresies against their law," and he claims that it was on this basis that he and Gregory IX had ordered the burning of the Talmud.[24] Popes and masters alike give the impression at least of being equally concerned with the correctness of both Christian and Jewish theology in its own terms. Nonetheless, it is clear that it was the books that were condemned, not the Jews themselves; the dispute was about ideas, rather than those who read or held them. "It is no less significant that, in the Talmud

Trial in Paris, neither Jewish witnesses nor the Jewish community were being prosecuted or at risk of punishment."[25]

The meaning of this whole affair, and William's role in it, is not easy to assess. Gregory's use of William to distribute his letters plunges him into the thick of things; but was Gregory putting everything onto William's shoulders because he knew he was keen to act against the Jews' books, or because Nicholas the convert lived in Paris, with an activist king who would undoubtedly be willing to act? No copies of the letter supposedly sent to the other rulers or churchmen appear in any of their contemporary records; and no action was taken anywhere other than Paris. It's tempting to suggest that William simply never sent them on. In his theological *summa* of around the same time, the Paris master Alexander of Hales, a Franciscan, asks "whether Jews who hold to the blasphemy of the Talmud" should be burned along with it.[26] He answers that only the books containing the offending material should be destroyed, although if the Jews themselves openly persist in their blasphemies, they should be given a suitable penalty by a judge. But the fact of his asking the question suggests that the issue was in the air at the time. One of the arguments he marshals in favor of destroying the Jews as well as the Talmud is that Christians have already killed nonbelievers who were in possession of the Holy Land. William was a secular priest, but he presided over a city that had welcomed the fervor of the mendicant orders, men whose vocation it was to promote orthodox Christianity in ways we would not condone today. He seems to have been a book acquirer and reader, rather than a book burner; but history also teaches us, as in the case of Thomas More, that the two personae can go together. More, staunch friend, family man, and Catholic scholar, burned people as well as books. In 1248, William was one of the many clerical and university signatories of a document confirming the conclusions of the commission headed by the papal legate, Odo of Châteauroux, which had revisited previous considerations of the Talmud.[27] In the modern edition by Denifle and Chatelain, it is bookended by Pope Innocent's foundation of a new, higher-level school (*studium generale*) in Piacenza, approval for Dominican scholars to be sent from the provinces of Europe to study in Paris, and funding for ten scholars at Paris to learn "Arabic or other oriental languages." Education was expanding everywhere, and in ways previously unimagined. It's perhaps not surprising that the Paris masters and clergy might think things were getting out of (their) control, and try hard to contain them.

Ironically, William himself was one of the most eager readers of the new "oriental" material when it became available in Paris. He appears to be the first Western theologian to cite the Jewish scholar Maimonides, and he (along with Philip the Chancellor in Paris) is the first to cite the polymath Islamic scholar from Córdoba, Ibn Rushd (d. 1198), known in the West as Averroes. We've already noted his considerable knowledge of Avicenna (Ibn Sina), whom he read for knowledge of Aristotle, despite the repeated prohibitions on the teaching of the newly translated works of Aristotle from 1210 to 1231. In addition, he shows knowledge of or cites by name other Arab and Arab-Jewish scholars, such as Avicebron (Ibn Gabirol; d. c. 1060), Al-Farabi (d. 950/1), and Al-Gazali (d. 1111). These Arabic thinkers were a treasure trove for his wide interests in astronomy and magic, as well as philosophy.

Maimonides (Moses ben Maimon) was an Arabic-speaking Jew, born in Córdoba but working mostly in Fustat or Old Cairo. He wrote on medicine and astronomy as well as philosophy and the Jewish Law, but he was best known in the West for his *Guide of the Perplexed* (*Moreh Nevukhim*). Maimonides was almost a contemporary of our thirteenth-century Paris scholars—he died in 1204—but his reputation was such that his works were relatively quickly available in Latin versions. The complete Latin *Guide*, known as the *Dux neutrorum*, is first quoted explicitly by Albert the Great, sometime between 1241 and 1246, and there is a tradition of early Dominican use, by Albert, Thomas Aquinas, and Meister Eckhart.[28] When exactly and where the complete Latin *Guide* first appeared is not known, and scholars are divided on the date at which William might have known it. The work was translated in separate parts, and William seems certainly to have known the earliest available of these, the *Liber de parabola*, which probably dates from 1223–24. This was a version rather than a strict translation of the section of the *Guide* that deals with the 613 laws of the Torah. It has no references to the Talmud, which probably means that it was prepared for a Christian readership; it was made for a certain "Romanus," thought to be Cardinal Romanus, the papal legate in Paris, who was known to William from their joint action in the university strike of 1229.

In William, the *Liber* had a very early and careful reader. He uses it in his treatise *On the Laws*, a comparative consideration of the Laws of Moses and Muhammad, which he wrote between about 1230 and 1236.[29] He seems to know something of Maimonides himself, whom he describes as writing for "Hebrews, mixing with Saracens, given to the study of philosophy"—a combination that leads them to falling into error and misinterpreting their own laws.[30] William wants to show that all the Jewish laws in the Torah, and not just the Ten Commandments, are there for a purpose. Although recognizing that the prohibitions of certain foods, animals, or behaviors may seem irrational, William argues that each has a logical meaning and purpose, even if it may not be immediately obvious, since nothing that God has given can be ridiculous and nothing can be ignored. He sets himself to explain the reason behind each of the 613 Mosaic commandments, including the rules for circumcision and sacrifices, and to do this, he draws on the *Liber*, which he cites anonymously. This may be because the *Liber* itself was anonymous (although the translation of the *Guide* is credited to "Rabbi Moses"), or it may be that William is simply employing the same rule of anonymous citation of contemporary or near-contemporary authors that he would have applied to Christian sources.

Although he doesn't always concur with the opinions of the *Liber*, William does accept that the laws have meanings beyond the literal sense, and he certainly agrees that the purpose of laws in general is to prevent the spread of paganism. In trying to understand the laws, rather than simply to ignore or condemn them as outmoded, William makes a serious attempt to get into the mind of a Jewish interpreter, an action in itself unlike that of almost any other Christian contemporary; and he goes to a Jewish source for help to do that—again, unusual if not unique. This is not to say that William is prepared to meet the Jews on equal terms, but the language he uses about them (common from at least Jerome) is that they are "children," who need help, rather than wicked people who are to be condemned.[31] The multiplicity of the Torah laws is an alphabet, he says, which is all they can take in—rather than the full sentences of the Christian Gospel.[32] They need so many laws to cover every eventuality because they can't be expected to think for themselves. William is undoubtedly rude about the Jews; we can expect nothing else of a man of his time and profession. But it is the rudeness that comes of paternalism, of the colonizer toward the native, and generally lacking in viciousness.[33] In comparison, we need only consider the language he uses about Muslims in the same work.

We have already noted William's particular admiration for Avicenna, as well as his use of other Muslim scholars, in his treatises from the first section of his *Magisterium* where he argues "in the mode of proofs and investigation." The treatise *On the Laws*, however, comes from the third section, where truths discovered by reason are joined by truths known through revelation. William's discussion of Muslim law, and in particular its concept of paradise, is long and detailed—the longest consideration of Islam in this period not simply designed as a polemic.[34] He spends considerable time describing and ridiculing Muslim ideas. He is incredulous that anyone could think that paradise could simply be *more* of the bodily pleasures that are available in this life. His arguments build to a crescendo as he mocks the idea of mountains of food and drink and children and—inevitably—excrement that he thinks this version of the afterlife would logically entail. And surprisingly, he chooses this point to criticize Avicenna by name:

> And for these reasons, some of the wise among the Saracens hold that Muhammad did not understand these promises literally . . . Avicenna, nonetheless, explicitly consents to these ravings in his first philosophy, where he says that bodily joys are found in our law which Muhammad gave, speaking of joys after death. On this point he clearly showed himself not to be a philosopher, but a partaker in this madness, and his condemnation is the more just to the extent that so great a philosopher could better see and neglected to see these ravings.[35]

Avicenna the Arabic intellectual has here been replaced by Avicenna the Muslim believer; and William's language is adjusted accordingly. The great philosopher is now a partaker in madness. The thinker who, in the first part of the *Magisterium*, which argued via proofs, can correctly formulate the name of God, has become, in its final part, which uses proofs only as a first step to faith, a Saracen who refuses to see that his faith is built on ravings. In comparison to this treatment, the language William uses about Jews is a model of restraint.

The final arena where we might expect William to speak of Jews is in his preaching, but of the almost 600 sermons, few mention Jews in more than a passing reference.[36] Two sermons are specifically on moneylending and usury, but don't refer to Jews in this, their traditional medieval role; he is much more exercised by Christian moneylenders and their business practices, and the general wrongness of charging interest.[37] Two, for the feast of the Epiphany, discuss the question of circumcision, which he also considers at length in *On the Laws*; but again, the sermons are entirely directed at Christians, and never mention Jews.[38] His concern is to persuade his congregation that the law still has some worth, because it's not really about the removal of superfluous skin, but the removal of the superfluous from all areas of your life. Christians should circumcise their mouths (by not gossiping or speaking ill of people), their ears (by not listening to wicked talk), and even their feet, by not walking in the devil's road rather than the paths of righteousness: today, he says, begins the renewal of our old skin, casting off the old like a dirty rag; we pay our debt for our redemption.

Two of the sermons are on the text from Luke's Gospel where a man gives a great dinner but, one by one, his guests cry off.[39] He sends his servants out into the streets to invite the poor and needy; and when there is still room, he sends to compel people to come in. The heavenly door, William says, is always open, and everyone is welcome. He contrasts the devil's tavern with God's hostelry, where you never have to pay the bill. Invitations are sent out again and again, by preachers, teachers, parents, good friends, by the persuasiveness of all good people: most people don't want to hear. Jews and Saracens are invited, but they don't come; after all, pigs called to eat good, flavorsome food don't come to eat. But neither do the majority of so-called Christians: married priests, those who are fond of luxury or greed, the avaricious and the proud, those with heretical beliefs—they prefer the devil's dinner and, like birds or fish, are caught in his net.

This conviction that the people of God are few in number turns up in another sermon, on a text from the Gospel of Matthew: Jesus will save his people from their sins.[40] Who, William asks, are Jesus's people? He lists them: obviously not pagans; not Saracens, "the people of Muhammad who are engulfed in pride, and who wish to be glorified like gods"; not Jews, who have hard hearts, and don't recognize Jesus for what he is. So far, so commonplace; but William goes on: the greater part of Christians are clearly in the devil's party—those who treat women badly; priests who marry; drunks; the idle; the envious and those who speak ill of others; usurers; anyone who doesn't stand up for good against evil. All these are the devil's servants, and they serve him very faithfully.

Two sermons are on Romans 15:4: whatever was written was written for our instruction, that we might have hope.[41] God has four ways to instruct humans, of which Scripture is one; and for this, unsurprisingly, William contrasts the Gospel and the Jewish law. God writes Scripture "from the outside," because what he put "inside" us naturally was lost with original sin. So humans now need "to beg from skins"—to scan the pages of parchment books—what they've lost from inside themselves. The Old Law was written for the Jews on stone tablets, in the same way that children have wax tablets to learn their alphabets. Jews are children who have the alphabet for their first lessons, but the New Law of Christ brings the refreshment of wisdom.

Finally, William preaches on Genesis 1:26, "Let us make humans in our own image."[42] If the eyes of a true Christian, he says, can't look without pain at even an image of the crucified Christ or the Virgin Mary being trampled underfoot, how much more should a whole Christian person, who is the true image of God, not permit himself or others to be trampled underfoot by demons? Alas, that's not what we see today. Heretics—specifically Albigensians—have deformed what we gave them; Jews would, if they had the power over us, take images from churches, mutilate them, and throw them out. But true Christians are few: people who admire the world and its works are so many more than those who love God.

William, of course, is preaching to Christians, and his focus is on *their* beliefs and behavior; even so, where there are obvious opportunities to denigrate Jews, he does not seem to take them. He holds the customary Christian position, that Jews are children whose Scriptures are only those equal to their level of understanding, although the comparison of the tablets of the Law with the wax tablets on which children learn to write is, I think, all his own. He believes Jews should be able to recognize Christ as the Messiah, but he doesn't single them out for special mention among the many others to whom this also applies: they're part of a line running from pagans to drunks and gossiping women. And where he might be expected to single out Jews for criticism or ridicule, when he talks about usury or circumcision, he's silent. Only when he discusses those who ignore the teaching of God, with a reference to Jews and Muslims, does he speak in the next sentence of their traditionally unclean animal, the pig. There's no linguistic link between the two sentences, but it must be the case that the mention of the one triggers the idea of the other in his mind. William admires Avicenna, but is shocked that he can believe in "the Law of Muhammad." He cites Maimonides, but regards him as belonging to a childish people. He reads Greek and Arab texts that the Church believed to be dangerous for students, but has a part in burning the books of scholars of another faith. None of us is consistent.

9

WOMEN

There ain't a thing that's wrong with any man here
That can't be cured by putting him near
A girly, womanly, female, feminine dame!

William lived in a male world. From school to university, from the cloister at Notre-Dame to the bishop's palace and the court, his life was spent predominantly among men. Such a world could be rough, both physically and intellectually. Walter Ong characterizes the medieval classroom as strongly "agonistic," that is, combative, as well as gendered. The "pedagogical violence" of the schoolroom was literal, with frequent beatings administered to students, and metaphorical, in the polemical method of argument that was encouraged increasingly during the thirteenth century. For Ong, it was part of male socialization that boys learned to give as good as they got.[1] Although William's treatises do not use the scholastic method of raising a question, then pitting arguments for and against, before coming to a solution, his language is often pitched at quite a high polemical register. If he doesn't employ the relentless cut-and-thrust we might associate with Thomas Aquinas, for instance, neither does he simply narrate his own position in coolly dispassionate terms. He has learned to argue as men were taught to do, if only in a different way.

Nonetheless, there were obviously women in William's life, starting with family members and certainly encompassing tradeswomen, servants, nuns, and prostitutes, not to mention his friendship with the queen and queen regent, Blanche of Castile. Aside from Blanche, however, everyone he knew who wielded any power was usually male. In this, of course, he was no different from medieval people who didn't live in academic and clerical circles: the age-old oppression of the physically weaker by the physically stronger, alongside the dangers and responsibilities of childbirth, gave rise to a society with men in charge. The man in the Parisian street may have rubbed shoulders with more women than William in everyday life; but he would still have taken little notice of them as equal members of society, even if he noticed them as objects of desire. Although the message of Christianity was intended to turn the hierarchies and values of this secular world upside down, this was not modeled in the institutional Church. As far as medieval women were concerned, Christ, whose apostles were all men, was still fighting a losing battle.

Our difficulty in understanding the lives of women at this period is one of evidence. Written evidence tends to cluster round the interests and actions of the literate classes, and even when women were comparatively rich, their interests were often represented, legally as well as practically, by male relatives or other agents. Where physical evidence survives, archaeology has often assumed it was produced by or lived in by men.[2] Often, those assumptions are reasonable: since we are reaching back eight hundred years, it's not surprising that the majority of what still exists is built in stone or written on the remarkably tough medium of parchment—the prepared skins of animals—and represents the remains of the world of the powerful and Latin-literate male elite. It's not that women did not create in the Middle Ages, only that what they created—food, textiles, conversation, the ambience of domestic life—is much less likely to have survived, either because of the medium in which they were made, or because of the use to which they were put. When their work does still exist, it can be difficult to unravel from that of men. For example, were it not for the extant records of the oaths required by the university of Paris from their licensed makers and sellers of books, we would not know of—and had not previously imagined—the work of Jeanne de Monbaston, who worked with her husband, Richard, in the first half of the fourteenth century, running a successful business copying and illustrating manuscript books in the very center of the city. Only because Jeanne continued on her own after Richard's death, and therefore had to swear the oath in her own name, was another husband-and-wife team able to piece together her career.[3]

No direct statistical evidence of women's work survives for William's lifetime, but we are fortunate in possessing seven tax rolls (*tailles*) for the city of Paris covering the years 1292 to 1313. Although their figures are centered to a large extent on households rather than individuals, they give us some idea of the work of the 14,517 people they record as liable for tax in 1292.[4] Of these, around 2,238 were women taxed in their own right, of whom 883 had occupational surnames covering 172 trades. It's uncertain whether these represent current work, or the work of husbands or fathers, but David Herlihy judges that women were probably practicing a wide range of the occupations listed. His calculation of the top fifteen trades for Parisian women is headed (by some distance) by household servants, followed by peddlers (street sellers of various sorts), dressmakers, laundresses, and hairdressers. Next comes working in the silk industry, which, as we know from the list of Paris guilds drawn up c. 1270 by the city's provost, Étienne Boileau, was dominated by female workers, and included five guilds open only to women members.[5] Women were well represented in the food, textile, and caring industries, but could also be found as barbers (who also did bonesetting and bloodletting), pharmacists/spice sellers, midwives, and even doctors: at least eight women doctors practiced in Paris in 1292; they may have trained in southern Europe and come north. There were women money changers and moneyers minting coins, along with smiths, shoemakers, and millers. Women could even train male as well as female apprentices. Few professions appear to have been exclusively male, aside from those relying largely on physical strength alone, such as porters and seamen, and the Church and the Law, both of which required a licence to practice, which women could not obtain. Although women were not confined to the poorer sorts of work, judging by tax liability they were as a group less well off than men. Nonetheless, Herlihy concludes that "the Parisian economy at the time of Philip the Fair [c. 1300] remained remarkably open to women." We can assume, then, that the buzz of the Paris streets included the voices of women; how much of it William saw will have depended on how regularly he left his

Notre-Dame enclave, and how well he listened when he did. How interested was a scholarly cleric in the lives around him?

Before we look down on William's world as unfeasibly distant, we might compare it to the upbringing and career of an upper-middle-class British man before, say, the 1970s. Sent at a young age to a private, single-sex boarding school, his contact with women, apart from mother and sisters in the holidays, would have been limited to the school matron or nurse and those who cleaned and cooked. Moving to an all-male "Oxbridge" college, he might see more women of his own class, in lectures and the library, but opportunities for social interaction were strictly controlled; between 1939 and 1960 he would have been conscripted into the armed forces, which might have expanded his social contacts, but only with other men. Finally, university graduates could then head into a profession—medicine, the law, or business, perhaps even the Church—where women figured largely in ancillary roles, and were denied entry into the social clubs and societies that helped cement success. These men would marry, certainly, and have families; but for many the daytime world of their work was completely separate from the liminal interaction with their wife, children, and domestic servants.

Nevertheless, although as a cleric William was supposed to be celibate, he was not a monk living in enclosure or under a rule. As a student and teacher, he would have been able to come and go much as he wished, in a city replete with taverns, gambling, and multiple other forms of entertainment, many of them involving women. The regulation forbidding women to stay overnight in the cloister at Notre-Dame did not apply to mothers, sisters, close relatives, and high-ranking women friends, which suggests that this was a formulation designed to catch sexual partners, whom it would otherwise have been difficult to define and legislate against. The repeated prohibitions of women as visitors and servants must make us think that they were not unknown in the cloister. As a bishop, William preached to mixed audiences of men and women, and to houses of nuns. We believe that he was the confessor of at least one woman, Blanche of Castile, and the rule of thumb in modern Christianity, that women are more likely than men to be regular church attenders, was probably also true in thirteenth-century Paris. As bishop, he was also the spider at the center of a web of priests who reported to him the concerns of their parishioners at twice yearly synods. William's written works certainly present a lot of women in a lot of situations. What might reading them tell us about his attitudes to and relations with women?

He himself asserts that his knowledge of at least one intimate situation is not merely book-learning. Discussing the strength of marriage as a sacrament, William argues that it offers "a cool refuge against the fires of fleshly desire"—that is, that marriage makes you less desirous of sex! Occasionally, even young men are less ardent with their wives, he says, even if they're beautiful; and with other women, again even if they're beautiful, they're almost frigid: "and we have learned this from women, not from gossip or conjecture but from women's experience and conviction, speaking from the testimony of those men to whom this was given by divine authority, and knowing it in person, in confession."[6] William's writing very often appears to reflect personal interaction and observation, but that could simply be the result of clever rhetoric; here, however, he's telling us that, even if he didn't learn these things from women themselves, he has heard them from the parish priests who did. He's had similar valuable personal communication about those who try to maintain their virginity and chastity, and even about the threatened corruption of children: "ask the priests of parishes that are in my territories and jurisdiction, and you will hear from their testimony."[7]

The sense of direct knowledge is very striking when William talks about the difficulties of pregnancy and childbirth. The Bible could have been his text, as God says to Eve, "I will greatly increase your pangs in childbearing; in pain shall you bring forth children, yet your desire shall be for your husband, and he shall rule over you."[8] William uses the pain of human childbirth (which he contrasts with the easy birth of animals) to chastise the ancient pagan scholar Aristotle, a thinker he admires, for not realizing that this difference must point to a particular punishment being inflicted on the human race; for "since the fruit [a human child] is more noble [than a baby animal], birth ought to be more pleasant for the mother, and it would be fitting that the birth itself be not only without pain, but that it should be even with joy."[9] The difference can only be explained by original sin. William's words elsewhere suggest he had more than an academic understanding, in the sense that he had listened to women talk about their own lives: "so great is the pain of childbirth, so hard the suffering of pregnant women, so difficult the hard work and misery of breastfeeding, that no woman, or almost none, once freed from these things, would return to the work of bringing children into the world."[10] Even for their husbands, it's "no easy job" to support wives who are pregnant, in labor, or breastfeeding; then they both have to look after, feed, and educate their children.

The physicality of bodies, even of women's bodies, is not something to be shied away from. The nature of Christian belief, in which the Son of God grows in and is born from the womb of a virgin, can at the best of times make for some surprising images: "the whole uncreated Trinity was in the bridal chamber of the virginal womb."[11] But in general William is much more literally physical. We noted earlier his allusion to the stratagem of the wet nurse, "who at the time of the weaning of the child she is feeding, sees that the little one is so attracted by the sweetness of the milk that it does not allow itself to be separated from her and refuses to be moved either to solid food or some more suitable for it. And so she sprinkles her nipples with something bitter, which the little one, sensing it on the nipples, spontaneously spits out."[12] In an extraordinary illustration, William likens the need for immediate repentance of sin to the swiftness with which women wash the cloths they use to catch their monthly menstrual blood, so that the cloths do not rot.[13] His phrasing (*pandentes mulieres*, in Latin), could be translated by the blunt, old-fashioned description of menstruating women as being "on the rag." He uses the image in another work to make the point that nothing is so foul it cannot be cleaned.[14] Some remarks are even stranger, but again are said with the air of everyday knowledge rather than being abstractions from books, such as his passing comment that the smoke and stink of a snuffed candle can sometimes make a pregnant woman abort the fetus.[15] In fact, William probably has this particular example from the Arab scholar Avicenna's *Canon of Medicine*—a reminder that his chatty style can disguise his wide and deep reading. The example may also have come to him through his awareness of language, since the Latin words *foetus* ("fetus") and *foetor* ("stink") are very close.

William is not afraid of using female imagery to describe God. Caroline Bynum has written of twelfth-century use of female metaphors to talk about Jesus, but William is unusual in using similar terms to talk about the first person of the Christian Trinity, God the Father: "the Father himself is so luminous that he is pregnant with light";[16] the "first intellect," God the Father, "is necessarily most perfect and most pregnant and most fecund in every manner and mode."[17] God can be both father and mother at the same time: "as a result of the birth [of goodness] the great paternal fecundity rightly shines forth and is reflected in the offspring."[18] But he seems to realize that this approach might be too much for some: "You ought not to shrink from calling the first potency the first parent or first father . . . and from calling the first father the womb of the first generation and the bosom of the first fecundity and the fullness of the first utterance. For he calls himself all of these in David: 'You are my son, from the womb before the light of day have I begotten you' [Ps 2:7, 109:3]. From the womb, that is, of course, from himself."[19] And although the concept of Mother Church was an ancient one, in a sermon on Proverbs 31:25 ("A capable wife, who can find? Strength and beauty are her clothing and she laughs at the things to come"), William details how this woman's body forms the Church: her head is Christ, her neck is the Apostles, her upper arm is the Martyrs and her chest is the Confessors . . . "and so on through the rest," he says, leaving us to imagine what his examples would have been.

Pregnancy—repeated pregnancy—was the lot of most medieval women, although contraception of various sorts, male and female, was practiced.[20] William was in something of a cleft stick here, upholding the Church's teaching but also counseling a limit on the number of children to match a family's financial resources; he doesn't want families to resemble litters of pigs, with unwanted offspring sold in the market.[21] On at least two occasions, he chooses a surprising setting to make reference to pregnancy, in sermons to communities of nuns celebrating the solemn profession of sisters—their entry into the community, when they became "brides of Christ."[22] Both sermons (on different biblical texts) use a similar extended metaphor of pregnancy. Like any husband, Christ expects his bride to be chaste, but in this case, physical chastity is not enough; the sisters must be spiritually chaste, too. A soul pregnant and swollen up with pride is not pleasing to her husband, nor is the woman who puffs herself by reminding everyone who her father or brother are, saying "I am his daughter—or sister." And the virgin pregnant with pride in her own virginity also needs to beware: a virgin worthy of the name is slim with humility. Pride is the devil's fetus, and proud sisters may be impregnated by him. In one of these sermons, William reminds himself to say how much they have given up for Christ: "father, mother, husbands, sons and daughters, and all the consolations of the world . . . These are queens because they are betrothed to Christ."[23] The psychology of these sermons is interesting, whether the sisters had left the world in order to avoid the dangers of married life, or whether they were unwilling participants in the religious life, "extra" women whose part in the family jigsaw was to be offered to God—"thrown into the cloister by parents or relatives, like puppies or piglets whom their mothers cannot feed."[24] Having praised them for renouncing the world, William continues in a more terrifying vein, warning against (even spiritual) fornication and adultery, counseling them to see themselves as imprisoned and chained in the cloister for their own good, guarded by the abbess and an angel, and warning that if they break their marriage vows, like any other adulterer they will be beaten to death—but for them the punishment is eternal.

But nuns were not the only women William preached to. Women people his writing as young and old, married and single, chaste and widowed, as entertainers and prostitutes, as shoppers and shopkeepers, as makers and menders, as wise and foolish, as good and not so good. It's hard to think that William was not an admirer of women, because of the number of times he warns his clerical congregations against them, just as Bernard of Clairvaux's encomium for plain Cistercian architecture describes in detail the delights of Romanesque sculpture.[25] At times, the beauty of women appears to be the single greatest weapon the devil has to hand. Over and over, William calls it the devil's sword, armor, burning brand, and snare.[26] On a few occasions, William adds male beauty to this devilish ammunition, but his greater emphasis on the attractiveness of women must reflect the number of all-male congregations, whether of masters and scholars, parochial clergy, monks or friars, that he customarily addressed.[27] To an extent these warnings become formulaic, said without thinking, but the variety of his expression and the particularity of the things he notes do suggest someone who has observed these things for himself. He knows that women pluck their eyebrows and the hair on the back of their necks, they wear fashionable fur coats with added tails, they bat their eyelashes, they laugh, kiss, embrace, and promise.[28] How innocent can a woman be, when every part of her is dangerous—her golden hair, her clear white complexion, the arch of her eyebrows, her fine eyes, her long white neck—even her dress and shoes are swords in her armory.[29] A beautiful woman goes through a crowd of men like fire through a parched city, and her clothes and other adornments are deceitful, in the way that a skinny horse is made to seem healthily fat by drinking water.[30] Women who are both beautiful *and* stupid do the devil's work for him.[31] Women have their beauty from God, but it leads many men to damnation—even those such as priests who ought to be guiding others to salvation.[32] It's not important whether or not they actively mean to do this: women are dragons, breathing fire over everything they see and burning it up; and unless their minds are entirely centered on God, they're responsible for the consequences: "however you're killed, you're dead, as the saying goes."[33] A man can be corrupted forever by a single sexual act or even a single sight of a woman.[34]

But though Eve is the enemy of Mary, it would be wrong to give the impression that William dismisses all women out of hand.[35] Many women lead good lives: they are more generous than men, have merciful hearts, are more likely to fast and do good, or to undertake other religious acts.[36] After a hard day, a man gets home and his wife washes his feet, sets the table, puts aside a portion for God, feeds her husband, and then takes care of the children and herself; and all along, though the man claims to be making money for the family, his pursuit of riches is playing into the devil's hands.[37] Even beauty can be managed: wise mothers make sure their beloved daughters appear ugly and badly dressed, to protect them from being taken advantage of.[38] If most of William's examples come from within marriage, that surely reflects the expectations of the period and where he feels he can do the most good as a preacher. Marriage is a sacrament, a medicine, an ordered life, a book in which we can read about God, and a full and faithful fellowship of body and heart, of spiritual and worldly things.[39] But it's also difficult—especially when it comes to bringing up kids. He is notably aware of the suffering that women receive at the hands of men. Men betray women, he says, as Judas betrayed Christ.[40] They drink away their money in taverns, leaving their wives and children to starve.[41] Marriage ought to be the nest where, like birds, a man and woman find comfort and bring up their offspring, but instead, many men despoil it with their behavior, and compel their wives to do bad things.[42] Men are duty bound to "pay the conjugal debt"—that is, to have sex with their wives—but some do so without moderation, as a farmer plowing a field, or they do it for pleasure rather than as their Christian duty, and this sort of excessive demand is equal to adultery.[43] Equally, not to embrace your wife at all is a terrible thing.[44] In what is clearly a response to the Cathar heresy, which regarded all sexual relations as irredeemable, and so to be avoided, William says, "They don't know what they're talking about."[45] His treatise on the sacrament of marriage gives a sharp taste of how important he thinks marriage to be: it is the "holy, sanctifying and perfect society of male and female in the human species, and the bond or necessity which makes them debtors to each other in this sort of society."[46] There's no higher example, because God is a husband and human beings are all his wives.[47] Marriage is intended to produce children, but that is not its only purpose; it is the place where men and women might live in true religion, honoring God, mirroring the relationship between Creator and creation, and sharing all worldly goods. To be valid, marriage has to be contracted with mutual consent, with the prayers and blessing of a priest; without this, any children will be illegitimate, without legal rights as heirs.[48] It is indissoluble, even if there is cruelty or adultery; in such a situation, a wife may leave, but there is no divorce. Instead, she should try, with the help of the Church, to reform her husband.[49]

Historians differ in their readings of medieval theologians on marriage.[50] We can't expect the impossible from an ordained representative of the medieval Christian Church. My reading of William's emphasis on marriage is that he is supportive of women. Men might be taken in by a pretty face, but it was the women who were left to bring up the result of a one-night stand. Marriage provided a partner in the practicalities of life and in childrearing, and crucially it provided *societas*, "fellowship." Without marriage, there might not be love between fathers and sons.[51] If women could not divorce husbands, then neither could husbands simply divorce wives—which isn't true for Muslims, he adds—in favor of a younger or richer model.[52] Girls could be at the mercy of their families when it came to choosing partners, but William counsels fathers to choose the poor but wise man over the rich but stupid one.[53] Marriage and children were, for most people, the inescapable reality of medieval life; William doesn't think he should change that, but knows he must do what he can to make it as happy as it can be.

The worst exploiters of women are priests who live with them as though they were man and wife. Clerical celibacy had a contentious history in the Western Church. It was not a Gospel precept, but it had long been a Church teaching, and the canons of both Lateran III (1179) and Lateran IV (1215) had specifically ordered it.[54] In sermon after sermon William warns women against such relationships and condemns the clergy who engage in them. The women will have no more standing than prostitutes and their children will be bastards; such clergy are agents of the devil.[55] Unchaste clergy are diabolical enchanters who turn innocent girls and good women into soiled goods without intelligence or sense.[56] The devil's hunters and birdcatchers are those corrupt clergy and gigolos who use money, promises, and gifts to achieve their rotten ends.[57] William is aware of the attractions: "a young priest asked to hear the confession of a young woman for whom he burns with lust can remove himself and leave her to another confessor on account of his own danger."[58] But he also knows that women can feel threatened by their own parish priest, if he is known as a lecher or a betrayer of confidences, or she may recognize her own attraction to him and fear the priest may exploit her weakness; and in these circumstances, she can take herself to another confessor.[59]

Good husbands make suitable provision for their wives and children so that they don't fall into penury, which might cause them to abandon their faith, blaspheme against God, and commit adultery.[60] But not all women had that level of security, and William was also deeply concerned for those at the other end of the sexual scale: prostitutes. It's startling how many times they appear in William's writing and hard to know what exactly this reflects: as Baldwin remarks, a male clerical and student audience may have felt an "irresistible fascination" for these transgressors of the social norm, or it may be that the linguistic net for who exactly constituted this group was cast wider than it would be today.[61] If the only sexual relations recognized as valid were those inside marriage—and not all of those—then it was important to defame every other sexual act outside this norm. But there were, of course, women who sold sex for money in the thirteenth century, from high-level courtesans to purveyors of a backstreet quicky.[62] William doubtless preached to the former, but his concern for the latter was longstanding and practical. Official treatment of prostitutes varied. The papal legate, Robert Courson, was a hardliner who advocated (and in 1213 implemented) their excommunication and physical expulsion from Paris; but the pope himself, Innocent III, had issued a bull in 1198 declaring remission of sins for those who removed prostitutes from brothels and provided means for them to marry.[63] According to the chronicler Aubri of Trois-Fontaines, William's own response dates from late 1225, while he was still a canon. William founded a religious house in Paris for former prostitutes, named the Daughters of God (*Filles-Dieu*), overcoming local clerical objections to provide land outside the city walls to the north; and he continued to support the sisters as the house expanded, while he was bishop.[64] He believed that it was poverty, not innate immorality, that forced many women into prostitution (although prostitution itself was certainly immoral), and he urged others to do what they could to provide them with support, so that they had other ways to go: "goods of a wealthy church can be given to prostitutes and actresses as to needy people or in some other guise of piety." Nevertheless, there is always a moral undertone: "And these alms are more excellent and more pleasing to God than those which meet the neediness of the body alone."[65]

If sexual sins were certainly not the sole preserve of women, does William associate the female sex with any other particular wrongdoing? Malicious gossip, backbiting, and disparagement of other people, although regularly noted in sermons to both men and women, do seem to me to be attributed predominantly to women: "Disparagers of others, by their tongues, arm the first woman [Eve] with bows and arrows against the second [the Virgin Mary] and against good people . . . Defenders and excusers of sins and the like give her a shield against the second woman [Mary]."[66] William is also worried about superstition and other "folk" or pagan practices. "Old wives' tales" lead to belief in astrology or fate, rather than God.[67] "When women lose their youth, they begin to use makeup; and when the makeup doesn't work, because age has made their teeth fall out, their hair go white, their breasts shrivel, their belly sag, and given them varicose veins, then they turn to fortunetelling and the like. And at last, they can only live by selling tripe, the unclean parts of animals, and finally, they become very poor."[68] An extraordinary passage of touching human observation, spoiled by the punchline: "and this is God's fitting reward," for abandoning faith and turning to such delusions. Even in the desperation of poverty and old age, William can't allow his flock to turn away from the faith, in case they lose their chance of heaven.

William's sense of responsibility as a theologian and a bishop is, I would judge, what drives his warnings to and about women, rather than any simple prejudice against the female sex as such. Indeed, William specifically rejects Aristotle's view that women are not quite fully human: "nor should one listen to Aristotle, who says in his book on the natures of animals, that the female is an imperfect male." He is clear that there are (and are meant to be) equal numbers of men and women in the world; and that making new human beings requires men and women as equal branches of a tree.[69] His pastoral theology is sociological at least as much as ideological, driven by his experience of human foibles and of economic status. Wealthy connections can make a nun proud; poverty can make a woman turn to prostitution: both effects need to be recognized and mitigated, dealing with individuals as they are, rather than systems as they might be.

10

THE WEAK

For better for worse, for richer for poorer, in sickness
and in health, so long as we both shall live . . .

The weakest in society—the unborn, the ill and infirm, and the physically and mentally disabled—are the subject of this chapter. Very often in the Middle Ages they were also the poor, since the ability to work was crucial in a society where practical support relied on disparate charitable provision rather than on any central state organization. Nevertheless, poverty and infirmity were not the same, and William discusses them differently. Poverty was inevitably linked to money, possessions, and your attitude toward them, with avarice—the desire to have more for the sake of having more—numbered among the most serious or "mortal" sins. William tries hard to persuade his audiences that poverty in this world is a sign of God's favor, a down payment on the entry price for heaven. Illness and affliction, however, were often seen as a punishment for sin, whether your own or that of your parents or grandparents, since the Ten Commandments spoke of God "visiting iniquity down to the third or fourth generation."[1] Like everything else in William's world, weakness and disability could be read on more than one level. There was the simple, literal level of this life, where the existence of those unable to look after themselves afforded an opportunity for personal charity, fulfilling the biblical command to love your neighbor as yourself. Beyond the literal, however, was a level—in fact, a series of levels—of "spiritual" interpretation in which what could be seen here and now was simply a clue allowing humanity to read a deeper lesson that could bring it closer to God. William is unusual as a theologian, in this as in many things, in not losing sight of the world around him while interpreting its meaning for the next.

Here, we are mostly concerned with William's attitude to physical and mental rather than spiritual weakness. In a subsequent chapter, we'll explore his response to a doubting master of theology, and his recognition that doubt was sometimes simply to be lived with.[2] For the human intellect,

> is weak in itself and does not stand by itself, and for this reason it [the human intellect] at times approaches doubt. But doubt is only its changing, by which it is now inclined to one side of a contradiction and now to another, but at times it falls into the darkness and emptiness of ignorance and at times into falsities and errors. But its weakness is supported at times by the evidence of the truth, often by proofs or persuasive arguments, at times by signs; and when a reason, that is, a proof or persuasive argument, is feeble or without weight, it does not lean on it with confidence, but holds itself back in some sense, fearing that it is not strong enough to support it. And on this account it is evident that it uses such support or props like a weak or fragile cane upon which one who carries it does not lean either fearlessly or entirely.[3]

The need for a cane—for proofs of the existence of God—merely demonstrates the inherent weakness of your faith. But the whole point of faith, as he says many times, is that, by definition, it involves believing something basically improbable; as soon as you have proof, faith, like the Cheshire Cat, disappears. It's like the merchant who will only advance you goods against security; where's the faith in that?[4] In the same way, when you see someone who can only walk with one or even two sticks, you immediately judge that "his power to walk is weak and feeble, and that his hips and legs or feet are injured or in some way impaired, so proofs, persuasive arguments, and signs, like a multitude of canes and props, indicate that the intellect that is . . . walking in that way on the path of the truth, is weak, impaired, and limping."[5] And just as a cane doesn't heal a weak leg, but only props it up, so this sort of belief, which relies upon proofs and arguments, can't heal doubt; it's just belief, not true faith.

The link between William's discussion of literal weakness and its use as a signpost to the spiritual is found in his treatment of the soul.[6] Such a theological question may seem far from this chapter's theme, but the common point lies in the question of whether an individual's exterior weakness was a proxy—an outward sign of an interior weakness or defect in their soul that made them less than human. The Latin word for soul, *anima*, had a wide field of reference that often renders translation difficult. Along with its masculine form, *animus* ("mind" or "spirit"), it could be used to speak of issues of human consciousness that modern philosophers speak of as a mind-body or mind-brain problem, and it is often at the root of discussions of what we would call psychology—what makes people think and act the way they do. The soul was the vivifying or animating immaterial or spiritual substance that is the image of God in creation, and which was infused by God into every living thing. It sat on the horizon between two worlds—those of the senses and the intellect.[7] Each soul was individual—indeed, it was what gave each plant or animal its individuality, rather like a SIM card in a modern-day mobile phone. Although as an idea it was an ancient one, Christian discussion of the soul was given an enormous boost in the early thirteenth century by the appearance of Latin translations of treatises *On the Soul* by Aristotle and by his Arabic commentator, Avicenna. Aristotle's theories were both a stimulus and a challenge to medieval Christian belief, and he was too much of an authority simply to be ignored. William was one of the first university theologians to respond to Aristotle's arguments, although it was only in the next generation of scholars, such as the mendicant friars Thomas Aquinas and Albert the Great, that his ideas and language were incorporated into an orthodox formulation of Christianity.

Questions about the architecture, purpose, and position of the soul had always been keenly debated, at least from the time of Plato and Aristotle. William responds to both thinkers, as well as to Avicenna and Augustine, but his conclusions and his methods of explaining them are very much his own. The soul inheres in its own body and survives its physical death, since once created, that soul is immortal. Nonetheless, a human being is not comprised of two parts, body and soul, for the soul *is* the whole human person, even though it needs to begin its existence by being united with a suitable physical body. A human soul can only inhabit a human body, just as a pig soul can only inhabit the body of a pig. Some heretical groups believed in *metempsychosis*, the transmigration of souls between species after death, but William is clear that this cannot be an orthodox Christian belief. The soul has fifteen powers, which include the five external senses for which a physical body is essential (sight, hearing, smell, taste, and touch), as well as internal senses, such as memory, imagination and desire, the intellective power (the power to learn and understand comprehensible things), and most important of all, the will. In the Christian universe, without an individual will they are free to exercise, human beings couldn't be held responsible for their moral choices, whether of sinning or of acting virtuously. As ever, William takes this complex theological doctrine and expresses it in everyday terms: the body is the house where the soul lives; it is the ship with the soul at the helm; it is the workshop where the craftsman-soul plies his trade.[8]

Plants, animals, and human beings do not have the same sort of soul. God created three different types: vegetative, which belonged to plants; sensitive, which belonged to nonhuman animals; and rational, which only humans possessed.[9] Although human souls incorporate the characteristics of these other two types, they are nevertheless single, simple entities. This is the case even though humans are themselves animals, but as humans they have rational rather than sensitive souls. Each type of soul is designed specifically for its particular function, which is why, unlike human souls, the souls of animals do not live on after death, since the purpose of an animal is to be of use to human beings, and once that is done, there is no further need for them. Using a thought experiment, the Flying Man, which he takes (with acknowledgment) from Avicenna, William argues that all human beings intuitively recognize the existence of the soul.[10] Avicenna imagines that "if we put a man in the air with his face covered and [who] is without the use of any sense and who had not used any sense, there is no doubt but that it is possible that this man thinks and understands. Hence he will know that he thinks or understands, and he will know that he himself exists."[11]

That knowledge of one's own existence can come from nowhere other than the inhering soul.

When and how did each individual acquire their soul? The discussion centered on that weakest of all human forms, the embryo.[12] "It is obvious that [the embryo] is alive for many days before the human form or figure has been perfected in it. The question, then, is what sort of an animal is this [and] how such a fetus is alive, since it cannot be living save by a soul or through a soul."[13] William is opposed to those who say that the embryo lives through the soul of its mother, because it's impossible for one soul to be able to vivify more than one body, "since the body is matter and the soul form."[14] If this were the case, the soul of the sow pregnant with fourteen piglets would herself be responsible for the form of them all; or "since one woman had seven children at the same time," her soul alone would have had to animate them all. This can't be the case, otherwise the embryo would only have the desires of the mother, wanting to eat "coal and ashes and every filth," as pregnant women do.

Even if it were true that the mother's soul at least initially gave life to the fetus, how long would that continue? Does it die, by losing its mother's soul, at the same time as it lives by gaining its own? This seems too risky: any slip in timing would mean either that the embryo had two souls at once, or that its own soul would have to enter a dead body. Neither of these arguments is convincing to William. The mere fact of growth does not mean that the fetus becomes something different, only that it is being perfected—and that in itself means it must have its own human soul. The fetus is "a human being, even at the time of its unformed state; hence it was a human being, even at the time when it [first] began to live."[15] For William, this means that if a fetus is killed *in utero*, it is an act of murder. This logic comes up against a difficult biblical example: how could Moses, who wrote the Hebrew Law, specify a lesser penalty for someone who makes a woman miscarry a child than for a murderer?[16] The terms, rather than the fact, of William's disapproval are interesting here: "Who would believe that a man of such great wisdom and endowed with the Holy Spirit did not know this bit of physical knowledge, namely, that such a man is a murderer of the unformed child if it is really a human being, especially since he had to establish a law on this point at the command of the Creator?"[17] William doesn't doubt that Moses meant to do his best, nor that he was a "confidant and friend of the most high God." To get something so basic so wrong can only mean one thing—Moses lacked an elementary knowledge of physiology. William is a little shocked at this unscientific approach.

Having established that the embryo has its own soul from the beginning, William's view of the type of soul it is given is rather nuanced. In the early stages, the embryo—which he calls the human seed, in a deliberate analogy to plants—has a vegetative rather than a rational soul. But even though it bears the same name, this sort of vegetative soul is of another genus (or at least another species) from the vegetative soul of plants, because it is the "vital spirit . . . appropriate to its body"—the body of a human being, not of a plant.[18] This soul is not a rational soul; the embryo is only infused with its final, rational soul when it is physically formed, with the development of the limbs that are suited to it "insofar as the possibility of nature goes. I say this on account of the mishaps and obstacles that occur to embryos for many reasons."[19] Crucially, physical deformity, which must have been a more common sight in the Middle Ages than it is in developed nations today, does not in itself hinder the reception of a rational soul: the imperfect are still full human beings.

But what happens to the initial vegetative soul when the rational soul arrives? Despite his earlier argument against the soul of the fetus taking over from the soul of its mother, in this case it's possible for one soul to give way to the next, because both souls belong only to the fetus or embryo, just at different stages of its life. The superseded vegetative soul simply "ceases to be"; it's now unnecessary, because the rational soul can effectively govern the body on its own. Interestingly, William is not dogmatic on this point: "if someone wants to say of the vegetative soul that the same thing happens to it at the arrival of the rational soul as happens to a smaller light when a far greater light overwhelms it, he does not say something improbable. For the lesser light seems to be, as it were, absorbed or extinguished by the greater."[20]

At what point does this greater light enter the forming embryo? William quotes Hippocrates ("a certain philosopher of the Latins") as saying that this happens "at the seventh hour from the entrance of the seed into the womb."[21] But Christian teaching was that it happened on the forty-sixth day after conception, which is when the formation of the embryo is sufficiently completed for the rational soul to take over. This number appears to come from Augustine of Hippo, who takes it from the number of years it took to complete the building of the Temple in Jerusalem.[22] William notes that forty-six days is almost seven weeks, a number that links this creation with the original creation of the world in seven days. He also takes the opportunity to belittle the beliefs of astrologers, who say that everything about a human being is set in the first hour.[23]

Not every child is born in complete working order. This is a matter of bad luck, not of the will of God—it happens by a "chance impediment." Some people say that the Creator ought not to infuse souls into such beings, or should perfect what has gone wrong; William disagrees. It's up to the Creator to give life to anyone he wishes, and if some are receptacles for his greater gifts, and sometimes very many of them, it's not unreasonable that others have fewer: sunlight is sunlight, even on a cloudy day.[24] Imperfections came in two sorts, physical and mental, of which the most challenging for theologians were mental disabilities and disease. William distinguishes between various sorts of suffering—among them, those without the capacity to learn (*moriones*), the frenzied (*frenetici*), the raving mad (*furiosi*), the demented who have lost the use of their minds (*dementes*), the maniacal (*maniaci*), and the simply insane (*insania*). While it's possible to follow his distinctions to some extent, and certainly they show an intention to differentiate between types of mental illness rather than simply lumping them together as one, it's still not always clear that he is consistent in his terminology or his categorizations. Yet he is concerned to make it clear that, although the rational human soul is equipped with a higher power of learning and understanding, it doesn't follow from this that those without the ability to learn (*moriones*) have no such soul, or that they aren't full human beings. Anyone who argues that they are not fully human would have to say the same about the blind or those unable to walk, he says, since walking and seeing are equally powers of the human soul, and their loss is as much an impediment as the lack of capacity to learn.[25] An even more interesting comparison is with those who seem out of balance—the frenzied or mentally disturbed who are prevented from learning in the conventional sense but nonetheless "often philosophize and see marvelous visions that cannot be seen by perfectly sane and most learned human beings."[26] Mental harmony in itself, he argues, has no effect on the perfection of the soul, or else the disturbances everyone experiences, which are brought about by anger, fear, sorrow, or joy, would somehow also affect the completeness of their soul.

How is this consonant with the fact that it's in the nature of the soul always to progress toward greater wisdom and virtues?[27] How can the "unteachable," the "frenzied," and the "maniacal" make any sort of progress, so that it's clear that they do indeed have a soul? William finds the answer in their potential for betterment. If by some chance medicine was able to free them from their chains, it would be clear that they could naturally progress toward wisdom and virtue, "as is evident in those who are naturally mute. For, when the chain on their tongue is loosened, they make progress toward eloquence."[28] The crucial implication of this natural potential is that all souls—all human beings—are fully human, and should be treated accordingly.

Our sympathy is perhaps less easily engaged with William's attempts to explain God's providence—the care that he has for all creation—in the face of the existence of human suffering, pain, and death. He's adamant that the Creator can do nothing that's not good, and can turn anything to good, although he acknowledges that people very often find it hard to understand where the good in illness or in natural disasters, such as famines or earthquakes, might be.[29] One problem is that it's not clear to those forced to suffer under poverty or oppressive regimes, for example, exactly how they can turn their bad luck to good ends; but oppression, he claims, acts like the rocks that weigh down a light roof so that it won't blow off in the wind, keeping the flightiness of sin from taking the upper hand.[30] William means to be comforting or reassuring, but it's hard not to see this as the complacency of a bishop in his palace. In a comment reminiscent of the fictional reprobate Harry Lime, William asks, "Who does not see that, if this world had only peace and delights, it would hold back human beings in itself with an inseparable clinging and would turn them away from future goods and virtues?" Mirroring a saying of Francis of Assisi, William thinks that the sweetness of this life had to become bitter, lest it turn humanity away from the good.[31]

William's argument on human suffering combines a Pollyanna-like optimism with careful observational examples. One such is the question of the insane. God makes sure that such people are cared for, he says, though from a variety of motives or benefits. Some are "bound or beaten so that they do not harm themselves or others, and . . . fed and clothed and given other things necessary for them. For, whether done out of the natural love or the piety of those offering them or even to protect the property or persons whom they could harm if they were released, all these things are done through the care and providence of the Creator." For those who are left to themselves, to wander if they wish, this again is done because it is "salutary against their madness." We can just about follow William's reasoning this far, but his next claims are more difficult. What if someone escapes from confinement? When caught, he has the "good of more careful custody," and those who have to deal with him when he is free have the good of the challenge to their own response to him. "Even if he harms someone before he is captured, this brings forth the benefits of which you have learned, and perhaps many others. But if he hurls himself into water or fire, this too is beneficial . . . because through his death comes the good of peace and security."[32]

Madness itself is "often, in fact always, beneficial to the mad. For if they are good and just, when they fall into madness, their holiness or goodness is secured through their madness, since they cannot sin at the time of madness, and so holiness and justice cannot be lost by them or diminished at that time, since justice and holiness can be either diminished or wholly taken away only by sins. But if they are evil or unjust, they are cared for through the madness so that their malice is not increased at that time, and on this account the punishments of future damnation do not increase for them."[33] For a believer in life after death, this is of course a logical position; the prize of life with the Creator is worth the struggle, however hard that struggle might be. But had William really never seen the insane treated badly? Had he never met anyone racked and tormented by their mental state? "All shall be well" was the teaching of the fourteenth-century English mystic Julian of Norwich, but the line between a deep sense that the universe would one day be put right and the motto of Voltaire's Candide that "all is for the best in this best of all possible worlds" is often hard to discern.

In the Middle Ages, *lepra* ("leprosy") was the name given to a constellation of symptoms that included those of what is now called Hansen's disease.[34] Although insanity was regarded as a worse affliction overall, since sufferers were not able to repent, confess, and ready their souls for God, leprosy was terrifying because of the (false) perception that it was highly contagious, and because of its dismal symptoms, which commonly included ulcerated skin, contraction of the limbs, loss of fingers and toes, and gangrene with its stench of decay. Lepers had to wear distinctive clothing and carry bells to warn of their approach, and they were isolated in *leprosaria,* often named after the biblical Lazarus: in Paris, the hospital of St. Lazarus was located on the rue Saint-Denis, to the north of the city walls. All sinners should be shut out like lepers, William says, because they, too, are contagious.[35] The fear of contracting sin from elsewhere recalls a punishment for gluttony or lust that he reports in passing—to be tied to a leper.[36] Voluntary association with lepers, as practiced by Francis of Assisi or Louis IX, was seen as a particular mark of sanctity.[37]

Preaching on the Gospel passage in which Christ heals a leper by touch, William takes the individual symptoms and turns them into common signs of spiritual failing, so that anyone could be a spiritual leper—not merely those with the physical ailment.[38] Spiritual leprosy is an excessive love of this world, neglecting prayer and proper devotion, speaking ill of others or flattering the unworthy, and ignoring all attempts by God to hold out the hand of healing. In contrast, the Gospel leper is a model for how to pray, not thinking himself worthy of healing, but throwing himself completely on the mercy of the Lord. Christ holds out the hand of pity at the end of a long arm—long enough to reach even to death, and always outstretched; anyone who chooses not to receive that health-giving touch must work hard to avoid it. They will have to run from the Lord as though he himself were a leper, while he tries to pursue them for their own salvation.

The souls of the blind, like those of the insane, are fully human.[39] In fact, "souls are most whole and most strong in bodies that have been mutilated and have suffered amputations in their large and noble members [limbs], as if what seems to have been removed or taken from them by the loss of members was compensated for them interiorly."[40] William gives two examples, apparently drawn from life, of a blind merchant who could distinguish all sorts of coin by touch alone, and a blind man who was nevertheless a renowned warrior, making up for his lack of sight by his power of imagination. Reading between the lines of this discussion, it is easier to see through to reality. Amputees or those have been mutilated will tell you, he says, that they are not diminished in themselves; in modern terms, this is the struggle of disabled people not to be regarded as subhuman or unable to make decisions for themselves: what they've lost is only mechanical and can be supplied, in medieval terms, by wooden feet or metal hooks.[41] And yet he admits this isn't always easy to remember. Their union is so strong that it's sometimes difficult for a soul to see itself apart from its body. It needs, as the prophet says, to "'separate the precious from the cheap so that it becomes like the mouth of the creator' . . . the soul itself is precious and the body is cheap."[42] Here at least, William appears to recognize that it's hard always to stay upbeat; but his advice is to remember what's really important—again, perhaps, easy for the bishop to say.

Although people regard blindness as exceptional, William reminds his readers that it's sight that is truly miraculous, whether as part of the everyday miracle that is creation, or the gift of faith that God has given to humanity. Familiarity has bred contempt for God's extraordinary provision, "for though each and every work of the Creator is worthy of admiration, by experience of them . . . they have become cheap in the eyes of human beings to the point that they have already ceased to be admired."[43] Of course, everyone is astonished by miracles, but such individual events are nothing compared to the regular course of nature: "for it is far greater and more marvelous to give sight to all human beings than to one, and to give life to all than to one."[44] It's a sad fact of human nature, however, that people are more impressed when some are born blind, or when others are cured of blindness, than by the vast majority who can see.

Physical blindness as a metaphor for a lack of spiritual sight is a biblical trope, so it's not surprising that William uses it regularly, too.[45] The parable of the blind man healed by Christ's touch affords him numerous parallels.[46] Just as the physically blind run to places where healing miracles have been reported, so the spiritually blind should run to the light of the word of God, which is there for everyone—pagans, heretics, Jews, and even the excommunicate—who doesn't wilfully reject it. Just as a blind person hates blindness and loves the light, so you must turn away from the delights of this world, and toward the light of Christ. Heretics aren't blind—they just refuse to see which path is the right one. They sit next to the true path but won't travel along it, and they'll only give directions to a blind man if he comes and sits alongside them. Parish priests are there to lead the blind to salvation, but they must themselves be prepared, or else when the blind leads the blind, both fall into a ditch; and the bishop who puts such blind men in charge is equally culpable. The spiritually blind will quarrel with those set to lead them, because they refuse to believe they can't see; but in Paris, where there are so many learned men, there's no excuse for not accepting help. For just as the physically blind use a cane or a dog or a boy to help them find their way, so they can go about by themselves where they can, so those who have poor internal sight should seek out guidance from such supports. Those who are literally blind are rightly careful, never putting a foot down until they've tested the ground with a cane, but the spiritually blind carelessly rush toward harm. Some people are blind in only one eye: they don't see what's wrong with buying preferment for their sons or, in the case of clergy, valuing their own ambition above their love for God.

Sometime before 1260, Louis IX founded a community for blind people in Paris, just west of the Louvre. The Quinze-Vingts (Three Hundred) was named after an obsolete counting system, with the number signifying the number of members the foundation could house, although it seems never to have been full.[47] The community was unusual in being not a type of hospital, with top-down religious care for the sick, but instead a society of blind men and women who pooled their property and lived together, rather like a house of mendicant friars. Although Louis gave an annuity, the inhabitants were to support themselves by licensed begging. His intention seems to have been social support, rather than any implication that blindness was a punishment, or that the inmates might receive a miraculous cure. William was dead by the time Louis, now returned from Crusade, founded the Quinze-Vingts, but he would have approved of the assumption that blind people were capable of being functioning human beings, able to decide for themselves. All human beings possessed full human souls, and so at the most basic level deserved to be treated as equals in the sight of God. William's response to bodily infirmity is not to regard it as a divine punishment, but simply to accept it as what God has given. His theology saw this life as short and to be endured; the real prize was the vision of eternity. For that, every human being, weak or strong, had an equal chance of success. His message was clear: no matter where you are, God will stretch out his healing hand, and if you take it, you will join him in heaven.

11

POVERTY

God who made the lion and the lamb,
Would it spoil some vast eternal plan,
If I were a wealthy man?

It's the question that rings down the ages. Why him and not me: why can't I be rich? It's part of the reason that poverty is probably the single topic that William most often addresses. In his world, the difference between being rich and being poor was often a matter of life and death. Money made possible better housing, food, and medicine; it allowed for better surroundings, cleanliness, and space; and it removed the need to do the hardest and most dangerous jobs. The rich lived in a comfortable world of servants, eating a varied diet of fresh local produce supplemented by the exotic imports of international trade The poor lived precariously on what was left. To survive, you needed to work; and those who couldn't work, whether because of age, illness, or inability, and who had no family to support them, had to fall back on the charity of the community. With no "state," and no state aid, the needy were visible, begging on the streets of Paris.[1] Some "seem utterly abandoned, like a dead body exposed to the dogs and birds, for whose deliverance from those who tear it apart and devour it, nothing is done."[2] William's vivid image jolts us into the reality of a pauper's death. He knows that the question people ask here is: where is God?

The absence of an organized state did not mean the absence of any organized help at all. As we shall see in a later chapter, with means came duties and responsibilities, and those at the top were to set an example for those of lesser resources. The monarchy of God was the pattern for the monarchs of this world, and along with order and justice, Christian rulers were expected to copy his gracious generosity. The Capetian kings of William's lifetime were all notable for their personal piety, which had its practical consequences in almsgiving and charity. Blanche of Castile, as queen, queen regent, and queen mother, was thought by some to be almost too openhanded.[3] Blanche had a system of royal almoners—almsgivers—who organized the distribution of funds; she kept a contingent of poor people at court, as a reminder of the poverty of Christ, and she supported hospitals, including the city's own Hôtel-Dieu. Her son, Louis IX, was ridiculed by some for the extent of his personal piety. His own extensive charity focused especially on making provision for lepers and underwriting the work of mendicant friars. He and his sister Isabella were particular friends to the Franciscans, and Isabella eventually founded her own Franciscan house for women, at Longchamps, which she joined.[4]

The older monastic orders had their own tradition of charity and care for the neighboring population, since hospitality was a central part of the Rule of St. Benedict.[5] The city's abbeys and religious houses fed and clothed the needy, and employed others for those tasks the monks could not do themselves. In addition to the cathedral, local churches would have provided help to their parishioners, depending on their resources. In the text of a sermon to an audience of monks, William writes himself a note: "Go through all the types of almsgiving."[6] According to the Dominican Thomas of Cantimpré, William refused to accept the hefty sum of 3,000 marks, the property of one of the Notre-Dame canons who had died intestate. The bishop could take the money by right; but William gave it away to be used for the needy.[7] The poor, then, had places they could turn to—but these were the result of individual or institutional charity, rather than universal entitlement.

Charity was the primary Christian virtue, but poverty was also central to its religious message. Not all religions find poverty attractive or important; wealth, after, all, is a far more obvious sign of divine favor. In the Hebrew Bible, prosperity—the "fatness" of the land, the flow of oil, milk, and honey—was the desired and desirable state of all. The widowed, childless foreigner, Ruth, marries the rich landowner, Boaz, and their union is blessed with a child; God's favor for Job is signaled by his return to his former fortunes, leaving the dungheap behind. But the Christian message was one of renunciation: asking Jesus how to be perfect, the pious young man is told, "Go, sell all your possessions and give the money to the poor." The young man went away grieving at this unexpected response; and Jesus's disciples were astounded at his own footnote to the encounter, that it was easier for a camel to pass through the eye of a needle than for the rich to enter the kingdom of God.[8] Christians would eventually have riches, but they would be in the next world not in this one, and their wealth would be of a different kind. William is aware of the change: "after the human race had been gradually educated both by the teaching of the law of the Hebrews and of the prophets [the Hebrew Bible] and by natural doctrines and other teachings and miracles of the Creator, lofty goods were promised in the law of the truth and perfection [the Gospel], namely, goods of the next life."[9]

Christian teaching had more than one message, with different emphasis being placed on different strands at different points in its history.[10] William's interest in poverty is grounded in a particular context. The centrality of poverty had not always been so evident, but the expanding monetary economy of the late twelfth and early thirteenth centuries gave rise to an increased interest in the virtues and vices associated with the acquisition, retention, and distribution of cash. Economies based on land and goods required workers, and only a certain amount of perishable goods might be accumulated before they would spoil; but unlike land, coins were not a finite resource, and an unlimited number could be stored for an unlimited period by an increasing number of people. The expansion of the economy brought with it a bulging commercial middle class, with the leisure time and resources to devote to religion, if religion had a place for them and their concerns. The more money talked, the more inevitable became a religious response that rejected filthy lucre entirely. Among the profusion of individuals and groups experimenting with new forms of life, many held that any ownership of goods, even in common, was against Gospel teaching, which made clear, in the formulation of the liberation theology of the 1970s, God's "preferential option for the poor."

As a southerner, William must have known or heard about a variety of these variously orthodox associations, since the physical and political geography of the region was so favorable to their evolution. As a student in Paris, he would have known the life of the poorer Left Bank of the Seine, where the schools were situated. As bishop of a swarming urban diocese, he was shepherd of a flock that took in the royal family at one extreme, and those so destitute their bodies were left unburied, at the other. His responsibility for the laity was joined to his care for the houses of professed religious—monks and nuns—whose first vow was one of poverty, and whose numbers had just begun to be swollen by the appearance of the new mendicant orders, whose dedication to poverty was central to their religious life, and whose members were predominantly those who had turned away from their roots in the new commercial class. These points on their own don't make a decisive argument for why William might be concerned with the poor; rather, they represent a coalescence of ideas, and an illustration of how William himself often ordered his material. Rather than moving progressively through a series of propositions, objections, and responses, he commonly preferred to throw links for a possible chain of argument onto the table, in a rough order of importance, joining them not by a tight logical sequence but simply by the word "further" (*amplius*) or "again" (*item*). The result is rarely a single knockout blow, but rather a string of jabs from many angles: "more extensive than profound" at times, and "as numerous as they are diverse," but his "disconcerting prodigality" of ideas can be hard to resist.[11] Similarly, none of these reasons for William's predominant interest in poverty is by itself irresistible, but taken together, they present a likely explanation. In his own words: "[Jesus] laid the foundation of the Christian religion, when he said in Matthew 5, *Blessed are the poor in spirit for theirs is the kingdom of heaven* [Mt 5:3]. But he spoke more explicitly in the Gospel of Matthew 6: *Do not store up for yourselves treasures on earth* [Mt 6:19], and in Luke 6: *Blessed are you poor for yours is the kingdom of God* [Lk 6:20]. Similarly, in chapter 10 of Matthew, he says: *Do not possess gold or silver or money in your purses* [Mt 10:9], and so on. And in Luke 10 he says: *Do not carry either bag or purse* [Lk 10:4]. For he was not otherwise going to found the Church on them, that is, on the apostles, unless he had first brought them to this nothing and established and confirmed them in it."[12]

What did this mean, "brought them to this nothing"? When William talks of poverty, what does he have in mind? His understanding is on three levels. The first and commonest idea is of "a lack or privation of riches, and this is penury [*peniuria*] from [the word] storeroom [*penus*] . . . but a poor person is properly said to be destitute [*inops*], as if without resources [*sine ope*], without the help of human beings or without riches." This is the poverty that is "best known to all and hateful and terrible for almost all, and the reason is that it is the privation and lack of those goods that are not only necessary in the judgment of many, but according to them also delightful, honorable, and desirable for many other reasons." Fear of this sort of poverty "rouses many to seek and save riches," which makes it the root of ambition, greed, and other vices; those who can turn away from the desire for these temporal goods achieve "one of the more perfect virtues," and this renunciation of worldly riches is his second definition of poverty. But the third and "most perfect" form of poverty is a positive love of the absence of worldly things, and it is very rarely found.[13]

We need to bear in mind that the audience for this threefold definition is clerical. William is always aware of whom he is speaking to, and he alters his language, his references, and his message to suit. Here, he is preaching to the converted, so to speak; to those for whom a basic inability to put food on the table was unlikely ever to be a problem, and who had turned their lives to God. If his introduction to the first form of poverty seems dry and definitional, it is not because he has no feeling for the reality of destitution, but because he knows the difference between the poverty of religious professionals, and the unintentional and unchosen poverty of the laity. His task here is not sympathy, but an attempt to explain to clerics how to turn a mere lack—a negation or "nothing"—into a full and positive virtue. Nevertheless, it is worth noting in passing that real destitution, for William, is not just the absence of goods, but the additional absence of other human beings to help you.

When William is speaking to ordinary people, rather than clergy, in his sermons, his language is rather different. In this context, he rarely speaks of poverty on its own, but rather as part of a terrible trinity of poverty, troubles, and shame (*paupertas, molestiae, ignominia*), the presence of which marks someone out as a friend of God.[14] These three are inseparable, since the presence of one, and most especially of poverty, so commonly brings about the other two. They are the "timbers" that support us in this life; the tools God uses to destroy weeds in his fields and vineyards.[15] Why does God let people live with these three grim companions? Without dismissing the grinding reality of a life with nothing, William's self-imposed task is to persuade his hearers to embrace their situation as a gift and an opportunity, to look beyond today's scarcity to tomorrow's riches. He does this while walking a tightrope. It is easy to leave a comfortable episcopal palace to lecture those living on the breadline about how lucky they are. But we have reason to think that he lived what he preached, at least as far as his office would allow, not only practically, in foundations such as the Filles-Dieu, but by advocating the virtues of poverty to all classes of people—something that surely would have produced little effect if he was not known to live simply himself. He recognizes seven evils of poverty that the poor know—hunger, thirst, nakedness, cold, exposure to the elements, debt, and servitude—and the tone he employs speaks of an awareness of the realities of life at the bottom; the sins of many, such as thieves and those who prostitute themselves, he says, are caused by poverty, rather than innate immorality, which was the more common explanation.[16]

The Gospel aphorism about the camel passing through the eye of a needle ends with another: "Many who are first will be last, and the last will be first," which sums up the paradoxical nature of much Christian teaching.[17] This is the line that William takes when trying to persuade the poor that theirs is the better part. "The world says that evil is good, and vice versa, but God's view is completely the opposite. The world thinks that poverty, troubles, and shame are bad things; God, on the contrary, thinks they are good."[18] They are present at the Lord's table, where it is an honor to be a servant, and they are the road to the joy of the heavenly banquet, for poverty will be turned to riches and troubles to delights.[19] His message to the poor is that God has surely not forgotten them; on the contrary, their situation is closest to his heart. The trick is in how you see it: in the terms of modern psychology, if you can't change your situation, then happiness comes in changing your response to it. For "poverty is treasured in heaven; the poorer you are here, the richer you will be there, for whoever makes himself rich loses the reward of the house of God, namely, paradise, which is only for paupers. So to be part of poverty and misery today is to make treasure for yourself there."[20] "As the saying goes, a man with good money in his pocket can go cheerfully to market. Paradise is had by doing good and avoiding evil, and troubles and shame are the money with which paradise is bought."[21] In one sense, given the extent of medieval poverty, this is a practical response; in another, it simply supports the status quo: "God made them high and lowly, and ordered their estate."

This world-turned-upside-down is depicted in a story recounted by the Dominican Étienne de Bourbon, who attributes it to William: A great king convenes a court in his kingdom to judge sinners and pronounce their just reward. He calls them to the court, as many rich as poor. The rich come on horseback, through fields, forests, meadows, vineyards, and villages, and seeing such beauty, they can't believe that anything could be any better than these. They ask the king if they can have them, and he agrees. Pleased with themselves, they mock the poor, who are coming, on foot, for nothing, since the rich have got it all. The poor ask the king if there isn't anything left that he can grant to them. There is, and he can; he has incomparably—eternally—better goods. The poor claim these for themselves, and the king agrees, on condition that they wait for them a little while, with patience. The king then convenes his court, and in front of everyone hands out the rewards that each group has claimed. The rich are given all the goods of this world, as they had requested, but in addition they demand the goods of eternity, too. "I've given those to the poor," the king says, "and I'm not taking them back; but you can buy them for yourselves, with what I've given you." We barely have to be told that the king is Christ, "who gives worldly goods to the rich who, in the Gospel, ask for the eternal goods of the poor."[22] Poverty now means riches in heaven; all you need to acquire it is patience, and trust in the word of the king.

Poverty, says William, is empowering; it makes you free by removing the dangers to body and soul that wealth, and the anxieties that accompany it, brings—to which, of course, the poor might well answer, "I'll take that chance."[23] Poverty, in contrast, is security: if you have nothing, you don't have to fear losing it. Nevertheless—a sort of double kick in the teeth—nothing in itself is not enough. Although it's a good start, not all the poor are destined for heaven: beyond having nothing, you must *want* to have nothing and be happy with your lot. A man is not reckoned to be "just" simply because he doesn't kill or steal out of fear or lack of opportunity, but only when he doesn't want to do those things. In the same way, no one is "poor" because he has nothing, but because he doesn't want to have what he could have. God knows the difference because he can see into hearts.[24] The purpose of poverty is to overcome greed, that of troubles is to overcome carnal desires, and of shame to overcome pride.[25] The test of poverty is not what goods you have in this world, but which goods you have in your heart; so lovers of earthly wealth cannot possess eternal wealth—only the other way round.[26] The poor man who has God in his heart is rich, but the rich man whose wealth means nothing to him may also be saved, and it's not always obvious which is which.[27] In some cases it's very evident who has heavenly riches, but others are concealed, "just as Saracens and others by their skill work gold so that it looks like ashes and embers."[28]

Many of William's sermons on poverty are preached to members of religious orders, in particular Benedictines, Cistercians, and Augustinians, whose first vow was always a vow of poverty.[29] His focus here is often firmly on the question of how those who are part of well-supported communities can be said to be—can in fact be—poor. Just living in such communities is not enough: a mouse can live in a cloister, but that doesn't make it a monk; a donkey bears a cross on its back, but it isn't a Christian; a bird may fly into a church, but only to drink the oil in the lamps.[30] So a monk needs to make sure that, in giving up his father and mother, his family, and his own chance at founding a family, he doesn't transfer those affections to the worldly life of his religious community and neglect the spiritual. Too many celibates turn their passion to their stomachs; they're in love with the kitchen and the refectory, not with God.[31] Some monks join precisely to avoid the physical poverty of life in the world, because community life provides square meals and a roof over their heads. They "do not enter religion, but a restaurant, so to speak . . . Such men are oxen tied to the feed trough . . . Because they bind themselves to this in order to eat, we usually call them kitchen or refectory monks, because the kitchens, refectories, and cellars are for them the reasons for profession in their heart and intention."[32] This isn't a change of life, just an exchange of one sort of comfort for another. There are those, in fact, who give up considerable wealth so that they can lay down the responsibility that comes with it: they embrace "a sort of childishness," like layabouts and wasters.[33] Some even become monks for the opportunities monastic life can provide to enrich themselves or their relatives. They "enter like thieves and robbers . . . They make their habit a hideout, because they steal temporal things, take them from pious uses, and turn them to harmful purposes. Like foxes, they pretend to be spiritually dead by reason of their habit and tonsure, in order to plunder."[34]

Not only individuals but also whole communities are in danger of losing their poverty. This is at least partly due to the ambition of their leaders, who want to build up their houses to great heights and lord it over people, when they should be living surrounded by a moat of worldly and spiritual poverty. That moat is encircled by the devil, who works hard to fill it in, by procuring wealth for religious houses and benefices for educated individuals, and he's aided and abetted by "insane" abbots and the like, who not only fill in the moat, but build earthworks out of heaps of riches. From these heights, ambition, luxury and avarice, and other enemies of the cloistered life—which includes the sons of the nobility—find their way in and overwhelm it.[35] Maintaining the moat of poverty requires a three-pronged defense: making sure that your heart is not given up to the enemy; being careful not to exalt worldly goods; and finally, putting property to good pious use, such as by giving alms and not allowing the rich too much influence over religious affairs. True monastic poverty, however, is something beyond goods; it involves giving up all your own will and aligning all your desires to God.[36] "He who has renounced his own will truly possesses nothing. For whatever is possessed is possessed willingly," and people are chained by what they love, as a glutton is chained by the table or the tavern, flatterers and gossips by their tongues, and even learned men by their books—tied to them just as drying parchment skins are tied to wooden frames.[37] So whoever would be a poor man in spirit must banish his own will and judgment from the storeroom of his heart.[38]

William is all too aware of the criticisms leveled at the clergy and the Church in general: it's wrong for the Lord's servants to ride when Christ himself went about on foot, or to live in pleasure when he lived in poverty. Clerics need to ask whether they are disciples and ministers, or lords and masters.[39] If poverty is so good, how is it that the institutional Church has amassed so much wealth? Again, as a bishop living next to Notre-Dame—already under construction for more than sixty years when William was first installed, and absorbing enormous amounts of money—he was between a rock and a hard place; neither could he afford to fall out with the well-endowed religious communities in the diocese. He certainly understood the problem: "do not be mistaken about those who profess poverty in words and dress, but are literally very wealthy . . . For the heirs of a rich and glorious kingdom are not poor, if they possess it in common, although they are also forbidden to sell or give something away in accord with the good pleasure of their will . . . The brothers are rich who own such great riches. How then are they poor?"[40] William backs up this question with a variety of rather convincing arguments that refuse to allow common monastic ownership to be counted as poverty, but in the end he comes down on the side of the traditional interpretation: the property of abbeys and churches belongs to God, and those who live there have only the use of it, not the ownership. And those whose job it is to look after these goods are not necessarily tainted by them: the administration of worldly goods doesn't by itself make you spiritually one of the rich, but sticking to your own will does.[41] Perhaps the bishop could hardly say anything else; but he does add a codicil: "wanting to avoid such evils, holy men have fled and flee riches, and knowing that this poverty is the safest refuge from so many and such great evils and dangers, they flee to it, and they get from this no small joy at the removal, or rather immunity from them."[42] Ownership in common, then, is not impossible, but the wisest will avoid even that, if they can.

William did not need to look back to the earliest Christian monastics, the Desert Fathers, for an example of those who had renounced even common ownership of goods, since it was during his time as bishop that the two mendicant orders of Francis and Dominic had consolidated their position in the city. The mendicants provided him with useful nonparochial help by educated men as dedicated as he was to the pastoral aims of Lateran IV. The two groups had settled at sites on the poorer Left Bank, just inside the city walls, with the Dominicans alongside the main southern thoroughfare, the rue Saint-Jacques (from which they gained their nickname, *les jacobins*), and the Franciscans slightly to the west, based in a squashed triangle of land that came to be known as Les Cordeliers after the three-knotted girdle or *corde* that cinched their habit. We have seen already William's support of mendicants in the university and his granting of teaching chairs to Dominican and Franciscan masters, but other evidence shows that he didn't merely think of them as a means to plug a short-term teaching gap; rather, he recognized them as sharing his reforming instincts. In his campaign of 1238 against pluralism, he worked with the Franciscan master John of La Rochelle and the Dominicans Guerric of Saint-Quentin and Geoffrey of Blèves to come up with the formula that condemned the holding of more than one benefice if any was valued at 15 *livres parisis*. Bonaventure, who was later head of the Franciscan Order and was a student at Paris toward the end of William's life, recounts a theological disputation in 1241 in which William took part with the Franciscan master Alexander of Hales, and also notes William resolving ("determining") a theological question on causality in the Franciscan school when Alexander was present.[43] We cannot be sure that Bonaventure was present at this occasion, but he does say he heard William give theological judgments at other times. The mendicants shared William's conviction about the importance of preaching, and his only definitely datable sermon was preached to the Dominicans on Tuesday, 21 May 1241, although it is clear from the content that many others were intended for one or other order.[44]

Not everyone was as enamored of the mendicant contention that to live a true Gospel life required the renunciation of all goods and property, and both orders were criticized for what was perceived as a holier-than-thou attitude, especially toward other clergy and religious. Mendicant begging was also seen as taking away much-needed alms from the "real" poor.[45] While the Dominicans were permitted to own goods, as long as this contributed to their fundamental vocation of preaching, for Franciscans the life of poverty was the goal in itself, and, especially in the context of their life as Paris academics, they were caught in a dilemma that left them open to the charge of hypocrisy: although they claimed to own nothing, they had the use of buildings, money, and much other property that was held in a sort of trust for them by the pope. These issues caused disputes within the orders, too, particularly the Franciscans. For Francis, poverty had also entailed powerlessness, but soon, friars were not refusing positions of authority. William is aware that religious movements often start poor but, undone by their own success, end up rich.[46]

As bishop, William had once again to walk a tightrope, since it was his duty to support all those living approved religious lives in the diocese. His writings allow the various arms of the Church ownership of considerable amounts of property and wealth, as long as they are used for Christian purposes and without sin; but his words seem warmest when he is addressing those vowed to owning nothing—always remembering, as we have seen, that poverty is primarily a matter of the heart. It's clear that William knew some of the stories about Francis of Assisi, even if he had never seen him. Speaking in the persona of Lady Poverty, he writes:

> That holy father preferred my nothing to all riches. For when a disciple said to him that he had books from which he edified the brethren and from which the brethren profited and for that reason he wanted to keep them, he replied: By no means shall you do so, because to have nothing is worth more than all of them . . . [T]he Order of Friars Minor has surpassed all others . . . My nothing has endowed these orders with outstanding persons.[47]

In sermons to the friars, William often seems concerned to reassure them about the life they have chosen. God respects little poor men, he says, not those bloated by sin and worldly goods who lord it over others.[48] The friars minor and those like them are said to be "like" paupers, when in fact they are rich and full—as full as a jar that can't contain another drop of wine. In the same way, the powerful of this world are really not, but are only "like" the truly powerful; their desire for riches and luxury only shows how far from true fullness they are.[49] But friars are rich, like jars from which the balsam of holiness flows, because they have the security that comes from knowing they already possess entrance tickets for paradise.[50] No animal, he adds, is as stupid as mankind, because animals obey the laws of their nature: "the donkey doesn't give up the pelt that nature has given him, for any amount of money," and that word "pelt" (*cardeum*) was one also used for the Franciscan habit.[51] No member of the order should exchange what he has for mere worldly goods, for the religious man has stored up treasure in heaven, although he has nothing in this life. In a mock syllogism, William ends, "The house of God is the poor man's home. But the house of God is the kingdom of heaven." Therefore, the poor man's home is the kingdom of heaven.

William's moral universe, in common with the theology of his time, is one of individual ethical choices. Humankind as a whole was sinful, and humankind as a whole had been redeemed. But the choice to accept that redemption was one that each individual had to make for themselves. God—omniscient and omnipotent—saw every sparrow fall, which left little room for thinking that the way things were was not the way things were meant to be. Like Pope John Paul II, or Mother Teresa, in our recent past, William makes no attempt to reorder the structure of the economic world around him, nor even to advocate such a rearrangement. His response to the afflictions of poverty is in terms of personal and professional charity, allied with a reading of the world that turned its rewards upside down. A more political response is beyond him. Persuading the poor that their current penury was a down payment on future riches was his psychological strategy—he would have called it theological truth—for making what had to be borne more bearable.

12

THE LANDED AND THE MONIED

The rich man in his castle,
The poor man at his gate;
God made them high and lowly
And ordered their estate.

Whether his own birth was rich or poor, William's career in Paris brought him into the very highest circles of society. He was probably too junior to have known Philip Augustus, who died in 1223, just as William was made a canon of the cathedral, or his son Louis VIII, who died only three years later; but he certainly knew Louis's capable and educated wife, Blanche of Castile, and their son, Louis IX. Indeed, Blanche and William shared the Île de la Cité for at least twenty-one years from his installation as bishop, and he is described in at least one source as her confessor.[1] They seem to have been on terms of friendship beyond the merely professional: it's possible that William's southern roots allowed him to mix with the Spaniards Blanche liked to have around her at court, and gave him entry into that trusted group.[2] A story from a Dominican collection of around 1285 tells of William using Blanche to solve a problem for him, while simultaneously solving one of her own. William was aware that the Dominican friars who lived on the rue Saint-Jacques in Paris had run up debts they couldn't repay. He went to see Blanche, who had vowed to go on pilgrimage to the important shrine of St. James (St. Jacques) at Compostela, a journey that would involve her in great expense, and he asked if everything was already well prepared. She told him it was. "My lady," he replied, "you've already shelled out a lot of useless expense on worldly goods so you can show off your magnificence in the land of your birth. You could put it all to much better use." "All right," she said. "I'm ready to follow your advice." "I'll give you one piece of good advice, and I'll commit myself to answer for you in front of the highest judge. The Friars Preacher, who are known as the St. Jacques brothers, are in debt to the tune of 1,500 pounds or thereabouts. Take the staff and scrip [carried by all pilgrims] and go to St. James—to their house on rue Saint-Jacques—and pay off their debt. I'll acquit you of your vow to go on pilgrimage, and promise as well to answer at Judgment Day that what you have done is a hundred times better than going to Compostela, with all that excessive expense and paraphernalia." The story ends: "And she, like a wise woman, followed the holy man's advice."[3]

The story sketches a picture of William as a shrewd operator with a smart line in humor used to good effect, and of Blanche as equally quick on the uptake. Like all the best twelfth- and thirteenth-century pastoral theologians, William was a psychologist. Both he and Blanche were supporters of the Paris Dominicans, and the queen was genuinely pious and charitable. But from Louis VIII's death until the mid-1240s, she was also de facto ruler of France during her son's minority, and the king's first counselor when Louis IX married and took over the reins of government. She had better things to do than undertake a lengthy journey to Spain. William's intervention got her out of a regretted promise, while also supporting a cause close to both their hearts. When, in 1237, Pope Gregory IX tried to persuade Blanche to make a pilgrimage to the Holy Land, for the good of her soul and to help the emperor Baldwin, he suggested she seek William's advice on what to do.[4] For whatever reason, Blanche stayed at home.

The same astute psychology is evident in another story from the same source, which has William deputed by unwilling courtiers, who dared not do it themselves, to tell Louis IX the tricky news that his first child—whose birth he and his wife Margaret had awaited for six long years—was a girl.[5] Going to the king, William innocently announced: "Rejoice, my Lord, for I bring you good news. Today, the crown of France has gained a kingdom, because you have a daughter. Through her marriage, you will acquire a kingdom, whereas if you'd had a son, you'd have had to give him part of *your* kingdom." "And so," the story concludes, "he cheered him up." Called upon as a safe pair of hands for a difficult assignment, William not only takes on the role that no one else wants, he manages it with skill and sympathy, leavened with a little wit.

From the other side, Louis's own chronicler, Jean de Joinville, retails a story which he says he had from the king himself. William had told Louis of a great master of theology who had come to him in tears, because he could no longer believe in the sacrament of the Eucharist. William asked the master if he enjoyed the feeling of being tempted in this way; he answered that he did not. Would he insult the sacrament in exchange for money? Again, the master said no. William told him not to lose courage, because there was no sin that God could not forgive; but it was clear the master was being seriously tested since this was more than a simple matter of gaining pleasure or money. So William changed tack:

> You know that the King of France is at war with the King of England; you know also that the castle nearest the boundary-line between their two domains is the castle of Rochelle in Poitou. So I will ask you a question: Suppose the king had set you to guard the castle of Rochelle, and had put me in charge of the castle of Montlhéri, which is in the very centre of France, where the land is at peace, to which of us do you think the king would feel most indebted at the end of the war—to you who had guarded La Rochelle, without loss, or to me who had remained in safety at Montlhéri? 'Why, in God's name, my lord', cried the theologian, 'to me, who had guarded La Rochelle, and not lost it to the enemy.'
>
> Sir, said the bishop, my heart is like the castle at Montlhéri; for I have neither temptation nor doubts concerning the sacrament of the altar. For this reason I tell you that if God owes me any grace because my faith is secure and untroubled, He owes four times as much to you, who have kept your heart from defeat when beset by tribulations, and have moreover such good-will towards Him that neither worldly advantage, nor fear of any harm that might be done to your body, could tempt you to renounce Him. So I tell you to be comforted; for your state is more pleasing to Our Lord than mine. When the theologian heard this, he knelt before the bishop, at peace with himself, and well satisfied.[6]

The Middle Ages is often characterized as an "age of faith," but here we have a window into religious doubt, expressed not by a heretic or someone with little knowledge of the Christian faith, but by a master in theology, and recounted by a bishop. William takes the master seriously; he acknowledges the reality of the temptation, but he doesn't attempt to argue him out of it, or debate theological points. His pastoral psychology tells him that's not how doubt is to be overcome. Instead, it must simply be lived with, albeit with the reassurance that God will not abandon the doubter, whom he trusts in fact more than the untroubled believer. But what's more remarkable about this story is that William told it to the king. The military metaphor, of castles and defensive lines, is an odd one to use with a classroom theologian, even in the thirteenth century where these things were more in evidence; it's much more appropriate to a king. It's tempting to speculate that Louis was here recalling a time when he himself had confessed doubts to William, and William responded with a story about a master theologian—an allusion to William himself, or at least a story that might be read that way? Whatever the circumstances of the telling, William comes out of the tale as a shrewd and sympathetic counselor.

Although he mixed with royalty, William didn't spend all his time in their company. The Capetians had made Paris their capital city, but their court was still somewhat peripatetic, to make sure they were known throughout the kingdom. William was not one of the "small but nebulous" group of churchmen whose names regularly appear as travelers with the royal entourage; it's more likely that he thought his place was in his diocese, where there was serious work to be done.[7] Moreover, although Blanche was a genuine friend to scholars and ideas, art, music, and culture, she was also fond of more traditional courtly pursuits, such as hunting, gaming, rich and exotic food and clothing, and conspicuous spending: in the 1230s, there was a court menagerie with lions. She and her husband Louis VIII had taken Philip's efficient but somewhat dull royal court and transformed it into the most glittering in Europe.[8] Even for her son, the pious Louis IX, there was regal magnificence alongside his genuine desire for humility—a tension that wasn't appreciated by all those at court. Although William was regularly trusted by the royal family to carry out negotiations and mediation on their behalf, he himself was only prepared to go so far with their glamorous life-style. The stories of William with Blanche and Louis IX show that he was not overawed by the royal mystique; his real job lay elsewhere.

We've already seen William preaching to the poor and extolling the virtues of poverty; but the diocese of Paris also contained more than its share of the landed and the monied. Indeed, some of them were Church professionals: William wryly remarks that it's easier for someone to gain entrance to a religious community if they're rich, and he writes at length about the wealth amassed even by orders that start out poor.[9] But he wasn't about to challenge the prevalent political system. The Bible made it plain that God was a monarch with a celestial court, and where God led humans should follow. Kingship as a form of government was thus clearly optimal (something Aristotle also taught), and the question for theologians wasn't to overturn the system, but to make it the best it could be. For William as a preacher, this was a complex matter: he spoke to the poor of their priority in the sight of God, but he had also to speak to the wealthy in terms they would recognize and understand. Using an image of a well-ordered royal palace, he explains how God cares for creation, incidentally describing for us how such a place should run:

> first the elders, that is, the wise men standing beside the king, secondly, the judges, thirdly, the treasurers, fourthly, the dispensers of royal wealth, then the chamberlains. After these there are the stewards; then the cooks; then those assigned to carry messages or legal documents, and after them cupbearers, bread-makers, and various table servants. Lastly, the keepers of the horses, whose task it is to prepare the horses whenever the king has to ride. And you will see in the whole royal palace that all the previously mentioned functions are carried out at the least sign of the royal will alone.[10]

The king stands at the head of this pyramid, which is governed by his will:

> Because of one royal will or command, therefore, you see that so many motions of human beings and animals, of wagons and other carriers are produced; you see that so many kinds of craftsmen and workers

> and occupied in various kinds of crafts, with all the workers and ministers knowing what art or work pertains to each of them, and you see that at one royal command, which they recognize by the slightest sign, the individuals undertake and carry out their tasks.[11]

With such wealth and power comes responsibility, whether that be a matter of money—"Woe to those rich people who have their riches from God, but who don't look to the needs of the poor"—or of setting an example: "Good matrons and burghers ought to beware . . . for if they set a bad example in anything at all, it is as though they are the devil's best horses, or carrying his standard. For others seize on what they do and follow it and wish to imitate it, and excuse their behavior because of it. And they do this, even if it is unintentional."[12] The whole point of the rich having money is to use it for the poor.[13] It's not enough to say that you're holding back something for a rainy day, like "certain people who under the pretext of piety have kept their money most impiously while, by retaining it, they kill those in need, as Ambrose said: if you did not feed them, you killed them."[14] It's true, however, that the proper use of money for good can come in many forms:

> those who keep their riches for pious uses and also those who honestly trade in them for pious uses have already transferred them to the heavenly storerooms, while keeping and retaining them for themselves. But we understand that pious uses are not only the feeding of the poor, the support of the churches and other pious buildings, and the foundations of ecclesiastical benefices, but also suitable provision for their wives and children when these actions are referred to the honor and glory of God and their salvation.[15]

While continuing to argue that poverty is preferable, and a sign of God's favor, William has also to acknowledge that, even among the wealthy, there is space for charity:

> The goodness of the creator also offers such goods to his friends and good servants for sharing with, helping, and defending the needy and good people against wicked oppressors. For when the abundance of riches is obtained by good people, it nourishes and supports the needy

and especially the good ones. But power defends them from unjust oppressors.[16]

It was not, after all, the fault of Blanche or her son Louis, both sincerely religious people, that they were born into money and power; the question was what they did with it. William acknowledges that humans naturally desire three things: honor, riches, and health—which, indeed, is what God wishes for everyone in paradise. The key is to use them for God, and not for the devil.[17] The very rich should give lots away.[18]

Nonetheless, just doing is not enough; as with poverty, intention is all.[19] In a sermon of Robert de Sorbon, William is pictured riding with King Louis and his son, the count of Artois. There was such a strong wind that William's hat kept blowing off, and repeatedly he had to put it back on his head. "Look here," said Louis, "can't you put it on so it stays on?" William answered, "Sire, I can't make it stay put—the wind snatches it from me! That's not surprising, when the wind sometimes rips the clothes off your back." "What do you mean?" asked the king. "Sire, the wind of vanity sometimes tears the coat off a knight, who then passes it on to some court jester."[20] Robert, who was regularly part of Louis's entourage, is using William here to denounce those courtiers who, in the guise of charity, dress even their servants in rich clothes, not out of liberality but out of self-regard and the desire to show off. It's not real generosity, he says, to let people pick up your windfall pears. Although this story isn't in William's own words, it has an authentic William flavor, even down to his tetchy impatience with the king. It accords with what he says elsewhere, that not stealing because you can't or daren't doesn't make you a just man; the point is not to want to do it.[21] And once again, it shows the bishop at ease with the royal family, with a snappy comeback pointing out to Louis a rather greater failing among his courtiers than an ill-fitting hat.

William works hard to persuade his hearers and readers that worldly goods not only have no true existence in themselves, but that they cause harm to those who possess them. He draws on the language of the senses to try to connect riches and physical repulsion in their minds, using a sequence of biblical passages to back up his points. Francis of Assisi also used this emotive sensory language and experience, making friars pick up coins in their mouths, rather than touch them with their hands, and place the money on piles of animal dung.[22] According to William, such temporal possessions, which seem like gold and silver to the greedy man, in fact taste like mud, like pitch that defiles all who come into contact with it, like bird droppings, like dung, like thorns, or like deception and like vanity.[23] The taste of thorns is the "countless cares, fears, and sorrows" that they induce; the taste of deception is that, "though promising satiety and abundance, they give only hunger and need and their increase"; the taste of the vanity of riches is their failure to "bestow plenitude on one who has them [or] support for one leaning on them [or] fruit for one laboring in them or for them."[24] Worldly riches also taste of the burdens of whose who have them, of the danger of protecting them against robbers, and of the strife that holding on to them brings: "All the courtrooms and consistories echo with uproar and shouting for this affluence."[25] "In the same way riches savor of wars and the dangers of all wars, on account of which a rich and wealthy man is exposed to every kind of ambush and attack for no other reason than because of the riches themselves. They savor of a sword because they pierce the hearts of men with the wound of their evil love. They savor of fire because they burn with the ardor of desires, and they savor of excessive water because they drown and extinguish the hearts of human beings with the waves or swells of harmful cares."[26] "What is lacking is food for the soul, the scent and sweetness of God": generosity tastes good.[27]

The rich have no true friends. "Dogs and birds of prey don't honor cadavers while they eat them: when the flesh is gone, they don't look after the bare bones, or as the saying goes, everyone at the king's court is there for himself."[28] Those with money can't let down their guard for a minute: a certain priest collected funds so he could cross the sea, perhaps on pilgrimage; but when his chaplain learned about the cash, he wanted to kill him and take the money.[29] "So there's no security in these things; for truly, the rich of this world aren't rich, even if they're considered to be so" according to worldly valuation. Others are the slaves of their purse; they have to work to keep it full, ordering their days, mistreating their animals, living as though in servitude and wretchedness, all on the orders of the wallet. In a madcap passage, William conjures up the specter of the purse personified—a sort of *éminence grise* of the wealthy: "who was doing this? The purse!" This enslavement drives some men insane, while others hang themselves or drown. And then what? "A corpse in a golden grave isn't considered rich." The power of the purse shows when the rich think what's in their coffers will allow them to make everything right, by giving and lending, as though by a few good deeds they can indemnify the rest of their behavior. But this can't happen unless they first make restitution to those from whom they've made their money. And here's the rub: the money needed to do this can't be borrowed from the purse; the rich man would rather go to Jewish moneylenders than deplete his capital. He's the most wretched of men: he's wealthy, but his wallet won't allow him to do what he wants. In a rather gruesome pun, William describes the man who has long guarded the purse hanging at his belt, drawing its strings tight until, having been drawn himself, he finds himself hanging on the scaffold, because of the deeds the purse has made him do.[30]

William quotes the Roman writer Valerius Maximus to claim that you don't possess your riches; they possess you. This is especially miserable because people are imprisoned in their own iron money boxes, as though in a coffin or a grave, and they don't notice. In reality, they're dead and they should say the *De Profundis* from the liturgy for the departed; after all, a mouse in a mousetrap isn't free, nor is a bear that's caught in chains, even when the chains are gold or silver.[31] A debt collector from Paris traveled to Rouen, wanting to stay in the finest lodgings in town; but he found none good enough. He asked himself in desperation, 'What am I to do to get the best lodgings in the whole of Rouen?' So, coming to the doors of the castle, he struck one of the guards on duty and was immediately taken in charge and locked up inside. Asked why he'd done it, he replied that he wanted to have the finest lodgings in Rouen. This is how the rich get what they want, is William's comment: they imprison their hearts inside what they truly love—their riches. But you are not your possessions, even though those who have them often speak that way. If their vines suffer a hailstorm, they say, "We were hailed on"; if their house is on fire, they say, "We're on fire": but this can only be true if your heart is set on what you own, rather than on God, and if you equate yourself to your goods, then you're valuing yourself as nothing. The greedy heart can't be satisfied by anything in this world; those who appear to be rich are, in truth, in the worst sort of poverty, cold, and hunger. What good is it to a soldier if his horse—that is, his body—is well fed, if he himself (his soul) is naked and starving. That soul needs the taste of God and that body the clothing of virtues.[32]

Better by far, then, to rid yourself of the burdens and anxiety of wealth. The only thing riches bring is more problems. If you have fields, you need animals—oxen for plowing, sheep for fattening, dogs and shepherds to guard them. If you have a castle, you need knights, arms, servants, victuals. If you're a prelate—a bit of heavily self-conscious humor, here—even though you may seem like an honorable man, you can't do your duty when you see the flocks committed to your care torn apart by the wolves of sin and have your hands full trying to rescue them. Gold and silver, clothes and plate—they appear to offer security, but really just bring work, danger, fears, and cares; the wise person rightly acts to throw them away.[33] William uses the example of Peter and the apostles, who gave up all their goods to follow Christ, and received in return the kingdom of heaven.[34] In fact, like a mariner in a heavy storm who throws his cargo overboard so that his ship will not sink, jettisoning your possessions isn't a loss but a gain. In these circumstances, no one would think that their life was a price worth paying to hold on to their goods, just as no one would claim a corpse possesses the water he drowned in. It's the same as a farmer sowing seed—he's not throwing it away, he's investing it for the harvest; or a thief who throws away his loot if he fears it's slowing his escape from his pursuers. No one buys dearly if he gives worldly goods for heavenly riches, whatever amount of gold and gemstones he gives in the transaction. Since riches are truly nothing, to give them away is to give away nothing except the strain of the greed they create. Once more, William warns that wealth can drive people to suicide: "sometimes because of this, people hang themselves. They have nothing, not even themselves."[35]

Some people worked with money professionally. Moneylending was the most common occupation for Jews in the medieval West.[36] The work hadn't come about through choice; rather, Jews were legally barred from many other types of employment and had to live as they could. Their situation was precarious: on the one hand, it made them creditors for the aristocracy; on the other, when the debts owed to them were too high, kings reacted by expelling them from their kingdoms. They were needed, but also despised. Lending money at interest, a practice known as usury, was a touchy subject for the Church, since the biblical book of Deuteronomy forbade lending at interest "to your brother."[37] Christians interpreted this as referring to those of the same faith, although there were, in fact, Christian moneylenders, particularly in Italy. In an economy increasingly focused on monetary transactions, cash flow and the availability of capital were pressing questions for many, from the king downward. It was simply not feasible to be unable to borrow. The issue had been addressed in Roman law, and from the twelfth century medieval canon lawyers made adjustments to its regulations to suit the times, while theologians fought a rearguard action to keep the practice within reasonable limits. Lending goods was not a problem, since goods were understood to deteriorate with use and it was reasonable to expect recompense; but with money, all that had changed was time, and time belonged only to God; human beings could not charge for it. If you got back exactly what you gave out, how could you expect to have more? The theologians came up with a solution centered on the risk taken by the lender, and the precise rate of interest levied and profit made. It could be difficult to define what constituted usury and what was fair dealing, but it was clear that the absolute biblical ban had to make way for the practical realities of commerce.

William's discussions of usury are brief and seem mostly to concentrate on the damage caused by lending to those who couldn't afford to repay: "woe to those rich men who hold their riches from God but don't look to the needs of the poor . . . but instead attack the poor and lead them into sin by lending at interest."[38] Moneylenders may seem innocent enough, but what they do is necessarily evil. A usurer has a mouth that is always full, because he's constantly stuffing things in; a hand that can never be emptied, because it holds on to everything it gets; and a heart that can never be full, because it's always wanting more.[39] Recalling those who judge the metal value of coins by testing them between their teeth, William conjures an image of money which itself "bites and devours" those who borrow it. Such coins eat the corn and drink the wine that God made for humans to enjoy, so that the hopeless borrower can only lament, "The £20 I owe to usury is eating me up!" "No beast devours men as cruelly as a usurer: everything he owns has teeth and a beak!"[40]

And yet, given all his strictures against the danger of money and possessions, it is impossible to ignore the language in which William so often addresses his audiences—the language of commerce. He speaks to them in words and images from their daily lives, characterizing the Christian message in their own terms. Preaching on Peter giving up his possessions so he can follow Christ, William wonders whether the apostle wasn't just a negligent businessman who didn't know what he was buying into. He finds three reasons why this can't be true. First, Peter got more than he gave: in return for his own belongings, he got God's own goods. Second, he had faith in the deal, and faith is factored into the price for which the kingdom of heaven can be bought, whereas a lack of faith doesn't count against the price you pay, and so the deal can't be completed. And third, God's goods have no tax on them, which means it doesn't have to be added to the price you pay, so your profit is higher. In addition, God is selling truth, and where truth is sold, there's no place for doubt about the deal, no place for fraud or deceit. God sells on a handshake, with one word, and he doesn't charge tax. Finally, God himself sets the price, so no one else can change it. All together, this proves that, in fact, Peter was a canny trader, who didn't, in William's words, "buy a pig in a poke."[41] But it's true, he says, that almost everyone wants to buy God at a cheaper price.[42]

The wise person prepares for what's to come. Just as a prudent dealer investigates the goods and resources and markets where he wants to do business, so the heavenly trader, seeking eternal riches, frequents spiritual markets and places of business. What is teaching and preaching but a spiritual plaza where God and his salesmen hawk his goods to sinners? This is a trade that God wants to have with humanity; this is the kind of wealth that, with careful looking after, with labor and skill, will be exchangeable for the kingdom of heaven.[43] But first there has to be loss, because no one can be ready to go to a different place unless they leave the one they're in now.

This world is like a market where it's not safe to leave without having first paid—otherwise, you'll be punished just like other thieves.[44] This is a market where no one leaves without buying, because original sin has enrolled everyone in the sale of their whole inheritance; Adam's debt is the price of heaven.[45]

Historians have commented on the use of this sort of mercantile language by the mendicant orders.[46] Franco Morenzoni, the modern editor of William's sermons, wonders if it was not his personal preaching style that impressed the Paris friars and influenced their own use of contemporary language, references, and proverbs.[47] The use of commercial language to describe faith goes back to the Bible, but it finds a particular renaissance at the time of William's episcopacy and just after, and not only among the mendicants. Robert of Sorbon (d. 1274) in the generation after William, was also an exponent of such images—and it may not be a coincidence that he possessed an extensive collection of William's sermons.[48] One of the recurrent images in William's preaching is that of the provident merchant who, rather than carry his money with him on his travels round the circuit of trade fairs, sends it on ahead.[49] This might make him seem poorer than he is, because he has less to spend in some of the places he visits; but it means he can travel with assurance, since he knows his wealth is already safe at home. Some merchants may even borrow on the strength of what they've got, to further invest in the future.[50] The moral of the story is clear, and William used it regularly, especially when preaching to religious houses, to demonstrate that outward appearances have no significance for judging interior riches. To the friars, particularly the Franciscan friars minor, he adds a grace note: "I asked a certain man what he was; 'A poor monk,' he replied. 'Brother, [I answered,] there's no such thing! It's the very opposite!' This story should teach you that the friars minor will all have slippers in heaven!"[51]

The definition of riches is very different for different people. The Franciscans were required to wear sandals, not shoes, and their regular mode of transport was walking. Footwear was a point of contention, with some brothers accused of cutting down the tops of shoes to make them appear to be sandals, while still having the comfort of their sturdier construction. William knew that for the friars, after a day on the dusty roads of the city, slippers were indeed heaven. In the economy of his Parisian pulpit, William matches wealth and poverty to his particular congregations. He asks much of those who can give, and makes promises to those who cannot. From each, we might say, according to his ability; to each, according to his need.

13

ANIMALS

Would you like to swing on a star,
Carry moonbeams home in a jar,
And be better off than you are,
Or would you rather be a pig?

A pig is an animal with dirt on his face,
His shoes are a terrible disgrace;
He's got no manners when he eats his food,
He's fat and lazy and extremely rude,
But if you don't care a feather or a fig,
You may grow up to be a pig.

This 1940s Bing Crosby hit, "Swinging on a Star," might have been William's favorite song. In fact, he might have written it, if the Roman philosopher Boethius (d. 524) hadn't gotten there already:

> The violent plunderer of others' wealth burns with avarice: you would say he was like a wolf. The wild and restless man exercises his tongue in disputes: you will compare him to a dog. The secret trickster rejoices that he succeeds in his frauds: let him be on a level with the little foxes. He that cannot govern his anger roars: let him be thought to have the spirit of a lion. The timorous and fugitive is afraid of things not fearful: let him be reckoned like a deer. The stupid sluggard is numb: he lives an ass's life. The fickle and inconstant changes his pursuits: he is not different from the birds. A man is drowned in foul and unclean lusts: he is gripped by the pleasure of the filthy sow. So he who having left goodness aside has ceased to be a man, since he cannot pass over into the divine state, turns into a beast.[1]

William knew the writings of Boethius well, and when he first made his own similar comparisons, would likely have had him in mind. Men should "live the life of a man, not a beast; not the life of a lion by his aggression or pride; not the life of a bear by his gluttony; not the life of a wolf by his rapacity; not the life of a pig by his extravagant excess."[2] "Our body is nothing but our donkey or our pig. You have to be out of your mind to give up your own food to immerse yourself greedily in a pig's trough."[3] His words illustrate the difficulty when dealing with any medieval author of judging originality. Medieval teaching was founded on a set of authoritative texts, to which teachers and students responded. Often what is common between authors is much greater than what is different, certainly in terms of content, questions asked, and range of reference. The well trained absorbed the language and imagery of the accepted authorities, and especially the Bible, until these exemplars became completely their own. They used phrases and paraphrases from the approved texts without conscious quotation and certainly without specific references; they were—as William says of sea fish in brine—so attuned to what they swam in that they no longer noticed it.[4] For modern readers, following behind, distinguishing what idea or expression comes from where is a minefield of unmarked paths and unexploded bombs. Indeed, to point specifically to a source may be to inject false precision, since the prevailing ideas were, by definition, so common to the milieu that they were merely the unnoticed water in which theologians swam.

A renewed interest in the natural world was another aspect of twelfth-century expansion and renewal. A series of writers on "the nature of things" (*de natura rerum*) took as their core texts the *Natural History* of Pliny the Elder (d. 79 in the eruption of Vesuvius), as well as Ambrose of Milan's (d. 397) commentary on the biblical six days of Creation, the *Hexaëmeron*, and Isidore of Seville's (d. 636) *Etymologies*. By the ninth century, much of this knowledge had been collected into the *Physiologus*, a compendium of material on animals, plants, and minerals, which circulated widely in a number of similar but varying forms.[5] In the twelfth century, one very particular type of work developed from a merging of the *Physiologus* and the *Etymologies*: this was the bestiary, in which types of animal were individually described both in terms of their natural history, as we would term it, and as moral subjects, to provide lessons for readers in how to behave.[6] In the thirteenth century, the bestiary was joined by new encyclopaedic works such as *The Mirror of Nature* (*Specu-*

lum naturale) by Vincent of Beauvais (d. 1264), and *On the Nature of Things* (*Liber de natura rerum*) by Thomas of Cantimpré (d. 1272).[7] New impetus was given to the study of animals by the availability from the 1220s of Michael Scot's translation of Aristotle's three treatises on animals, *The History of Animals* (*De Historia animalium*), *The Parts of Animals* (*De Partibus animalium*), and *The Generation of Animals* (*De Generatione animalium*), later joined by his translation of Avicenna's commentaries on them.[8] William was an avid and early reader of these new Aristotelian and Avicennan translations. The important works on animals by the German Dominican Albert the Great (d. 1280) were written too late for William to have known them, although he may have met Albert himself when Albert was a student in Paris in the 1240s.[9]

Perhaps it should not, then, come as a surprise that William's pages teem with animals of all sorts, from the all-too-real lice and fleas that live in clothes, to the fictional basilisk that can kill with a look.[10] Did he write about animals mostly from his personal observation, or was his knowledge derived from literary sources—or was it some combination of the two? Was he interested in animals for their own sake, or only to provide moral examples for his teaching? We can at least be sure that William would have encountered animals very regularly: there was "probably no period, other than human prehistory, in which animals and humans shared space, food, famines, work, and weather conditions more intensely than the Middle Ages. Wherever one looked, there were animals: the forests, fields and farms, towns, fairs and markets, and the household itself."[11]

William takes his cue from Scripture: "I shall act in accord with the counsel of the wise man who says, 'Question the animals, and they will teach you, and the fishes of the sea will make it known to you.'"[12] William often prefers to speak of the deity as the Creator or even simply the First, rather than as God, and this Creator overflows with being like water over the basin of a fountain.[13] If they know and understand creation, human beings can come closer to knowing and understanding God: "For there is no creature that—to the extent it can—does not offer itself to, and in fact thrust itself upon, everyone who looks at it, and that does not reveal itself and all it has, and that does not speak by its own truth, the power, wisdom and goodness of the creator."[14] "Look to the tiny animals. The ant teaches you prudence . . . The birds and beasts which make themselves nests and burrows, to build your home in eternity . . . The fish, which never leave the water, except by force, teach you not to leave your true life . . . O preacher, the spiders teach you how to spin your net to catch sinners."[15]

The Bible demonstrated the dual position that animals occupied for medieval theologians. It is packed with real animals acting as animals, from sheep and goats to snakes and bees, and it is equally full of animals as metaphors, from the sheep that represent those people beloved by God and the goats that exemplify those who are not so lucky, to the snake that tempted Eve in the garden of Eden and the dove that is the sign of the Holy Spirit. The four evangelists, Matthew, Mark, Luke, and John, are equated with the four animals of the book of Revelation—the Man, the Lion, the Ox, and the Eagle—and in art these symbolic beasts became a shorthand for the Gospels themselves. Everyone should have the properties of these four, William says, roaring like a lion against sin, working at good works like an ox, flying in contemplation like an eagle, and using reason, like a man.[16] Central to all is the image of Christ as the lamb of God, the *agnus Dei*, an image of helplessness and sacrifice, but also a theological sign that after the sacrifice of his only Son, Jesus, God would no longer require or accept the animal sacrifices (*holocaustum*, in Latin) that were an integral part of Jewish worship in the Temple in Jerusalem. Jesus's own parents, Mary and Joseph, had celebrated his birth by presenting the prescribed pair of turtle doves or young pigeons to the Temple to be sacrificed to God;[17] but when that son had himself been crucified, Christian theology declared an end to the sacrifice of animals as a necessary element of religious belief. The physical offering of animal flesh and blood was replaced by the ritual offering of Christ's body and blood, in the form of bread and wine, in the Eucharist.

Christianity had similarly abolished the notion of clean and unclean foods or clean and unclean animals; nothing was any longer out of bounds. This meant that, whereas pigs were still shunned by Jews and Muslims, for Christians, especially in Northern Europe, the meat of the pig was a staple food, since unlike beef and mutton, pork was if anything enhanced by salting or drying or a host of other preservative techniques. The rules for ritual behavior, which included the dietary laws, were laid out in the Torah—the first five books of the Bible, traditionally said to have been written to God's dictation by Moses, "the Lawgiver." Judaism, Christianity, and Islam all regarded these books as sacred, but held different views about how far the regulations prescribed in them had still to be obeyed. Although the laws are not codified in the Torah, long-established convention reckoned a total of 613, including the central Ten Commandments, or Decalogue, which all three faiths retained. Rather unusually, William is particularly interested in the remaining 603 laws discarded by Christians, which gave detailed instructions for daily living, including the relationship between humans, animals, and food.[18] In his paired treatises, *On Faith* and *On the Laws*, William contrasts the approach of the three Abrahamic religions to the concept of law and offers explanations of the purpose and rationale behind the precepts, using the contemporary Jewish scholar Maimonides (d. 1204) as his guide. Instead of simply dismissing these regulations as having been "superseded" by the sacrifice of Christ, and suitable only for the "childish" Jews, which was the position of most Christian biblical commentators, William argues strongly that the laws were underpinned by a logic that was reasonable for the Jews' situation at the time they were given, and which demonstrated the practicality behind God's injunctions.[19]

The eating of animals was problematic in a different way for some heretical groups. Those who adhered to dualist religious beliefs saw the world in terms of two warring principles or gods—good and evil, light and darkness, spiritual and fleshly.[20] Orthodox Christianity was certain that the final outcome of this battle had already been decided, since only the good principle was truly divine, but dualism was not so sure. To be on the side of light required believers to renounce as much of this corporeal earthly life as possible, so that they could embrace the spiritual. For full initiates, this involved abstaining from sex and following what we would call a vegan diet—giving up eating both meat and food (such as eggs) that was the result of any sexual acts—since sex served only to trap good spirits inside evil flesh. William begins his treatise *The Universe of Creatures* with a sustained argument against these beliefs, represented in his time by the Albigensians or Cathars of his native South, although he also refers to them as Manicheans, after the dualist sect to which

St. Augustine of Hippo had once belonged. Although we noted in an earlier chapter that, as bishop, William demonstrated a preference for peacemaking over aggression, he nevertheless stands firm against this "pestilential" error, and is supportive of action that "does not cease to pursue with sword and fire and to exterminate it right up to today," asserting that the "Hebrew people and the Saracen people would do no less, if they [dualists] were found among them."[21] And he's not sympathetic to the idea that flesh cannot be food: it's the law of nature that some creatures are born to be food for others, he says, and "by the authority of God human beings have dominion over the fishes of the sea and the birds of the sky in order that they may eat them as they want, as we read in Genesis"—and this permission extends to "a deer or a boar or even an elephant, because even an elephant is merely chaff among so many good things of God."[22]

This isn't to say that animals should simply be seen as human fodder. The other end of the spectrum to dualist beliefs was manifest in William's lifetime by Francis of Assisi. It's hard to overstate the rock star status that Francis held in the medieval world, even during his lifetime. From the twelve followers who accompanied him on his visit to Pope Innocent III in 1209 or 1210, it's estimated that the Franciscan Order had 30,000 members by 1250.[23] Beyond numbers, Francis's message of Gospel poverty and penance had galvanizing effect on the rest of the Church, as did his incorporation of the whole of created nature into the worship of God. He addressed other creatures on terms of equality as "brother" and "sister," and stories from his close circle, recorded soon after his death, assert both his refusal to allow living creatures to be killed—he released fish and rabbits from traps, for instance—and his recruitment of them as fellow proclaimers of God's goodness.[24] In one of the best-known stories of his life, when he was unable to find people to listen to him preach, Francis turned instead to birds: "My brothers, you have a great obligation to praise your Creator. He clothed you with feathers and gave you wings to fly, appointing the clear air as your home, and he looks after you without any effort on your part."[25] God was concerned for each creature, no matter how small; in biblical terms, "not one is forgotten in God's sight."[26]

This sense of the providence of God, the care that God has put in place for every part of creation, is the subject of one of William's works. It may seem ridiculous or laughable, he says, that the Creator takes such care of these tiny things, but the fact that he does is proof that this isn't the case, for God would make nothing simply as a joke.[27] "The wisdom of the Creator in no way extends to the smallest things less than to the greatest or those in between, and on the other hand, he knows the uses, although they are very small, of the smallest no less than those of the greatest, although they are the greatest . . . so he has care to order individuals to their ends and uses."[28] "In this way, then, he cares for the number of insects that are captured by spiders and little flies devoured by swallows and for the whole order of their being captured and devoured. For he sees all things by his fixed and most lucid gaze, along with their uses and ends. For the eating of one little fly is part of the feeding of one swallow, and the little fly is part of the totality of its food."[29] This concern for the entirety of the picture has a surprisingly modern air:

> But do not doubt that, just as for all the fishes or all wild animals to be caught at the same time would mean the universal destruction for the fishes and wild animals, so for some fish or wild animals to be caught and eaten now and then would mean the destruction of that particular nature in them, in terms of one body of water or one region . . . It is not surprising, then, if by his care and providence the Creator and preserver of natures watches out for particular natures, as he does for them all so that they are not totally destroyed and do not perish, until their use or usefulness has to cease . . . But if the princes of lands and their lesser lords at times forbid hunting and fishing in waters and lands under their jurisdiction, intending by this to look after only their own greed, and not to provide for the conservation of nature, for how much better reason does the goodness of the creator not disdain to look after the conservation of the natures he created for such great benefits so that they do not perish completely?[30]

If God takes care of every single thing he has made, William is still clear that this does not extend to eternity. Animals were created by God not for their own sakes, but for human use. Since they won't be needed in any world to come, then along with everything else—animal, vegetable, or mineral—made for human utility, it will be necessary for their "creation and degeneration" to cease: no animals will be needed in heaven—or hell.[31] The utility or usefulness of animals to humanity is only made possible by the care and providence of the Creator, who has given people the "skills and arts" to use animals for good.[32] This means that, although all God's works should be loved, because "each in its way proclaims his power, wisdom, and goodness," it doesn't preclude killing them, if that is the use that God intended for them.[33] This doesn't excuse cruelty, however, such as hunters inflict in killing wild animals, the "torments" that butchers inflict on sheep and cattle, or the chariot driver who takes out his anger on his horses.[34] Indeed, in comparison to humans, animals ought to be admired, because their souls have not been corrupted by original sin. They are what they are, full of the natural virtue instilled in them by their Creator; they have a prudence humans have lost.[35] Drawing on common tales, William recounts the piety of lions that lead lost travelers back to the road and the magnanimity with which they spare those who humble themselves before them—unless the lions are *very* hungry. Wolves, too, are pious, and will feed abandoned children. All animals have natural gratitude.

> Countless examples of these occurrences can, however, be read about and seen by those who are willing to see. After all, who would not admire the faithfulness of certain horses, if we may speak in that way, which in the middle of battles fight against the enemies of their riders with hooves and teeth with an incredible boldness and courage, and rescue and set their riders free from the hands of the enemy . . . There are also found in animals amazing examples of prudence, providence, medical knowledge, the art of architecture, and the cunning of the hunt.[36]

This passage is not from a sermon, but from his treatise *On the Virtues,* intended for an educated audience.

The sheer variety of animal usefulness for humans in the Middle Ages mustn't be forgotten. Animals were for eating: they provided meat, offal, brawn, bone marrow, and blood for black pudding; their milk (from sheep and goats as well as cows) was used for the range of dairy products; their intestines and other internal membranes made skins for sausages; and their eggs were gathered from many kinds of domesticated fowl as well as wild birds. Parts of some animals were used to make medicine. Their dung and urine were prized as manure. Their bodies rendered up oil and fat, which had many uses, including as fuel for tapers and household lights, as well as for lubrication and softening. Their skins and hides were worked into parchment for writing on, and into leather for clothes, shoes, and other useful goods. Their hides, fur, wool and hair could furnish textiles, bristles for brushes, insulation, and high-quality clothing; horsehair was made into rope. Feathers were used as pens for writing, and together with down made excellent stuffing and insulation. Flattened horn was used to make window coverings that let in light, or in its own shape, to make containers for liquid. Hooves were boiled down to make glue. Bones could be fashioned to a variety of uses that needed light but strong materials, or used as fertilizer, along with blood. Animals could be employed for riding, for haulage, or for plowing. Dogs and birds could be trained to be excellent hunters, as were cats on their own terms, and some pigs could sniff out truffles. Inedible creatures could be used as bait to catch others, such as worms to catch fish. Eminently willing and teachable, dogs made excellent shepherds, and along with geese could be trusted to sound an alarm. Animals furnished entertainment, too, in the form of trained apes, bears, horses, birds, or dogs; exotic animals in menageries established the status of their owner. Some animals were scavengers, tidying up unwanted remains. Even insects were valuable: bees gave honey and wax for the best quality candles; silkworms provided the highest quality fabrics; and some insects and shellfish could provide dye and coloring for textiles and pigments used by painters. Not the least important, animals were valued companions.

This variety is mirrored in William's writings. Animals, he says, are killed to feed us; their hides are used to clothe and shoe us; their hair and fur are taken for our clothing; they are plucked for our sleeping [in pillows], softly and sweetly; animals are even flayed and plucked for our learning, to provide parchment and pens for books and writing.[37] Red dye comes from the blood of purple fish;[38] wool garments are warmer and more comfortable than any others, though women wear fur coats, from ermine or squirrels;[39] pack animals carry burdens through towns;[40] snakes, scorpions, and bears can be used for medicine.[41] Sheep in Flanders are tethered so they can only stray so far.[42] Skinny horses are disguised to look fatter by making them drink water, and there's a difference between the sorts of horse a knight might ride and those of the lower classes.[43] Bears are chained for baiting, and birds are kept in cages, which they constantly try to escape.[44] Crows scavenge corpses, but can also mimic human speech and have a "cleverness in borrowing and lending."[45] Cranes can be caught by the beak, though all birds avoid glue or pitch, in case they get stuck.[46] Old women burn their cat's fur to keep them close to home.[47] Apes "ape" humans for entertainment, sometimes too well: he recounts the proverbial story of the barber who gets fed up with being mimicked by an ape, and so mimes running a razor over his own throat for the creature to copy; the ape's fine motor skills, alas, let him down.[48]

Alongside the everyday are the oddities, the exotic, and the frankly miraculous. The legendary phoenix constructs its own pyre from spices, and dies so that another phoenix might rise from its ashes.[49] Some unnamed creatures are said to be fed "only by odors," or to "fashion dwellings for themselves out of cinnamon";[50] the salamander is said to feed itself from fire;[51] the basilisk kills using sight alone.[52] The sea furnishes some of the strangest examples, such as the stingray, which "makes the hand of the one who touches it so numb that it can do nothing at all for a whole hour"—even if the hand is at the other end of a metal lance; and the sucking fish, which attaches itself to the outside of a ship, "no matter how big," and stops it from moving. He is prepared to believe that ostriches have such a ferocious power of digestion that they can ingest iron, but not convinced by reports that they can incubate their eggs just by looking at them: "it is more probable that [the gazing] is done . . . to guard them rather than some other reason. For the warmth of the sand is sufficient to warm or incubate the eggs."[53] His remarks on elephants might be thought to come from book-learning, but Louis IX sent an elephant as a gift to Henry III of England, so William may indeed have seen one. He is impressed by the inflexibility of their knees, which means they cannot bend down; so that, as the bestiary would have told him, when a big elephant falls over, it needs to be jacked up by the smallest one getting underneath it, since the other adults cannot stretch down to help. The moral—reminding us that all his remarks about animals are made for reasons other than natural history—is that by being born on earth as a baby, Christ the Lord "like the little elephant among the big ones . . . puts himself under each sinner who cries out because of his fall, in order in some sense to pick him up and carry him."[54]

William's favorite exemplary animal is undoubtedly a spider. They scuttle, tiny, clever, and intrepid, across many of his pages. They teach him about God's provision for creation, about foresight and innate knowledge, and about the nature of the soul. The skills that spiders exhibit are proof that the Creator gives all creation the skills it needs to thrive. A spider does not need to *see* what is happening to *know* what is happening. "From the striking of one thread of its web or net, the spider imagines the fall of a fly and that it is prey or food for it."[55] Where, he wants to know, does this spidery imagination come from, if not "from the art with which the Creator endowed the soul of the spider so that by it the spider both weaves webs and hunts flies by them. There is, then, an art of skill, in such living . . . since, before the spider sees or apprehends the fly in any way, it proceeds to produce its threads and to weave a web from them. It is obvious that, as soon as it was hatched from the egg, it practiced such skills."[56] The industrious spider, which fights for its food with "ferocity and stealth, even with trickery and skill," lives its life in accordance with its nature, following the natural knowledge and moral goodness it was given to live in obedience to the divine will.[57] It does this because each new being is "created with its law, and as if with a book in which it reads what it should naturally either do or avoid . . . [and] with a lamp or light showing it the paths by which it should walk and the path that it is necessary to avoid . . . It is, therefore, evident to you that in this way a spider is born with such a law, a book, and lamp . . . an indication and sign of the will and good pleasure of the Creator."[58] With so much baggage, it's no wonder they have eight legs.

Unlike humans, who "have turn[ed] their souls aside from the rectitude of their natural laws," animals obey the light of their natural knowledge.[59] Though that light be small, in comparison to the light the Creator vested in humans, they follow it more closely, and "rightly ought to be held in our admiration."[60] William describes the spider with such engaging charm that it's hard to think he wasn't speaking from direct observation; but the image of the spider was one he took from the Stoic philosopher Chrysippus, known to him from Chalcidius's commentary on Plato's *Timaeus*.[61] He discusses Chrysippus in comparison to Plato and Aristotle when considering the exact position of the soul in the body. Plato thought the soul was in the head, and Aristotle placed it in the heart. But Chrysippus puts it in the middle of the animal, like the spider sitting in the middle of the web, sensing from that central place all the things that happen elsewhere. William, however, takes the image further: "It is not . . . probable that Chrysippus understood that middle point in terms of place. For a spider is never seen there except perhaps when its prey, that is, a fly or other insect, is there. He understood, then, in that case a middle point in terms of power, and I mean a nest from which it could sense all the movements . . . and for which it extends and stretches out its web like a net . . . they lie in wait for flies as if from a watch tower, and look forward to their capture."[62] In this addition of his own, we can perhaps see William's real-life observation.

And then there are the dogs. The medieval pleasure in dogs is an interesting example of biblical precedent being put to one side in favor of lived experience. Almost all scriptural references to dogs are negative, but that is so far disregarded that the Middle Ages even provides us with a greyhound honored as a saint.[63] Dogs are everywhere in William's sermons, whether hunting for game or for souls. Preachers and teachers were the hounds of the Lord (*Domini canes*), which came to be a pun on the name of the Dominican (*Dominicani*) friars; and unlike wild, country dogs, these well-trained breeds follow trails and retrieve the quarry without eating it.[64] Not only is the dog's sense of smell "more noble than in many other animals, but it is also like a certain light of prophecy or divination naturally given to certain dogs by the Creator so that they search out, recognize, and apprehend by this light both thieves and men in hiding."[65] But the devil had his dogs, too, or could even be likened to one himself, tied up during the day but let loose at night, raging round, devouring anything he could find.[66] Best to throw it a lump of meat, so you can get away.[67] A rabid dog might bark itself to death.[68] Dogs are William's common metaphor for "detractors"—the biters who become backbiters, speaking ill of others for their own ends.[69] Priests and prelates were sheepdogs guarding their flocks, though one priest he mentions lived surrounded by his sixteen dogs, to stop him visiting his mistress—and even so he killed eleven of them trying.[70] Those people only interested in others for what they can get are like dogs only interested in bones with meat on them.[71] Some people are cruel, like those who throw a dog a stone instead of bread, so that it breaks its teeth; little use that the dog can learn from the experience.[72] Others indulge their dogs too much, for dogs are very likely to see a bone or food on the other side of the road and run off; and it's crazy to be a slave to your own dog when it does absurd or loathsome things, such as throwing itself into water or a latrine, or injuring itself by some stupidity.[73] But perhaps it's worth it when they "do much out of love of their benefactors," and fawn upon them with "adulation and tail-wagging."[74] Dogs were created for human protection, and show it "by their solicitude and a certain friendliness," "their barking and bites, by which they try to ward off the things they see will harm their human masters or their possessions."[75] "Love me, love my dog" was not original to William, but it's a phrase he uses again and again.[76]

"I saw a cat absolutely refuse the meat of the bird, which common folk call a plover."[77] William's references to animals run the gamut from his own lived experience to information he had garnered from the considerable medieval literature on the natural world. To our ears some of it sounds utterly incredible, so that anyone who believed in such tales must have been particularly gullible or naïve. Yet, as we continue to learn more about the workings of nature, perhaps we shouldn't be quick to rush to judgment; after all, no one who hadn't seen a giraffe would believe a description. While William had certainly read all the theoretical authorities on the natural world, it's difficult to think that he did not also observe it for himself and appreciate it, if not for its own sake, then for the sake of its Creator:

> Who can sufficiently admire the skins of many serpents and reptiles delightful to see in their most beautiful variety? Likewise, who can sufficiently think of how great is the variety and beauty of flowers? . . . No intelligent person fails to know that these arise, are fashioned, painted, and decorated in so many ways by the one wisdom and one teaching of the Creator.[78]

Even pigs.

14

FOOD AND DRINK

O, for a draught of vintage! that hath been
Cool'd a long age in the deep-delved earth,
Tasting of Flora and the country green,
Dance, and Provençal song, and sunburnt mirth!
O for a beaker full of the warm South . . .

A bunch of grapes is always better pressed."[1] William liked good wine and liked to drink it full strength, unwatered. Dining at William's episcopal palace, Jean de Beaumont, Louis IX's chamberlain, noticed that, although he kept a jug of water near him on the table, the bishop never added it to the excellent wine he provided: "That water serves no purpose," Jean mocked. "Not at all!" William replied. "[It has the same purpose as you.] When you're at the palace, if a prince or a count wishes to raise his voice, you silence them immediately, with a warning. If a knight or anyone else speaks too boldly, your order immediately shuts him up. In the same way, if the good wine on my table from Saint-Pourçain or Angers or Auxerre encourages me to do something wrong, the water standing there immediately contradicts it, and in a minute, everything's calm again."[2] The story neatly exemplifies the place of food and wine in William's writings. Although he's always talking about eating and drinking to teach a moral or pastoral lesson, the frequency of his references and the detail he offers along the way tell us much about his kitchen and table, and their role in his happiness. It's God's intention that eating and drinking are delicious, of that he's sure: there's a joy that comes from food and drink, from the sheer physical sensation of eating, when it's done with pleasure, and from the simple delight in enjoying the drink go down.[3]

William saw the world as the book the Creator had written so that humans could understand him. This gave him free rein to use anything and everything to shed light on the workings of God, drawing lessons from the most surprising everyday things. His images are startling in the directness with which he approaches the most complicated theology by means of the most common experience: "I have cooked him on the stove of his Passion for the refreshment of my poor and starving. I roasted him on the spit of the cross like a paschal and spotless lamb"—so says the personification of Piety about Christ.[4] But in making these theological points, William tells us about the reality of food and its preparation: "Benevolence offers a sacrifice from a stove," cooking the heart with sweet love and pious desires; "piety offers a sacrifice from a frying pan, frying with oil and fire"; but "zeal offers a sacrifice from a grill, that is, roasts that are only roasted with heat and burning."[5] The most delicate dishes, are "ones that are baked," and cooking itself "is a drying of the raw and impure moisture in meats, and meats cooked in water seem drier than those baked."[6] Cooking is hard work, so a cook's hands are hard and calloused;[7] different foods need different seasonings.[8] In a sermon to nuns who are clearly feeling the trials of the religious life, he likens them to olives, for the harder olives are squeezed in the press, the better the oil that flows from them.[9]

If you often find yourself becoming angry, you may be a cook—but of yourself. People like this

> not only spiritually feed, nourish, and fatten the devil from themselves, but also, like his chefs, cook and prepare themselves for him. Those who become angry set a new fire of their anger, for baking, grilling or—what is truer—for charring themselves, as if the fire of tribulation were not enough for cooking and preparing them in that way for the evil. These people are properly the grilled or burned meat of the devil that is called braised [*braleim*] in the vulgar tongue. They delicately and lavishly feed the devil who make themselves grilled, burned, and baked meat for the devil. But those who readily yield, as if softened and melted by the difficulty of tribulation, make themselves sauces for the devil, such as are often made from cheese melted at the fire and from many other things. These people seem to take pity on the devil who has lost weight and is unable to chew hard food. For sauces are

> prepared and set before only children who do not yet have teeth or old people whose teeth were removed by old age or some other cause.[10]

A sinner can only be cooked in his own sins, piecemeal, just as sins are committed one by one; so the vice of gluttony will cook your tongue, the vice of lust, your genitals; and the desire for other people's goods will cook your heart.[11]

In a sermon to the "people of Paris," he weaves an extended metaphor of food.[12] The city is a mill where all God's corn is ground to feed the world, "milled by the teaching and disputations of the masters." The city is an oven where bread for the whole world is cooked and a meal prepared. God gives more spiritual bread here—more preachers and teachers—than in many whole provinces, so woe betide those who don't eat when so much has been provided. Everyone should be the Lord's bakers, since Christ is the flour from which we can bake the bread of penance or the tart from his pastry.[13] Bread and wine were the basics of the Christian liturgy, and William uses both repeatedly in the endlessly creative analogies he comes up with to explain the life of faith. Food has both a corporeal and a spiritual self, "for what is sweet to the palate of the mouth seems good to the palate of the heart, and what is bitter to the palate of the body likewise seems evil to the palate of the heart."[14]

For William, wine is a gift of God, and in itself a good thing; which only goes to show that humans can take any good thing and make a bad thing out of it. In the case of wine, this is drunkenness. This isn't just a vice of the poor, who are regular customers at the string of pubs the devil seems to own in William's sermons; in fact, the better the wine, the easier it is to get drunk from it.[15] "Off" wine and nasty-tasting food defend themselves against being eaten, but vices draw us to themselves in the same way that the deliciousness of expensive wine attracts us to drink it.[16] In the Middle Ages, the alcoholic content of wine and beer made them safer than water, even for children. It's his expectation that rich men will have many vats of wine in their cellars, and will adapt it to those drinking: what father of a family would not temper a very strong and intoxicating wine if his children were at table?[17] Don't be caught sleeping like a drunk when the devil's out to get you, he warns, for drunkenness takes you beyond sense, beyond wisdom, which is your defense against him.[18]

But God can take apparently bad things and made good things from them, in the same way as you add good wine to bad to make vinegar, which is so necessary for pickling and seasoning or even medicine.[19]

The drawing of wine from barrels is a path to considering the habits of the soul, which, unlike the wine that decreases as it is drunk, are enhanced and expanded with use.[20] Methods of judging the quality of wine illustrate different types of knowledge: you can know "scientifically" how good it might be by looking at its color and subtlety and clarity; but only through smell and taste can you know in a deeper way, "sapientially" (from the Latin word for "flavor"), what it's really like.[21] The justice of divine punishment is apparent when human beings take God's gifts and misuse them, turning them into occasions for sin:

> It is, therefore, most just that drunkenness or some other punishment, according to the good pleasure of the Creator, follow upon the misuse of wine, as at times dropsy follows, at times a fever, at times a deep sleep, which gives thieves the opportunity to rob or even strangle drunks . . . Justice is clearly seen in all these punishments, that is, of those who misuse the benefits of the Creator, but his abundant kindness is seen in those who use them well.[22]

"What is a soul sobered up from the drunkenness of any vice or sin by bodily infirmity but one changed from bad to good . . . ?"[23] In such a case, the tears of human compunction—that prick of conscience when someone recognizes they have done wrong—are the wine that gets even God drunk.[24]

Where the only refrigeration is natural ice, salt is crucial for the preservation and flavoring of food, and the properties of salt are one of William's favorite and recurring images. God would accept no sacrifice without salt—a sign of its value and importance, and the Bible described Jesus's disciples as the flavor-giving "salt of the earth."[25] In desperate times, a dove's droppings were used as salt, for the bile from its gall bladder is said to be excreted this way—but don't try it at home.[26] Meat kept in "sweet"—unsalted—water will rot, William warns, so salt your delicacies to preserve them.[27] This is at the same time culinary and theological advice: make sure you dedicate everything that is dear to you to God. Salt heals, so when you feel that itch of lust, bathe it in the salt water of tribulation.[28] In sermons on the text, "Bring me a new cruet and put salt in it," William understands this salt cellar to be the Virgin Mary, for the salt is the first thing placed on the table, just as Mary, as its queen, is the salt of heaven as well as the earth.[29] But the cruet could also be an individual faithful soul—not the filthy old thing from the kitchen but one properly clean—and it holds three types of salt: the salt of temperance, the salt of wisdom, and the salt of the memory of Christ's passion. Everyone should be cooks for the Lord, and look out in case they don't lay down enough of this salt for their dishes. Let's remember, he adds, the salt we've eaten, in a palace, in a church, and in baptism, when a child has salt put on its tongue as a sign of offering to God.[30] Spiritual salt is one of the signs of the second coming of Christ, recognized by devotion, which is the Lord's salt cellar, mixing salt with ground aromatics such as the pepper of burning love, the ginger of tempered zeal, and the cinnamon of humility, all bound together with the bitterness of sins and the fresh green herbs of holy meditation and blended with the vinegar of tears. When this is done, discretion serves this salt to all.[31]

This is salt as it's used on land; but the landlocked William is also interested in the briny sea and the difference between marine and freshwater fish; in fact, he tells us that salt is made by boiling up seawater—still true in some places today.[32] All men except Gascons, he claims, fear the sea, which is salty, smelly, and restless.[33] The fish that swim in this water don't notice these things, and, remarkably, their flesh doesn't taste of salt. Once again, his meaning is simultaneously of both the physical and the spiritual world. This salt sea is the world of earthly delights. Those who live among these worldly pleasures are unable to be salted—to become the salt of the earth—unlike those saints who are dead to these delights, in the same way as flesh can only be salted when it is dead meat, not while the animal is still living.

God sends preachers out to fish this world, using their sermons as nets. Often, they only catch tiddlers—the simple folk; but some others can be put into the salt of penitence, or the fishpond of the cloister, and some are roasted over a little bowl, when they are angered by those things they did against the Lord. Some are taken by the devil, who keeps them down in deep water, in case they might show their heads; others are eaten by other, devilish fish—by sins such as avarice and lust. Some fish just aren't caught in the net, either because it's not big enough, or they swim over it, or it's not wide enough to span the river, or the fish are too small, or they live in the mud at the bottom. Kings and other secular lords will swim right over; pleasure seekers are stuck in the mud; some say they can't get to the sermon, so they swim right through; and others who declare that the preacher just doesn't speak to where they're at are fish that bite their way out of the net. Some fish allow themselves to be caught, but are too scaly to be eaten, such as those who think they're too aristocratic to join religious orders. Even those who *are* religious want a silk lining for the cowl of their habit. And those who do allow themselves to be both caught and eaten won't let themselves be eaten raw—some want to be boiled, others roasted but unseasoned, others to be cooked in bile or poison: such people refuse to give up their own wishes or quarrels, or they just want to make life difficult.

The medieval food supply was at the mercy of the weather, and famine was a concern for many. Paris was fortunate. Surrounded by fertile agricultural land, situated on a river, and with wide-ranging trade links, the city could provide, for those who could afford it, food that was varied and wholesome. William has Lady Poverty describe true riches: farms, fields, vineyards, and gardens, which give wines, grains, and fruits.[34] He appears very aware of where food comes from and how it is produced. He speaks of farms, orchards, and vineyards, forests where animals could be hunted and rabbits snared, holding pens for animals until they were ready to be slaughtered, and fishponds, which many large houses and religious communities would have possessed so that they could provide fish for the meatless Fridays, and other fasts, that Christians were supposed to observe. Birds of all kinds were domesticated and reared, or hunted and shot. His writings are peopled by those who sow seed; pull weeds, thorns, and thistles; harvest crops; and pick grapes. It's everyone's duty to look out for miscreants: if you see someone fishing in your secular lord's pond or hunting in his forest or stock pens, you've got to raise the alarm. But your parish—and even the neighboring parish, too—is God's fishpond, and if you spot trouble, such as the prostitute spreading out her nets, or other such unlicensed hunters, you must let the priest know. For from the fishpond that is the waters of baptism, via the grace of teaching, the fish are farmed for God's table. God wants sole rights to fish in his pond or hunt in his forest, through his preachers and teachers, and if you see a band of the devil's dogs—those married priests, again—out hunting there, denounce them to the bishop or archdeacon.

The threat of famine brings out God's generosity in the shape of miracles of abundance. The divine provision of food had a long biblical tradition, and in uncertain times it was reasonable that God's care for humanity would manifest itself in that way:

> Nor is it surprising since he has also multiplied in their time grains and vegetables by his omnipotent power and generosity, even in the barns themselves, in time of famine a hundred times and more than that, at the same time satisfying the pious desires of the religious, when the people were in danger of famine, and showing compassion for the necessities of the needy . . . It is admitted that in my own time fishes that were already cooked were multiplied at the table of a certain holy man by the kindness and generosity of the Creator. For, although scarcely six of those dining could have been served from those on one platter, the whole multitude of those dining festively were served by individual plates <from those> on three platters. And the remnants of the fishes that were left over were far greater than the fishes prepared and set on the tables.[35]

We will read this as gullibility or credulity, but in William's world, the line between what we would call the supernatural and the natural was porous. In fact, he does not commonly recount such outright miracle stories; like Augustine, he saw greater wonder in the everyday miracle that turned a grain of wheat into a loaf of bread. On the whole, rather than a God of miraculous interventions, William preferred to see a Creator who was the ultimate steward of his creation.

All this good food didn't come to the table without ceremony; part of the pleasure of eating was the circumstances that surrounded it. Boys from families who could afford it, or who had connections, might be sent to grander households to learn how to behave, which could involve learning to wait at a lord's table, as well as eating and conversing in an approved manner. The twelfth and thirteenth centuries produced books of etiquette to teach just these skills.[36] The better households had dining tables lit by wax candles and tapers, and servants to present the dishes. Again, William's descriptions are both physical and spiritual: chastity serves at table, lighting the candles with the spark of conscience, while flies are driven away by those getting on with God's work.[37] One of William's remarks seems to set standards at quite a low bar: "the heads of households sitting at their tables usually have sticks or scourges at hand to drive off dogs that at times wrongly intrude at tables." Even so, having the proper cutlery and table linen was an important mark of status.[38] In God's household, "there are the whitest napkins, clean dishes of foods, handy washing of the hands and mouth, the kitchen quiet and not cloudy with steam, nor terrifying with the fires of various flames or with the exquisite tortures of animals, and not noisy with the slaughter of animals and preparations of salty foods. With me, taking food is refreshment, neither diving in nor gorging."[39]

Domestic standards, along with the variety of diet, are similarly evident in William's elaborate metaphor of the Virgin Mary:

> This trinity of the highest Trinity made a feast in a Virgin's womb. At this feast, the table was the Virgin's heart; the tablecloth, her spotless mind; the cutlery, [the virtues of] providence, careful understanding, and reason; the bread, a pure conscience, a sincere mind, contempt for the world, and love for God; the gold vessels are clemency, grace, piety and patience. These objects don't reject what's poured into them, but rather they accept the wine of charity. The fowls to be eaten are perseverance, forbearance, constancy, and patience. The sea birds are faith, hope, and charity, which are nourished by the water of baptism. The land birds are compassion, consolation, sympathy, and other such humane qualities.[40]

Meals should begin and end with prayer—a blessing at the start, and a thanksgiving at the finish; anything else is eating not like a Christian but like a pig.[41] "It is the custom of great men to summon pipers after eating a meal to induce sleep or to make the meal more pleasant and longer"—*chacun à son goût*, is all we can say.[42]

Food can, of course, be a trap: if food is your god, then "woe to those who, via their stomach, throw all their goods into the latrine!"[43] We saw in an earlier chapter William denouncing those "kitchen monks" whose hearts are set on the refectory rather than on God,[44] but he is equally concerned about those who are too fussy:

> Bodily food, therefore, is food that conceals a hook, that is, the pampering of dainty pleasure; because while the dainty eater believes that he is the hunter and trapper, in fact *he* is caught by *it* and, as the saying goes, hooked. Hence it is that all who feast, all gluttons and drunkards, are like fishes caught by a hook, that is, pierced by the briefest pleasure in their mouths and throats . . . Alas, how wretched a spectacle for the eyes of the pious is the countless multitude of men so hooked, horribly bound by their gullets, men who are dragged off to a hellish hanging.[45]

The response to both gluttony and fastidiousness has to be temperance—finding a middle way—rather than any extreme. "For some persons fast to the point of making themselves lightheaded and of weakening their body, which makes them incapable of and unsuited for other holy labors and sacred exercises."[46] Fasting is neither good nor bad, as long as its aim is to enable the individual better to obey God, rather than remaining fixed on the lack of food for its own sake.

After eating comes digestion, which William claims as a form of cooking, since it purifies what the body has ingested.[47] But sometimes, things go horribly wrong. On a number of occasions, William uses the act of vomiting to detail what happens in the sacrament of confession, with the stages of illness related to the contrition, confession, and restitution that the confessing person experiences. His meticulous description of nausea is worth recording at some length:

> Vomit, literally speaking, is the emptying of the belly, either partly or fully, via the mouth or by the agency of the mouth; the emptying of the belly partly or wholly, which an upset of the stomach or belly or something inimical to them inside the belly usually induces. In the same way, the belly of the heart or conscience is emptied or relieved from vices or sins by the agency of the mouth, by speaking or revealing those things to a priest. Therefore, just as someone with an upset stomach, straining to expel what is harmful or unsuitable to it, distends his belly and opens his mouth wide to get rid of it, so too someone with an upset to a noble and holy conscience strains and searches the belly of his heart to throw

out and expel detestable and filthy vices and sins, opening his mouth wide for them to leave via the words of confession. Therefore, since the noxious humor of vices and detestable sins is pushed toward the mouth, because of this upset and disturbance of the spiritual belly or conscience, and leaves via confession, this confession is rightly called spiritual vomit, because of the similitude with bodily vomit.

You already know that vomit is sometimes one of the bodily purgations, and it happens in the belly when nauseating material is at the opening of the stomach, or near it; for at that point the awfulness of this material comes to the taste buds, and on account of this, the mouth of the stomach distends, together with a forceful widening [of the esophagus] all the way to the throat, so that it might be expelled. But when such material has sunk deep into the stomach or into the intestines, vomiting like this is rare or doesn't happen at all; and in this case it is clear for the healthy to see that since the excrement of vices of sin will have sunk deep by habit, or through ignorance, or simply because of the passage of time, that the vomit of confession rarely or never happens. Similarly, when the appetite or the digestive system have been mortified or weakened so that they are unable to sense detestable flavors or unhealthy liquids, vomit is reduced or stopped altogether. However, when these functions are strong and healthy, vomit increases and is more frequent . . .

And in the same way as when bodily appetite and taste becomes upset and disturbed and out of sorts, and desires things that are not natural or good and contrary to the body's health, and has a loathing and disgust for the health-giving delights of food, they want to eat ashes and charcoal and other filth that shouldn't be mentioned, so when the appetite or taste for spiritual virtue has been corrupted, it brings on vomiting and disgust and a loathing for the health-giving delights of spiritual food, and wants to eat ashes and charcoal and nameless filth, as Numbers 21[:5] reads, "We loathe this insubstantial food," when in fact it was the most delicious bread with the sweetest flavor.[48]

Surely everyone has been sick at some time in their lives, but rarely can the experience have been recalled to such effect. Confession, along with attendance at the Eucharist, was one of the devotional practices ordered for the laity by Lateran IV, and William shared a belief in its usefulness with the friars who developed a reputation as skilled confessors. The basic idea of "better out than in" as a metaphor for confession takes little imagination; but to capture an audience with the grisly details takes a particular skill. The taste of bile in the mouth, the distended throat, the sense of muscular force as the unhealthy matter is expelled are all unnecessary for making his central point, but by describing them with such immediacy, William establishes a bond of complicity between himself and his audience, a shared humanity that leaps the chasm of eight hundred years as it would have leaped from the pulpit to the pew.

In one of the few personal remarks he makes in his writing, William appears to describe being himself indignantly rejected by an unnamed someone—"a notorious sower of sodomistic abomination"—as being vomited out by them, "not without cursing and spitting." This happens, he says, because a weak spiritual stomach will nauseously reject the good. "And we experience this in ourselves because we who are thought to be or to have something good in ourselves are rejected by someone with indignity and abomination . . . something that we ourselves heard from the lips of someone who did not know or advert to this."[49] The memory obviously still rankled, and clearly he was not above a little public retaliation; was this another run-in with Chancellor Philip?

The Jewish faith embraces life's sensual pleasures by surrounding them with ritual. The weekly sabbath meal uses shared food and drink in the context of family prayer to celebrate the gifts of God, which in the Hebrew Bible is a promised land flowing with milk and honey. Although the human story begins in Genesis with the eating of forbidden fruit, with disastrous consequences, for Christians it ends in the book of Revelation with a heavenly banquet; and that banquet was foreshadowed by the institution by Christ, in the days before his crucifixion, of the blessing and sharing of bread and wine with his disciples, a ritual that became known as the Eucharist or the mass. As the Church organized, it marked out special days as "feasts," a word that comes from the same Latin root as a "festival" or holiday. Every Sunday (*dies Dominica*, "the Lord's day") was technically a feast day, balanced by Friday as a fast, when meat should not be eaten. Feast days included both smaller commemorations dedicated to individual saints, and the two major festivals of the year, Christmas and Easter, in preparation for which the seasons of

Advent and Lent spelled out more extensive fasts. Toward the end of William's life, there was a movement to recognize that first Eucharist on Maundy Thursday, four days before Easter (also known as the Last Supper), as a major celebration, to be known as the feast of Corpus Christi, or the Body of Christ.[50]

The Gospel text read on Maundy Thursday was the story of the man who put on a great feast and who, when his guests didn't all accept their invitations, told his servants to go out into the streets and compel people to come and eat.[51] Even in the Gospel, the text is a parable—a story told to make a moral point—and the lesson here is clear: God invites everyone who wants to eat, and he sends servants out to make sure they know they can come in. William preached on this text several times, with more or less complexity.[52] He notes that the meal is a *cena*—the Latin word for the evening meal, the last meal of the day—because this is the heavenly banquet before the joy of paradise. There'll be no eating after it, not only because there will be no eating and drinking in heaven, but also because this meal will completely satisfy all hunger and thirst. There will be an enormous amount of food and a huge number of courses—"beyond comparison"—full of sweetmeats and delicacies, so it makes sense that those invited eat less, or even fast entirely, before they go. Be careful you don't stuff yourself so full of the pleasures of this world that you can't eat any of this great supper.

The invitations are made by God to all who believe in Christ; no one is excluded. His messengers are preachers, teachers, parents, good women, good prelates—any good person, in fact, who by doing this is doing the Lord's will. Moreover, all people, whether Christian or not, have the knowledge of the invitation; we carry it about as though it's written in us. Those who don't want to sit down aren't excluded by God—it's they who kill themselves by refusing to come and eat. The compulsion of the invitation is displayed by the presence of those old friends, the poverty, troubles, and shame that God bestows on those he particularly wants to summon. The feast can't start until Christ has been crucified, because he—the sacrificed lamb of God—will provide the food and pay the bill; he is first to the dinner and leads all the other guests in. It's a celebration, so come in your wedding clothes. But beware: no one is allowed to sell this food on. This last point is a reference to the selling of

Church positions, known as simony, which was forbidden by the decrees of Lateran IV and which, like pluralism, William was keen to stamp out.[53]

In one sermon on this text, William particularly addresses the preachers and teachers who are God's appointed heralds with the invitations to the meal. They are the birds called by the angel of the Apocalypse to flock to the Lord's supper, and by the prophets Ezekiel and Hosea to eat flesh and drink blood, to eat up the sins of the people.[54] But some of them are not as hungry as they should be: faced with people they regard as unworthy, their stomachs turn, and they're too fastidious to gobble up the souls that God regards as delicacies. William chides them for their picky appetites: "Miserable preacher, why open your jaws and prepare your teeth, if you're not hungry and don't want to eat! These aren't Christ's jaws if there's no hunger and the meal has no flavor." The preacher or teacher who has a mouthful of honey, but who doesn't want to eat souls, is spiritually dead. Alas, few come to the Lord's supper, They prefer the invitation to the devil's tavern, where heretics, "married" priests, and all those who prefer worldly pleasures to heavenly joys think they can go for a good time. In reality, they'll be caught in his net, like birds or fish, and eat filth and poison. The hunger and thirst of avarice, gluttony, lust, pride, and their like won't be sated by this kind of meal—they'll just leave wanting more. Only God can fill the human heart, but the Lord's tavern stays closed to those who've chosen to take their business elsewhere.

Jacques Le Goff has remarked that his evident love of food and wine shows William to be a true Frenchman—ignoring the fact that the earliest surviving cookery book is Roman, and a variety of medieval recipe books have survived, even from England.[55] The pleasures of the table cross national as well as temporal boundaries; William's good red wine is enjoyment we can share with him today.

15

DEATH AND BEYOND

We'll meet again, don't know where, don't know when . . .

William died in Paris in 1249, either on Palm Sunday (28 March) or a day or two later: as is so often the case with medieval dates, the sources don't quite agree.[1] He was buried in a modest tomb behind the choir in the abbey of St. Victor on the south bank of the Seine, a journey of about one and a half kilometers (about one mile) from his episcopal palace. St. Victor was the burial place of a number of the cathedral clergy, possibly because Notre-Dame, still in the process of completion in the first half of the thirteenth century, had little burial space of its own; certainly, it was not "prominent as a burial church."[2] St. Victor was secularized and its monuments destroyed at the French Revolution, but there are records of two memorial plaques to William: one brass, from the fifteenth century; another, marble, rather grander, from 1668.[3] The epitaphs are short, but note his dedication to pastoral care and the brilliance of his writing. His last wishes were carried out by his executors: his chaplain, Henri Tuebeuf, and Master Raymond, both canons of the cathedral, and Brother Raoul, the former prior of St. Victor. William left money for a mass for his soul to be celebrated in the cathedral on the Thursday of Holy Week each year, the anniversary of his becoming bishop. His goods, left to the treasury at Notre-Dame, were not extensive, and comprised his episcopal vestments, including his staff and ring, his table silver, an iron chest, two carpets, three embroidered leather cushions, two cruets for the oils used in anointing the sick and the chrism for them, a reliquary of silver-gilt and precious stones with the relics of St. Elizabeth and some hairs from the Blessed Virgin Mary, and finally, a bell, which bore the name "William."[4]

Bishops were appointed till death, so William died in harness. He was certainly working in 1247, when he tried to persuade Louis IX not to undertake yet another Crusade, and he signed Odo of Châteauroux's condemnation of the Talmud, in 1248.[5] He continued writing into the 1240s, when he was still working on *The Soul*. We know nothing of the state of his health before his death—or indeed, during his whole life. In language reminiscent of Francis of Assisi, he regularly refers to the human body as simply a donkey or a mule—the pack animal that carries the soul and makes God's work possible.[6] But he is clear in *The Soul* that illness was not part of God's original plan for humanity, and was the result of original sin:

> Who is so foolish or mad that, when he sees a man stricken with disease and sores, now with gout, now with boils, now with cancer, or now with lupus, that is, with the disease that arises from the whole body as a wolf, and does not on the occasion recognize that these evils are adventitious and inflicted and in no sense come from the primitive composition or constitution of that body? And I mean by the primitive constitution that which has only natural elements without any admixture. Who, therefore, would not see that the injuries of disease and wounds are from a foreign source, not from one's own primitive [state], since one also sees that such diseases should not be neglected or allowed to last, but rather that one must fight against them with every kind of medicine and by every art of medicine?[7]

The language of medicine and remedy was common in medieval metaphors for the work of the priest or of sacraments, and it occurs in a number of William's sermons, mixed up, as ever, with glimpses into everyday life. The shrewd doctor drinks the medicine before the patient, to show that it will do no harm; the insane have been known to kill doctors who are trying to help them; when a doctor cures you, you're indebted to him forever—although whether this is a matter of honor or money is not quite clear.[8]

Miserable though illness and pain might be, William could not believe that God would let them exist without some purpose: "On this account, the greater from among the wise men of the Christians said that the goodness of the creator does not really cause such actions . . . but tolerates or permits them on account of the goodness and benefits of the sufferings."[9] As we saw in an earlier chapter, his confidence in God's providential care for the whole of creation, at least as he presented it to the outside world, was absolute. Illness and infirmity are aimed at "education and salvation"; they tame the proud and goad others to turn to the right path, "for it is very rare that bodily infirmity does not change bad folks into good ones and does not bring them to the grace of repentance."[10] He quotes Ecclesiasticus 31:3, "Grave illness makes the soul sober," with the comment:

> What is the soul sobered up from the drunkenness of any vice or sin by bodily infirmity but one changed from bad to good and freed from debts by God and, although neither security for entering upon a promise nor credibility for lying had been left for it, it is freed of all debts and at peace and also enriched in the possession of grace and in the hope of glory?[11]

One sermon gives away the plot of Dickens's *A Christmas Carol*:

> Tell about that good Englishman [he reminds himself] who, shown by an angel, saw himself dead in hell with its punishments, or in paradise and its joys, and who, when returned to his body, was untiring in penitence, so that he would avoid the punishments he had seen and could gain the everlasting joys.[12]

Not everyone, however, learned the lesson, no matter how old they lived to be:

> bodily age shows that they ought to yearn more for lofty spiritual and eternal things. Alas, how shameful and how ridiculous are white hair and old age in the body and such foolish infancy in the mind. As Seneca says: How shameful it is that we have the titles of elders and have the vices of children.[13]

However, if age brought infirmities, it could have compensating strengths:

> It is natural that the higher and more noble powers of human souls are vigorous in old age and are and become stronger, more unhampered, and quicker in their noble operations, [and] it was granted that this naturally belongs to all human souls. Hence it is not only apart from nature but even contrary to nature that the opposite happens to some human souls. But it does undoubtedly happen to souls who neglect themselves and do not seek and care for their noble perfections. In them their chief and most noble part is clearly asleep, as it were, and buried . . . [T]he human soul naturally becomes young when the body grows old.[14]

> Moreover, in the approach of bodies to death, both wisdom and the virtues are found to be strengthened and increased in them and illumined for seeing those things that they could not see during the health of their bodies.[15]

Why, then, if age brought wisdom, did death have to occur at all? It had not been God's intention that it should. When God created Adam and Eve in Eden, their sinlessness made them immortal:

> Adam was immortal before [original] sin . . . For if someone wanted to kill Adam before the sin, by sword, spear, or fire, divine justice would not permit this, which does not permit punishment to precede sin, but rather orders punishment after sin. Adam, therefore, would not have a natural inability to suffer by a sword or fire in that state, which he in fact did not have, but the order of divine justice that, as we said, did not permit the punishment to precede the sin. For just as sin was the cause of death and, if sin did not precede, death would not be inflicted, so it is the cause of the whole present penal condition.[16]

The whole sorry mess, it seems, is our fault. It didn't have to be this way:

> because human nature was going to be made everlasting and man was going to be transferred to immortality since it belonged to the con-

> dition of his creation. For he was created for this . . . But the fact that death intervenes in it between the life of nature and the life of glory is not a matter of natural order . . . The moment of death, therefore, is a departure from the rectitude of natural movement. And all natural movement is correct. Every departure then from rectitude is against nature and custom. Therefore death is contrary to human nature . . . The fact that we die, therefore, is not proper to nature, but rather is extraneous and inflicted.[17]

The unnaturalness of death is evident in our resistance to it, and in the universal taboo against cadavers:

> a person is hard to find who is not almost intolerably horrified to look upon bodies of the dead after their souls have withdrawn from them. For as a result of the presence of the souls, that is, when their souls are in them, our bodies are pleasing and attractive to sight.[18]

When the soul has gone, the body is seen for what it is, with all its insufficiency.

During the development of the fetus, as we saw earlier, God places an individual soul into a particular body, and that soul is that body's animating principle. During a single lifetime, the soul inhabits the body and determines its manner of living, as the captain commands a ship or a musician plays an instrument. Before the Fall, this cohabitation could have continued indefinitely, the soul and the body living on together in corporeal immortality. The sin of the first parents put an end to that, but opened up the possibility of a greater, noncorporeal life in the divine presence, thanks to God's graciousness in giving the gift of his Son, Jesus Christ. This theology was the Christian rationale for why a God who was only goodness created and presided over a world where so much that was not good was allowed to exist and even flourish. The "happy fault" (*felix culpa*) of the original disobedience of Adam and Eve in the garden of Eden brought about bodily mortality but paved the way for spiritual immortality and a life of blessedness. The only downside to this obviously superior outcome was that getting there involved dying first, because human beings in their corporeal selves were simply not strong enough to bear the brilliance of the sight of God. Even Moses could endure only the sight of God's back as he retreated; for everyone else, the situation was quite clear: "a human being shall not see me and live."[19] This transformation of the donkey that is the human body into a thing than can fly with the friends of God, and enter paradise, is truly miraculous. All it requires is that your heart be set on the heavens, not the earth.[20]

Original sin resulted in the body's mortality, but the soul that was so carefully matched with it was not so fatally impaired. In the soul, the effect of sin was the introduction of vices, but unlike the illnesses that plague the body, these aren't diseases that alter its essential immortality.[21] Since "the union with the body does not bring life to souls or confer life upon them, it ought to be evident to everyone with intelligence that the separation from that body does not take away or remove life from souls"; this is because souls were created not for their life and actions in and through the body, but for the purpose of worshipping God, a task that can never end.[22] And just as the captain doesn't lose his seamanship when he's not on board ship, or the musician still knows how to play, without an instrument in her hands, so the loss of the body in death doesn't take away the abilities of the soul.

This isn't to say that the process of death itself is easy. It's hard enough for those who have a sense of what's to come, but for those who are wedded to the pleasures of the world, it's frightening to give up what they know: "For few human beings fully see what death is. After all, if death is the separation of human souls from bodies, it is clear that death does not fall within their estimation."[23] Fear can itself cause death, and the soul flees, as a householder abandons a house he thinks will catch fire.[24] William also describes what seem to be near-death experiences, from the testimonies "of those souls to whom it has been granted to experience their life after the death of their bodies":

> as if their souls were impeded and expelled to some extent from their bodies, they immediately draw near to and are carried into the region of light, and from there they receive revelations and divinations . . . For some, when the death of their bodies is close, similar things occur on

account of the nearness of the region of light . . . But they come down suddenly, as if vapors rose to the brain to produce the most overflowing and most ridiculous states of alienation.[25]

But although dying might not be easy, death itself is only good: "there is no one for whom bodily death is not beneficial."[26] The soul is freed from the misery of human frailty, like a prisoner released from captivity, and no longer has to fear "the whole bitterness of this life."[27] For the just, it is the point of departure to the "kingdom of future happiness"; and for "the evil and for those for whom the punishment of hell looms immediately after death, death is beneficial insofar as they would accumulate the punishments of a greater damnation by persisting in their evil merits from which they do not propose to come to their senses."[28] Death, in fact, is proof of God's providential care for his creation, for no good Christian is dead; they have simply left a house that's daily falling into ruin, to move to a better life.[29] This doesn't mean that anyone should seek out death. He condemns as "demented love" the desire of some heretics to "embrace it [death] with delight." He's on shaky ground here, as he argues that one can come to love one's own death, if it is seen as part of the honor and glory of God; but in these heretics, such love can't be real but only "madness," the actions of those possessed by demons "and nothing else."[30]

These arguments are characteristic of one strand of William's approach to the difficulties of the Christian faith. He doesn't deny that the difficulties exist; his strategy is to persuade the reader to see them in a different light. He recognizes that the tenets of belief are at odds with the values of the world—and that those values are often attractive and easy to desire; the way forward is not to ignore them, but to turn them upside down. The world is not the site of pleasures but the home of bitterness; death is not a sign that God is uncaring, but confirmation of his providence; mortality is not the feared end, but the gateway to a life lived closer to God.

As bishop, William's job—and the task of all clergy—was to prepare his flock for death. For medieval saints death represented a birthday (*dies natalis*)—but a birthday in heaven rather than on earth. Although no one could presume to fully understand God's justice, nevertheless, the Christian faithful believed that he had given some pointers toward a happier outcome. Ideally, having received the sacraments of baptism and confirmation, an individual was also a regular communicant at mass, having first been absolved of their sins in confession. These were four of the seven recognized sacraments—places where God had promised to be present for humanity—and along with matrimony and extreme unction (the anointing of the sick and dying), they acted as mileposts on the journey through life. The final sacrament, ordination, was only applicable to those entering the priesthood. Good works or, failing that, good intentions were also recommended. Those who had lived this way, who had repented of their sins and done penance for them, could make a "good death": they had done all they could, while recognizing that they were still reliant on the "grace"—the freely given clemency—of God. Even for those who had not lived such an ideal life, God was prepared to grant a last-minute reprieve: he calls and calls again to invite everyone to his feast.[31] It was the job of the preacher to make sure that the ways to God were proclaimed to all who would hear.

God had created time; but Scripture taught that Christ would come to earth once more, the dead would rise from their graves in a new sort of spiritual body, all human beings would be individually judged and consigned either to an eternal life with the Creator in heaven or eternal punishment with the fallen angel Lucifer in hell, and time would come to an end. Christian theologians had long speculated on the meaning of this *eschaton*: the nature of the judgment, its rewards and punishments, and the place of heaven and hell. William follows Augustine of Hippo in situating heaven at the summit of the universe (the Empyrean) and hell or gehenna in an underworld—height and depth having moral as well as physical dimensions. His immense work *The Universe of Creatures* is concerned with understanding the whole created universe, from the visible corporeal world of the stars and planets to the invisible spiritual world that included angels and demons; it included discussions of time and eternity and the nature of creation itself.[32] Considerable parts of his argument are concerned with refuting the non-Christian positions of Plato, Aristotle, Avicenna, and others, who argued for the eternity of the world, for a single world-soul to which the souls of individuals reintegrated at death, and for the world as a microcosm of a set of archetypal perfect "forms," alongside a number of other complex technical and philosophical questions. For our purposes, the key understanding is that the entirety of this world, from dirt to angel, from planet to human soul, was the creation of God. Everything in both the visible corporeal world and the invisible spiritual world was a creature, had been given its own created nature—and was therefore natural. The question of whether spiritual beings such as angels had some form of body, albeit immortal, was still in dispute, and William regards it as a point too difficult to decide, as things stood.[33] What he did not doubt was that each human soul, although entirely spiritual, had an individual and indivisible existence that included its own particular nature and powers, and continued as an individual after death.

Only the holiest individuals might make their way to heaven without the need for some additional cleansing or purgation from the sins accumulated during their lifetime. Equally, only those who had, without any sense of contrition or desire for forgiveness, committed the most serious, "mortal" sins, such as murder or denial of God, were destined for hell. A small group of souls comprised infants who had died before their baptism; they had not committed any sins of their own, but they were still infected by the original sin of Adam and Eve. William rejects Augustine's view that such children were destined for hell, and instead places them in limbo, "a place between gehenna and purgatory," where they live in "perpetual mansions" in a state of great happiness, although without gaining the ultimate glory of the sight of God.[34] The great majority of people, however, were somewhere in between the best and the worst: their "venial" sins, although lighter than the most serious sort, had still to be repented of and punished since, for various reasons including sudden death, the slate had not been wiped entirely clean while they were still alive.[35] Not all sins are equal; but the penalties of purgation represent justice, not malice or revenge. For this group there was the possibility of purgation, a preparation that should enable them eventually to enter into life with God.

William's discussions of this purgation, and his situation of a place, purgatory, where this cleansing would happen, mark him out among medieval theologians.[36] To begin with, he sees the punishments of purgatory as a continuation of the interior penitential judgment begun on earth, where

> the sinning souls accuses itself, testifies against itself, hands down judgment against itself as being worthy of infernal torments and punishments for what it has done wrong, afterward carrying out its own sentence against itself, by tormenting itself, not only in spiritual ways (which I've explained before), but by afflicting the body with fasting, hard labor, self-flagellation, and other such things which are called sacred exercises.[37]

It makes sense to him that where these penances are insufficient, they must be completed after death. He thinks it reasonable that the interior, spiritual penance of the postmortem soul would please the Creator more than the exterior penance of the body, since it would be closer to the place of vice, which is also interior to the soul.[38] He admits, however, that questions about the reality and location of purgatory are somewhat speculative. For the existence of purgatory at all, he brings as evidence the long Christian tradition of premonitions, along with a variety of the ghosts and apparitions of those detained for purgation, who appear as warnings to the living to change their ways. These aren't just funny stories, he says; they're actually useful and salutary lessons.[39] As to the place of purgation, he admits that "no law, no Scripture" marks out a place as having this sole purpose. Thrown back on the evidence of visions and revelations, he argues that there must be many places on earth for such purgation. This is reasonable, he thinks, because these purgations are a supplement to the penitential satisfaction that has already been undertaken, and so they should be at the places where the penitents are. Wherever you find a man, you also find his hands and his feet; so wherever a man's penance began, his purgation should be able to be completed, since they are part of the same whole.[40]

How is purgation achieved? Purgatory, like hell, was a place of fire—an element associated with purgation from the destruction of Sodom and Gomorrah or the cleansing of the lips of the prophet Isaiah.[41] But how could the corporeal fire we know on earth be effective as a punishment for the spiritual soul? William begins by reminding readers that fire takes many forms other than the ordinary sort we encounter every day; he gives a run of examples, from Greek fire, an ancient incendiary mixture not extinguished by water, and used as a weapon, to a Sicilian fire that was reported to make hair glow like a torch, while leaving it untouched.[42] If these are fires we already know, he thinks it is not impossible that hell and purgatory have fire-types of their own: in hell, a fire that burns forever without consuming the bodies of the damned, so that its pain is endless; in purgatory, a fire that burns only sins, and comes to an end when their purgation is complete.[43]

But how can fire—or indeed, any other corporeal affliction that purgatory may offer—be effective on the spiritual soul? William argues that, although the soul itself can't be hot or cold, it can nevertheless burn or freeze through its imaginative apprehension of the effects of fire and ice. In fact, this imagination—in the medieval sense of the mind's active creation of an image of something—can produce in the soul a keener response to stimulus than the body feels, since imagination is closer to the substance of the soul than of the body. We might even say that the soul doesn't *really* suffer from anything done to the body because its essence is untouched by that sort of activity.[44]

William offers several interesting examples to make his point. Nightmares and dreams can be much more "real" than reality, and are sometimes very useful in changing behavior. People of strong imagination can enjoy things at least as much by imagining them as they can by seeing the real thing. We've all known, he says, the situation where a man or woman has gotten more pleasure from looking at a member of the opposite sex, and the thought of their touch, than from the actual embraces when they come. "Reality" can be disappointing in comparison to what the mind can conjure up. And this is not just theory: "I've even seen a man who was moved to physical purgation [up or down? he doesn't say] simply by looking at the medicine, without having to take it. What could have moved him so much except the appearance, that is the likeness impressed on his soul, when neither the substance nor the taste or the smell of the medicine were with him?"[45] Here and elsewhere, William is aware of something that modern medicine is only just accepting—

that psychosomatic illness is no less physically real than illness with a clear physical etiology.

Alan Bernstein's reading of this explanation is that William saw the fires of purgatory as metaphorical, which leads him to argue that William kept one solution for the learned and another for the simple believer.[46] But only the examples he uses are metaphors; the purgatorial fire itself is reality. The key is in remembering that *everything* is the creation of God, whether visible or invisible, corporeal or spiritual. One is not more real than the other; both have their own reality and, in some way he cannot explain, are able to apprehend the reality of the other and suffer pain or experience pleasure through it. The fire itself plays a part, otherwise it would be superfluous to creation; but in fact, "it corporeally and really torments the bodies of such souls, and even the souls themselves."[47] However, Bernstein is surely right in thinking that William's insistence on the orthodox Christian belief in postmortem purgation and hell are arguments against the dualist Cathar heresy, which taught that sin could be entirely expunged either during this lifetime or, failing that, by metempsychosis—the transfer of your soul to another body at death.[48]

In the complexities of William's explanation, it's easy to lose sight of his pastoral purpose. William's insistence on the reality of purgatorial cleansing is fundamental to his argument that it's possible for all those who desire it to be received by God. Purgatory should be busy, since it's a kind of staging post for better things. The early Christian theologian Origen (d. c. 254) was anathematized for his belief that no punishment could be eternal, since divine purgation must eventually clear away all sin.[49] William doesn't quite go so far as to leave hell empty, but he's clear that the way is open, if anyone wants to take it, even though in *On the Laws* he laments the very great number of the damned compared to the scarcity of the saved. The choice is theirs: God's desire is for justice, not punishment for its own sake.[50]

William's remarkable talent is his ability simultaneously to explain Christian belief in terms of the highest sophistication and the most common experience. Nowhere is this better seen than in illustrations of heaven and hell, God and the devil. Hell, a place of pure misery, designed only for endless torment, is yet a shield to those who fear it. They hold it in front of their eyes as a shield against the assaults of the enemy. "For who suffers harm when he has hell before his eyes?"

> And what is more amazing, in fleeing from it, I flee to it, and to the extent that I flee from it, it is a stronger and securer refuge for me. For the more I fear it, the more secure I am. For no one is sent into it unless he runs to it or hurls or plunges himself into it by the leaps and bounds of evil desire.[51]

The devil is the parish priest of hell. He lives there like a watchdog chained up in the day but let loose at night; he apes God; he has dentures, is skinny rather than fat with spiritual food, but his breasts suckle unbelievers; he has bakers, hunters, gardeners, and cooks (who use the devil's frying pan to make the devil's dinner); he has many, many taverns, each full of punters eating, drinking, singing, dancing, and whoring their way to hell.[52] The familiar language of these descriptions is not a way of talking down to the laity; it is a reminder for himself as much as anyone that the devil is never far away. It's precisely the everyday nature of his evil that makes the devil such a dangerous opponent. He can trap you in the complex formulation of the Trinity; but he's far more likely to get you thinking about that woman in church, gossiping about a fellow monk, or working out how to make just that little extra profit: this whole world is the mouth of hell."[53]

God, too, is in the everyday. He has a limping donkey and boys when he needs men. But William's God is much simpler and greater than any metaphor, though his formulations are influenced by his knowledge of Avicenna and Arab philosophy. God is the "being that not only cannot not be, but also cannot be understood not to be": God so much *is* that that is-ness is unthinkable.[54] Such a being cannot help but bring other things into existence, so that "the life by which I live is God."[55] That such being is itself good is shown by the love of life found in all created things: "By the favor and choice of all things that are, being is shown to be both something other and better than all the things that are."[56]

> The universe cannot be universally in error in those things which are through nature or by nature. By its own love and desire and by its own choice the universe cries out that this being is best since the universe prefers it to everything else. He is incredibly deaf if he does not hear the cry of the universe. There can be no doubt that [this being] is everywhere and essentially whole, since wherever there is a being, the being of the First is necessarily there also.[57]

God is; and that "is" is an unceasing creation acting from a brimming flow of love. Those who die with this faith, will live with this being.

16

FACE TO FACE

Live in fragments no longer. Only connect . . .

> One and the same person is a man, on account of which he is owed love by every other human being, and he is a prince or a prelate, on account of which he is owed honor, reverence, and obedience, and he is a subject, on account of which he is owed instruction, discipline, and defense, and he is at times an opponent of the truth, on account of which he is owed, so to speak, contradiction, and at times he is in misery, either spiritually or corporeally, on account of which he is owed pity and also help, if the ability is present, and he is himself the companion of all other human beings, at least in nature, but at times also in fortune and at times in grace, on account of which he is owed faith, truth, and equity.[1]

All of us live as many people. We unconsciously alter our behavior, language, and expectations, depending on who we are at any one time: a mother becomes a daughter again, a teacher a pupil, a doctor a patient. The many faces we turn to the world make the pursuit of biography difficult at the best of times. Where our sources are as limited as they are for William, basic questions about his life and the consistency of his personality become even more intractable. Identifying and unraveling the strands that make up the skein of his life is a task with many broken threads and missing colors. In this final chapter, my aim is to reflect on what we can make of the fragments of his world.

A different biographer would certainly have produced a different portrait; we write about ourselves, even as we write about our subject, and an awareness of that fact doesn't mean it can be entirely avoided. Each choice always involves the rejection of another, and each chapter in this book could certainly have been a book of its own. My method in this book has been to shy away from the construction of a single narrative life—a style of biography that is a matter of dispute among those who theorize about life writing—in favor of a series of glimpses into William's world. This was less a choice against narrative than a response to the available sources: the themes discussed across this book surfaced from William's own preoccupations, from the material that he recurrently chooses to address. His literary world is always that—a construction aimed at an outside audience; no personal writing remains—but it can sometimes offer tantalizing glimpses of his interaction with life beyond the page. We see the world through his eyes: "We remember seeing . . . ," he says, or "I myself saw . . . ," or "Those who know have told me . . ." Other people are spoken of in ways that suggest they were more than examples made up for teaching and preaching. Writing of the burdensome nature of having too many belongings, William remembers how "a certain friend of ours whose spacious and magnificent house was destroyed by fire . . . summoned us, not for his consolation, as he said, but to hear what we would say about such a fire."[2] On the pretext of wanting sympathy, the friend was issuing a challenge to William about the providence of God: how could he—the friend—have suffered such a loss, if God was good? William is briskly unsympathetic: "if he had not had that house, he would not have lost it, and would not now grieve over its loss, nor would he have to be involved in the worry and cost of rebuilding it so that a similar danger would not threaten it once it was rebuilt." Problems of the rich, is William's response—but still the exchange with the friend sounds authentic.

Perhaps the most startling of these real-world asides is the case of "that man who believed he was a chicken and imitated the speech and sound of a chicken according to his ability, unwilling to use another speech or sound, for it seemed to him that he could not use another speech or sound at all, because he thought he was a chicken."[3] This appears as an example in a passage about the soul's knowledge of itself, and it's clear from the context that William knows his readers will recognize just who he means, so he doesn't need to expand on his illustration. The man is a well-known local character who can simply be mentioned in passing and, indeed, linked to similar cases that William recounts having seen with his own eyes.[4] Remarkably, as I was writing this chapter, newspapers reported a study by Belgian psychiatrists of a woman who believed she was a hen; zoanthropy is a rare condition thought to be related to depression.[5] Would medieval sufferers from these delusions have been brought to the bishop for his blessing, hoping for a cure? William doesn't say.

Another glimpse offers a teasing sense of the younger man, as he alludes to the lessons of age and experience.

> In my youth, it seemed to me that it would be easy to acquire the spirit of prophecy and of divine illumination, since our souls stand on the threshold of both of these worlds or regions. It seemed to me that it would be easy to cleanse our souls of the stains of vice, and easy to break free of the snares or chains in which our souls are restrained, like a neck twisted in a noose. I thought that abstinence would gradually free the soul from the cares and pleasures which held it captive and submerged in this lower world, the world of the senses . . . so that, strong and free, it would soar upward of its own accord to the highest regions of light. Now I know from long experience in the practice of divine worship that only grace and virtue can purify our souls from the stain of sin.[6]

In other words, although William started out believing that he could reach God by his own efforts, life has taught him that this is only possible with the gift of grace from God. No matter how much he might try, he has learned that without God he can't escape the shackles of this world. This realization was important to him because knowing God, achieving the presence of the divine, was the purpose for which humanity was made; it's what brings human beings joy. But this joy is not the end of life—it's only a kind of by-product of closeness to the deity: "joy is an almost continuous serenity of the heart from the presence of God who dwells in it, which even adversity does not cloud or obscure."[7] "We must, therefore, first ask this, namely, of what sort human life must be or should be. We say, therefore, that human life ought to give honor to God, its giver, be beautiful in itself, and useful or beneficial to others," "for it has become known so far only to a few human beings that the glory of God is the principal end and perhaps the only end of truly good actions."[8]

We have glimpses, too, of William's theological opponents—or at least, of his exasperation with those who take positions he regards as idiotic, who use spurious arguments, or who blindly follow so-called authoritative texts. He's short-tempered with those he regards as fools or who he thinks should know better, and in these cases his language is frequently intemperate and abusive:

> And since the blindness of certain people has become heated and their feeblemindedness has prevailed to the point that they have denied and still deny that the human soul exists, I shall first establish its existence, and I mean that I shall make you know that it exists—you as well as every misguided person who can see that the opposite of every contradiction is necessarily true.[9]

His frustration with the "misguided" and "feebleminded" springs from many pages in *The Soul*, along with their belief in "incredible absurdities that are rather to be mocked than destroyed by proofs," for they have not attained even "the childish rudiments of logic."[10] "Who would put up with someone raving of things so impossible and unthinkable?"[11] "This is one among those things that a new and as yet unheard of foolishness has dreamed up"; "such a man is in error and labors under an intolerable feebleness and shortsightedness of the intellect"; "and there are even right up to the present those who, because of the slightness of their training and the smallness of their intellect, follow [these] errors."[12] The careful discussion elsewhere in William's work of the limits of language that could be used in referring to God is strikingly different from the accusations of feeblemindedness and stupidity he repeats so often here. These examples are all taken from the treatise on the soul, which was probably the last of his major works to be written, still in progress around 1240. As Teske notes, while "here as in many places William offers no clue to the identity of his opponent; the abusive language would seem to indicate that such opponents are not merely imaginary." That's to say, these condemnations aren't general, but are directed at contemporary individuals or groups, which (unfortunately for us) he doesn't identify; the specificity of the accusations he sprays about suggests that he has particular thinkers in mind.[13] Perhaps they were those who, as we saw in the chapter on teachers, liked to keep a coterie of students as personal followers rather than as followers of truth. Perhaps he is too tired to go through the same old arguments yet again. William was a relatively elderly man by the time he wrote *The Soul*, which runs almost 450 pages in Teske's modern translation, and he was still a busy working bishop. At other points in his work, William is capable of generous assessments of other scholars; he speaks of even a non-Christian believer like Avicenna as a great philosopher. His impatience at the need to refute positions he regards as almost wilfully incorrect is evident at many points. Truth to tell, patience seems never to have been his strong suit, as we recall from Louis IX's tale of the windblown hat.

Situating William in his medieval landscape is made more complicated by one of his more certain characteristics—his independence. His actions in a variety of situations, his breadth of reading, and his decided opinions are always the result of his own thinking and choices. Thanks to his wide-ranging interests he's never unaware of what others believe, but that alone is never enough for him: he has to work things out for himself. Whether this was an innate personality trait, the result of his upbringing, or his southerner's sense of being an outsider in the North, we shall never know. What does seem evident is that in many facets of his life he straddled a line between two worlds: those of twelfth- and thirteenth-century scholarship; of university theory and episcopal practice; of the royal court and the poverty that surrounded it. He stands with both and neither, not entirely part of any group.

William's professional world was hierarchical, and for all the time we meet him in his writings he is close to the top of the tree; he looked up to very few superiors. The pope, as bishop of Rome, was the most senior prelate in the Church. William's lifetime spanned at least eleven popes, including Innocent III and Gregory IX, two of the most important reformers of the Middle Ages.[14] Gregory IX was personally responsible for appointing William as bishop of Paris, and so must be credited with the biggest direct impact on his life and career, on the influence he was able to exert. William's keen sense of the duty of his episcopal role is evident in everything he wrote and did as bishop. It was his highest loyalty, since he was answerable for it to God. Any sense of obligation or indebtedness he might have been thought to owe to Gregory, who had taken a relatively junior professor of theology and put him in charge of an important diocese, disappeared at its first test. William's actions over the university strike of 1229, which infuriated the pope, show that quite clearly. Neither did he feel bound by professional loyalty to the university masters, his erstwhile colleagues. One way to read this is that his head was turned by his newfound power; another is that his actions were motivated by the simple belief that violence should not go unpunished. His sense of responsibility as bishop meant putting old loyalties aside and doing what he thought was right; his wider obligation was now to the ordinary powerless souls in his care. In future, William worked with Gregory when he could, but he didn't always come when called.

Although Gregory gave William his platform, it was perhaps Innocent III and his vision for the Fourth Lateran Council in 1215, when William was still a student and full of intellectual adventure, that had the greatest effect on how he would pursue his life's work. Innocent's conception of the Church as an outgoing ambassador for Christianity, an institution to inspire admiration, with an educated and principled clerical workforce promulgating a message that spoke to all humanity, was one that William was prepared to endorse and promote. But does claiming a central role for Lateran IV on its own allow us to understand his motives? William objected to the manner of the election of a new bishop of Paris—the process that produced two candidates before he himself was given the job—because it didn't follow the rules set down by the Lateran Council; but was he objecting because those rules weren't followed, or because he thought candidates willing to accept the post after an uncanonical election were also less likely to be assiduous in following the Council's legislation and the spirit behind it? Might this have been particularly true in the case of the election that gave the post to the nephew of the cathedral chancellor, Philip, who perhaps already owed his current ecclesiastical position to his influential relative? Or did William just want to be bishop, as Philip's lyrics written in response to the election appear to claim? This is an episode in William's life for which we have comparatively many facts, and yet several readings of the situation are still possible. However he got the job, William subsequently earned a reputation as a notably conscientious prelate, and his reorganization of the diocese and promotion of the ministry of the mendicant friars, along with his own regular preaching, speaks of a pastoral energy and sense of responsibility for those in his care.

If he was unafraid of annoying the pope or his former university colleagues, William appears to have displayed a similar independence from the royal family. They were, after all, his parishioners, and in that way just another part of his flock. Blanche of Castile and Louis IX were both genuinely religious, and William and the king shared an admiration for the friars and their mendicant form of life. The story of William relieving Blanche of her pilgrimage vow, and redirecting the money she would have spent on travel to the Paris Dominicans, is an example of a pragmatism that also seems to be part of his character. Practicality led him to create a new home for reformed prostitutes that did more toward the alleviation of their poverty than the condemnation of their sin; and the same impulse allowed university masters who became Dominicans and Franciscans to hold on to their teaching positions, thus solving the problem of how the bishop could provide for students' teaching when their own secular masters were on strike. The tale of William being sent by courtiers to tell Louis that his first child was not a son reminds us that, unlike the courtiers' own position, the bishop's was not dependent on the king's favor; so however tempestuous the meeting, William's neck was not on the line. But the story also demonstrates William's smart way with words and his underlying humor—never far from the surface—as well as his genuine sympathy for Louis.

William also displays a particular academic independence. The range of his reading, beyond the usual Christian and classical texts, marks him out from his peers. The shape of his own academic writing, which conforms neither to twelfth-century models nor to the developing thirteenth-century scholastic conventions, is very specifically his own. Although he was a considerable figure in his own time, William's reputation did not long survive his death. The creativity, individuality, and fearless approach to new texts and traditions that made—and make—him so interesting to his readers left him outside any recognized school of thought. The practical intelligence that let him see the useful possibilities of the mendicant orders in his diocese did not go so far as persuading him to join them as a brother. William allowed the mendicants in Paris to hold university chairs in theology, and within twenty years almost all were held by mendicant masters, not least because their orders could afford to support them through the long years of study needed to reach the top. The scholars we know best from the thirteenth century—Thomas Aquinas, Albert the Great, Bonaventure, or John Duns Scotus, for instance—are those whose reputations were nurtured and burnished by their orders. William simply slipped between the cracks.

His pervasive sense of his audience, whether in his treatises or in his sermons, gives his writing a singular feeling of someone focused on communication, for whom considerations of style and solemnity are less important than the need to teach and explain. It's not possible to think about William without thinking about his language. It illuminates who he is, but also, perhaps, erects a barrier between his inner and outer selves. Like many thirteenth-century theologians, he wrote a great deal, and can often seem prolix. The Christian God, by orthodox definition, is inexpressible, but theologians and mystics nevertheless tried, in more and more writing, to say what could not be said. William struggles to make language come close to explaining the fundamentals of the faith. Sometimes he does that by admitting that language is merely an approximation of truth; elsewhere he invents new words in an attempt at greater precision. William's independence shows itself here in the unusual way he frames his approach to Christianity. Like Aristotle, he has looked out at the universe and asked himself how it came to be. Like Aristotle, he sees an unmoved mover—the First, in the term William borrows from Avicenna. His common name for the deity is Creator, and the miracle of creation and being is at the center of his faith. While he is undoubtedly Christian, in that he believes fervently in the person of Christ and his role in salvation, nevertheless the God who appears most often in William's writing is the sophisticated abstract idea of the being that cannot not be; the being whose will is to make other beings; the being whose existence and creativity is entirely good. Although medieval Christianity abounded in illustrations of the Trinity that anthropomorphized God the Father and God the Son, the theology behind these images was a much more highly developed and conceptual set of beliefs, which grappled with the difficulties of understanding an eternal being made manifest through the contingent and specific circumstances of the created world and the Bible. William holds his own, even among the most renowned medieval theologians, because his reading of Arabic and Jewish sources gives him a conception of God that at times can seem curiously a-Christian, which stands outside specific religions. He's searching for ways to describe a God that every human being can and should believe in; a God whose person is in itself existence.

But the abstraction of being was instantiated in the realities of worldly creation. As we've seen throughout these chapters, William's favorite way to talk about God is by describing the world around him—each new creation a page in the book God has written for human instruction. Only William, speaking in the *persona* of Piety, could write:

> I have made something amazing, namely, soap from [Christ's] blood. In this I clearly showed how much God loved the cleanliness of the human race and how much he hated its defilements, when on account of washing away the latter and replacing it with the former, I made the blood of his only-begotten Son into soap.[15]

The image works by the startling juxtaposition of two apparently incomparable things. Soap was understandable by all; whereas the theology of the blood sacrifice of the Son of God, repeated in the daily celebration of the Eucharist, was so complex it remained the subject of scholarly debate more than a millennium after the crucifixion. William's analogy, that Christ's sacrifice washes away human sin, is instantly comprehensible; as is his explanation that the soap is made by the piety of every individual's adherence to the Christian faith. The image is not simply a metaphor—that's to say, it's more than a figure of speech. For William, God created soap simultaneously as a means of getting things clean *and* as a means of explanation of sacrifice and atonement for sins. It has resonance for him (and his readers) precisely because the notion of cleansing is one and the same, whatever the context: the spiritual world and the physical world are not separate or distant—they're part of the same created whole. William's God is soap; but he is also, as we've seen, pure being and boundless creativity.

William found it impossible to imagine that anyone looking at the marvel that was the created world would not also see its Creator; and the only reasonable response to such a being was worship. This was the ultimate purpose of human existence. No one can have any true end that is not this one, since every adult person with the mental capacity to understand must necessarily be religious. A lack of understanding or education is no excuse for a lack of faith, since all that is required is to follow those who know:

> There is no sort of human being naturally so slow in intellect that it cannot grasp at least by a universal and general belief whatever pertains to the foundation of true religion. For there is no one at all in all human beings who cannot believe that whatever is contained in the sacred writings is true, that whatever human beings taught by the Spirit of God have taught is to be believed, and similarly that whatever the prophets believed or prophesied about God is true.[16]

The fact of one's own creation entails a debt to God that must be paid in worship or reverence to him:

> No one is permitted not to pay to the Creator or refuse the due worship and honor that is to be paid, so no one is permitted stubbornly to disbelieve or contradict, that is, to deny with the heart or the mouth, his truth or that of the things pertaining to him or to his worship and honor. And for this reason no one is permitted to withdraw or stubbornly to wander from the common faith and common worship . . . It is necessary that every intellect capable of religion be religious lest it be injurious to God and deservedly incur the punishment due to so great an injury. Therefore, it is necessary that religious belief be founded in every human intellect, that is, in every intellect that is capable of it,

> which we say on account of children and others that are impaired . . . Religion . . . is the whole beauty and dignity of human life and the whole merit of remuneration and eternal happiness.[17]

It's not possible to opt out of this particular contract; nor, when the chips are down, does he think anyone would want to:

> For fear has the greatest strength to drive out sins and to break human beings away from their evil ways and perversity of habit . . . This will become more evident for you from the testimony of those who frequently sail and journey on the seas. For they clearly report and testify that their vices and sins were never so displeasing to them, that they never so grieved over and repented of them, and that they never so loved justice and holiness as when they saw that the peril of shipwreck threatened them.[18]

As the saying goes, everyone's a believer in the trenches.

It would be wrong not to admit that I have come to like William, whether because of his vivid imagination and language, his love of learning, or his evident diligence in his episcopal role. It's easy to relate to parts of his world: his obvious enjoyment of food and drink or of the natural world, for example, establish a direct bond of human sympathy and give the sense that it's possible for us to understand him. His insistence that all individuals in some way share an equal humanity is very modern and compelling. But in other ways he seems very distant, for example when his response to the potency of the threat of drowning we've just read is to conclude "that it benefits and is most salutary for many sinners to perish by shipwreck." There's nothing in William's world that God cannot turn to good, whether it be mental illness, grinding poverty, or sickness and death, and his insistence on this universal providence can read as either naïve or heartless. His reaction to social evils is an acceptance that they must exist, combined with a strategy of mitigation, whether by individual charitable acts or resignation on the part of the sufferer. The structure of society is God-given, and political action is not part of his thinking. His views on sexual relations also run in line with the orthodoxy of the Church of his day; it would be impossible for a bishop to have expressed other views. To be free from sin, all sex must be within marriage and according to rules of moderation and consent. Divorce is not permitted outside of rare and exceptional circumstances. We spend our lives in a net of relationships that spread up, down, and sideways, and which tie us in to society. *Societas*, in Latin, has connotations of equality, and interestingly it is the word William often uses to describe marriage. As a cleric, his private life contained no wife or, as far as we can tell from the sources, "significant other" of either sex, although he speaks warmly of true friendship, for "friendship is a relation of equality."[19]

There can often seem to be a contradiction between William's attempts to systematize, especially in matters of theology and moral behavior, and his evident humanity. Is this a contradiction within William himself, or is it a matter of the limits of what we can know? At such points, the strength of his religious belief—in common with that of all medieval theologians—is a reminder that we are dealing with people who saw the salvation of the whole of society as depending on a unity of belief in an orthodox Christian faith that must be upheld by every single person.

This was an attitude that could lead, for example, to Inquisition or Crusade. We noted in an earlier chapter how William lauded the activity of peacemaking, especially among clergy, and we saw his attempts in the 1240s to dissuade Louis IX from undertaking another Crusade in the Holy Land. Early in his career, however, with the background of the Albigensian heresy, he reveals a different facet of his character, employing the strongest language to condemn those who refused to conform to orthodox belief:

> And because no human being has an excuse from belief in the articles of faith or from the confession of them except incapacity alone, as we already said, it is necessary that the totality of human beings be united and made one in the harmony and confession of belief in the faith of such articles and that the stubbornness of the disbelief and denial of them is to be wiped out by fire and sword and removed from the midst of human beings like the most accursed insult to God, like the most pestilential root of perdition.[20]

The treatise *On Faith* from which this comes was written sometime around 1228; in 1229, the Treaty of Paris paved the way for the incorporation of Languedoc, the heretic stronghold, into the lands of the French king, after the military victories of the Albigensian Crusade. Theologians often likened heretical belief to a gangrenous limb in the body of the Church, which had to be amputated before it could infect the health of the rest. William in the 1220s was ready to approve a military solution because this was a question of heresy against the faith; whether twenty more years of experience of the world had simply changed his mind, or whether his older self thought the king's role was primarily to be at home ruling, not abroad endangering his life, is an intriguing question. His younger self put uniformity of belief and conformity to a set of religious rules above individual conviction. As a bishop, that remained the case, but he had also learned that life was complicated—full of situations not always easy to shoehorn into readymade answers. What is striking in William, unlike many other medieval theologians, is that we can always see the humanity through the orthodox insistence on uniformity. The world is messy; and not to see the grubby muddle in which most people lived would be to miss the point. To minister to God's people, he had to start with them where they were. It's our luck as historians that he recorded this teeming reality in his writing, giving us a window on his world.

Would William have minded his relative historical obscurity, or would he simply have accepted it with a wry smile? When it comes to it, he says, we all cling to life, "and we don't perceive how much we love it until death knocks."[21] William's life was as real to him, as individual, modern, and immediate, as ours is to us. Through the fragments he has left us, we can begin to see the variety, the complexity, and the sophistication of his thirteenth-century world, and his own individuality within it. But the fragments must remain fragments; there's a barrier we cannot cross. William was an authentic individual, but we cannot be his authentic audience. Deeply as we might immerse ourselves in his world, it remains his world, not ours; we're always looking back. Try as we might, we can only know him as he is reflected in a smoky mirror.

ABBREVIATIONS

AUTOUR	*Autour de Guillaume d'Auvergne († 1249)*, ed. Franco Morenzoni and Jean-Yves Tilliette (Turnhout: Brepols, 2005)
CUP	*Chartularium Universitatis Parisiensis*, ed. Heinrich Denifle and Émile Chatelain, 4 vols. (Paris: Ex typis fratrum Delalain, 1889–97), vol. 1: *Université de Paris* (cited by document number)
DE LEGIBUS	William of Auvergne, *De Legibus*, in *Opera omnia*, vol. 1, pp. 18a–102b
DE SACRAMENTO MATRIMONII	William of Auvergne, *De Sacramento matrimonii*, in *Opera omnia*, vol. 1, pp. 512b–28b
DE UNIVERSO	William of Auvergne, *De Universo*, in *Opera omnia*, vol. 1, pp. 593a–1074b
DE VITIIS	William of Auvergne, *De Vitiis*, in *Opera omnia*, vol. 1, pp. 260a–93b
THE IMMORTALITY OF THE SOUL	*William of Auvergne, The Immortality of the Soul [De immortalitate animae]*, translated by Roland J. Teske, Medieval Philosophical Texts in Translation 30 (Milwaukee: Marquette University Press, 1991)

ON FAITH — William of Auvergne, *The Treatise on Faith and the Laws,* translated in Roland J. Teske, *William of Auvergne, Selected Spiritual Writings,* Medieval Sources in Translation 50 (Toronto, 2011), 74–120

ON GRACE — William of Auvergne, *The Treatise on Grace,* translated in Roland J. Teske, *William of Auvergne, Selected Spiritual Writings,* Medieval Sources in Translation 50 (Toronto: PIMS, 2011), 63–73

ON MORALS — *William of Auvergne, On Morals,* translated by Roland J. Teske, Medieval Sources in Translation 55 (Toronto, 2013)

ON THE VIRTUES — *William of Auvergne, On the Virtues: Part One of On the Virtues and Vices,* translated by Roland J. Teske, Medieval Philosophical Texts in Translation 45 (Milwaukee, 2009)

OPERA OMNIA — *Guilielmi Alverni . . . Opera omnia,* 2 vols., edited by F. Hotot, and *Supplementum,* edited by Blaise Le Feron (Orléans, 1674; reprinted Frankfurt am Main: Minerva, 1963) (cited by volume number, page, and column)

THE PROVIDENCE OF GOD — *William of Auvergne, The Providence of God Regarding the Universe: Part Three of the First Principal Part of The Universe of Creatures,* translated by Roland J. Teske, Medieval Philosophical Texts in Translation 43 (Milwaukee: Marquette University Press, 2007)

SERMONS — *Guillelmi Alverni Sermones,* ed. Franco Morenzoni, 4 vols., Corpus Christianorum Continuatio Mediaevalis 230, 230A, 230B, 230C (Turnhout: Brepols, 2010–13) (cited by CCCM volume number and sermon number)

THE SOUL — *William of Auvergne, The Soul,* translated by Roland J. Teske, Medieval Philosophical Texts in Translation 37 (Milwaukee: Marquette University Press, 2000)

TESKE, *STUDIES* — Roland J. Teske, *Studies in the Philosophy of William of Auvergne, Bishop of Paris (1228–1249),* Marquette Studies in Philosophy 51 (Milwaukee: Marquette University Press, 2006)

THE TRINITY	*William of Auvergne, The Trinity, or The First Principles [De trinitate, seu de primo principio]*, translated by Roland J. Teske and Francis C. Wade, Medieval Philosophical Texts in Translation 28 (Milwaukee: Marquette University Press, 1989)
THE UNIVERSE OF CREATURES	*William of Auvergne, The Universe of Creatures* (selections), translated by Roland J. Teske, Medieval Philosophical Texts in Translation 35 (Milwaukee: Marquette University Press, 1998)
VALOIS, *GUILLAUME D'AUVERGNE*	Noël Valois, *Guillaume d'Auvergne, évêque de Paris. Sa vie et ses ouvrages* (Paris: Librairie d'Alphonse Picard, 1880)
WHY GOD BECAME MAN	William of Auvergne, *The Treatise on the Reasons Why God Became Man*, translated in Roland J. Teske, *William of Auvergne, Selected Spiritual Writings*, Medieval Sources in Translation 50 (Toronto: PIMS, 2011), 19–62

NOTES

CHAPTER ONE

1. The only biography of William is Noël Valois, *Guillaume d'Auvergne, évêque de Paris (1228–1249). Sa vie et ses ouvrages* (Paris, 1880). The invaluable translations of William's theological works by Roland J. Teske, given in the list of abbreviations preceding the notes section, all contain sketches of his life, as do Teske's various encyclopaedia articles on William, such as that in Jorge J. E. Garcia and Timothy B. Noone, eds., *A Companion to Philosophy in the Middle Ages* (Oxford: Blackwell, 2003), no. 131.
2. Colin Morris, *The Discovery of the Individual, 1050–1200* (Toronto: University of Toronto Press, 1987); Caroline W. Bynum, "Did the Twelfth Century Discover the Individual?" in Bynum, *Jesus as Mother: Studies in the Spirituality of the High Middle Ages* (Berkeley: University of California Press, 1982), 82–109.
3. The extent of such millenarianism has been a hot topic in medieval studies since at least Norman Cohn, *The Pursuit of the Millennium* (New York: Secker and Warburg, 1957; rev. ed., 1961); and see Michael Frassetto, ed., *The Year 1000: Religious and Social Response to the Turning of the First Millennium* (New York: Palgrave Macmillan, 2002).
4. William discusses one such prophecy of the End, by Ps.-Methodius, in his *De Legibus*, chap. 18, in *Opera omnia*, vol. 1, pp. 49b–50b.
5. C. H. Haskins, *The Renaissance of the Twelfth Century* (Cambridge, MA: Harvard University Press, 1939); R. W. Southern, "The Place of England in the Twelfth Century Renaissance," in Southern, *Medieval Humanism and Other Studies* (Oxford: Blackwell, 1970), 158–80; R. N. Swanson, *The Twelfth-Century Renaissance* (Manchester, UK: Manchester University Press, 1999). All the essays in Robert L. Benson and Giles Constable, with

Carol D. Lanham, eds., *Renaissance and Renewal in the Twelfth Century* (Oxford: Oxford University Press, 1982), repay careful reading.

6. The aphorism was attributed to Bernard of Chartres (d. c. 1130) by his pupil John of Salisbury, *Metalogicon*, book 3, chap. 4, but it may already have been a common saying.
7. Peter Abelard, "Historia calamitatum: Abelard to a Friend: *The Story of His Misfortunes*," in *The Letters of Abelard and Heloise*, trans. Betty Radice, rev. M. T. Clanchy (London: Penguin, 2003), 3–43; M. T. Clanchy, *Abelard: A Medieval Life* (Oxford: Blackwell, 1997). Although the lives I discuss here are all of religious figures, some secular biographies also exist, such as Einhard's Life of Charlemagne.
8. John F. Benton, *Self and Society in Medieval France: The Memoirs of Abbot Guibert of Nogent* (Toronto: University of Toronto Press, 1984); Jay Rubenstein, *Guibert of Nogent: Portrait of a Medieval Mind* (New York: Routledge, 2002).
9. William of St. Thierry, *The First Life of Bernard of Clairvaux by William of St. Thierry*, trans. Hilary Costello (Collegeville, MN: Liturgical Press, 2015).
10. R. W. Southern, *St. Anselm and His Biographer: A Study of Monastic Life and Thought, 1059–c. 1130* (Cambridge: Cambridge University Press, 1963); Southern, *Saint Anselm: A Portrait in a Landscape* (Cambridge: Cambridge University Press, 1990).
11. C. Stephen Jaeger, *The Envy of Angels. Cathedral Schools and Social Ideals in Medieval Europe, 950–1200* (Philadelphia: University of Pennsylvania Press, 1994).
12. M. T. Clanchy, *From Memory to Written Record: England 1066–1307*, 3d ed. (Malden, MA: Wiley-Blackwell, 2013).
13. "We accept certain things in a lecture that we would not accept when writing it down": this and other examples in Lesley Smith, *The "Glossa Ordinaria": The Making of a Medieval Bible Commentary* (Boston: Brill, 2009), 8.
14. *On the Virtues*, chap. 11, p. 189.
15. Nancy Partner, "The Hidden Self: Psychoanalysis and the Textual Unconscious," in Partner, ed., *Writing Medieval History* (London: Hodder Arnold, 2005), 44.
16. Recent discussion of the nature of life writing have tended, with a few exceptions, to exclude medieval figures, precisely because we lack the sort of narrative detail that would normally be considered essential for weaving the texture of a life. See, for example, Zachary Leader, ed., *On Life-Writing* (Oxford: Oxford University Press, 2015).
17. Beryl Smalley, *English Friars and Antiquity in the Early Fourteenth Century* (Oxford: Blackwell, 1960), 1.
18. Caroline W. Bynum, "In Praise of Fragments: History in the Comic Mode," in Bynum, *Fragmentation and Redemption: Essays on Gender and the Human Body in Medieval Religion* (Cambridge, MA: Harvard University Press, 2012), 11–26.

CHAPTER TWO

1. Lesley Smith, *The Ten Commandments: Interpreting the Bible in the Medieval World* (Boston: Brill, 2014), 107–20.
2. *The Trinity*, chap. 21, p. 145.
3. *The Trinity*, chap. 21, p. 145.
4. *Why God Became Man*, chap. 7, p. 38; this chapter also has many matrimonial metaphors.
5. *The Trinity*, chap. 23, pp. 152–53.
6. Valois, *Guillaume d'Auvergne*, 4–5; Déribier du Chatelet, *Dictionnaire statistique du Département du Cantal* (Aurillac, 1824), vol. 1, p. 33.
7. Valois, *Guillaume d'Auvergne*, 4n1.
8. Stephen of Bourbon reported in A. Lecoy de la Marche, "Saint Louis, sa famille et sa cour d'après les anecdotes contemporaires," *Revue des questions historiques* 22 (1877): 478; and see *Compilatio singularis exemplorum*, no. 11, reported in Jacques Berlioz, "La voix de l'évêque. Guillaume d'Auvergne dans les exempla (XIIIe–XIVe siècle)," in *Autour*, 12 and 33 (Latin text).
9. I am indebted to the Press's second anonymous reader for this excellent suggestion.
10. *Augustine: Treatises on Marriage and Other Subjects*, ed. and trans. R. J. Deferrari and C. T. Wilcox (Washington, DC: Catholic University of America Press, 1999); D. L. d'Avray, *Medieval Marriage: Symbolism and Society* (Oxford: Oxford University Press, 2005); C. N. L. Brooke, *The Medieval Idea of Marriage* (Oxford: Oxford University Press, 1994); Georges Duby, *Medieval Marriage: Two Models from Twelfth-Century France*, trans. E. Forster (Baltimore: Johns Hopkins University Press, 1991).
11. *De sacramento matrimonii*, c. 2, in *Opera omnia*, vol. 1, p. 513a–b. William condemns *sodomia*, which can mean homosexual sex, and might possibly here refer to women who have sex with men who have sex with men, but is more likely, I think, to refer to anal sex or other non-missionary-position shenanigans. One of the few points that William found to approve of in Islam was its condemnation of homosexuality: *De Legibus*, chaps. 18, 20, in *Opera omnia*, vol. 1, pp. 50b, 54b.
12. *Sermons* 230A.163.
13. *The Soul*, chap. 5, pt. 10, pp. 211–15.
14. *The Soul*, chap. 5, pt. 10, p. 211.
15. *The Soul*, chap. 5, pt. 10, p. 212.
16. *The Trinity*, chap. 22; *The Universe of Creatures*, pt. II, chap. 4; *The Soul*, chap. 5, pt. 1.
17. *The Soul*, chap. 3, pt. 11.
18. *The Universe of Creatures*, pt. II, chap. 4, p. 149. For the need for both father and mother, see *Sermons* 230B.28.
19. *The Soul*, chap. 5, pt. 1.
20. *The Trinity*, chap. 43, p. 237.

21. *The Providence of God*, chap. 5; *On Morals*, chap. 2, p. 14. William warns parents they mustn't simply laugh if nurses teach their children incorrectly: *Sermons* 230B.23.
22. *Sermons* 230.70–71.
23. *De Matrimonio*, chap. 8, in *Opera omnia*, vol. 1, p. 524b.
24. *De Matrimonio*, chap. 8, p. 524a–b; translation quoted from Peter Biller, *The Measure of Multitude: Population in Medieval Thought* (Oxford: Oxford University Press, 2000), 72.
25. *On Morals*, c. 11, p. 206; *Sermons* 230C.41; *On Morals*, chap. 5, pp. 68–69.
26. *Sermons* 230B.34, 230B.27, 230A.321.
27. *On the Virtues*, chap. 9, p. 84.
28. The note is at the end of Paris, Bibliothèque nationale de France (BnF), MS lat. 15,756.
29. *The Providence of God*, chap. 24, p. 138.
30. Joseph Strayer, *The Albigensian Crusades* (Ann Arbor: University of Michigan Press, 1992), 1. In addition to Strayer, for this section I am reliant on André Bossuat, "L'Auvergne," in F. Lot and R. Fawtier, *Histoire des institutions françaises au Moyen Age*, vol. 1 (Paris: Presses universitaires de France, 1957), pp. 102–22; Gabriel Fournier, *Le peuplement rural en basse Auvergne durant le haut moyen âge* (Clermont-Ferrand: Presses universitaires de France, 1962); André-Georges Manry, ed., *Histoire de l'Auvergne* (Toulouse, 1979); Elizabeth Hallam, *The Capetian Kings of France, 978–1328* (New York: Longman, 1980); Robert Fawtier, "L'Auvergne," in J. Favier, ed., *Dictionnaire de la France médiévale* (Paris: Fayard, 1993); Linda M. Paterson, *The World of the Troubadours: Medieval Occitan Society, c. 1100–c. 1300* (Cambridge: Cambridge University Press, 1993).
31. Population figures are taken from Paterson, *The World of the Troubadours*, chap. 7.
32. Paterson, *The World of the Troubadours*, 161. William refers to Saracen slaves in *On the Virtues*, chap. 17, pp. 241–42; he also claims that they bred children to be sold as slaves in markets: *De Matrimonio*, chap. 8, in *Opera omnia*, vol. 1, p. 524b.
33. Bernard Craplet, Gérard Franceschi, and Pierre Belzeaux, *Auvergne Romane*, 3d ed. (La-Pierre-Qui-Vire: Zodiaque, 1962), with excellent church plans and photographs; see also Manry, *Histoire*.
34. Strayer, *The Albigensian Crusades*, 18–19.
35. Peter Biller, *The Waldenses, 1170—1530: Between a Religious Order and a Church* (Aldershot, UK: Ashgate, 2001); Gabriel Audisio, *The Waldensian Dissent: Persecution and Survival, c. 1170–c. 1570* (Cambridge: Cambridge University Press, 1999); Malcolm Barber, *The Cathars: Dualist Heretics in Languedoc in the High Middle Ages* (Harlow: Longman, 2000); Emmanuel Le Roy Ladurie, *Montaillou: Cathars and Catholics in a French Village, 1294–1324*, trans. B. Bray (London: George Braziller, 1978); Malcolm Lambert, *The Cathars* (Oxford: Blackwell, 1998).

36. Population estimates from Paterson, *The World of the Troubadours*, 175.
37. M.-Th. d'Alverny, "Translations and Translators," in R. L. Benson and G. Constable with C. D. Lanham, eds., *Renaissance and Renewal in the Twelfth Century* (Oxford: Oxford University Press, 1982), 421–62.
38. G. I. Langmuir, "L'absence d'accusation de meurtre rituel à l'ouest du Rhône," *Cahiers de Fanjeaux* 12 (1977): 235–50.
39. Strayer, *The Albigensian Crusades*, 22.
40. Paterson, *The World of the Troubadours*, 189.
41. W. A. Hinnebusch, *The History of the Dominican Order*, 2 vols. (New York: Alba House, 1966).
42. The best medieval source is Peter of les Vaux-de-Cernay's *History of the Albigensian Crusade*, trans. W. A. Sibly and M. D. Sibly (Woodbridge, UK: Boydell, 1998); Strayer, *The Albigensian Crusades*; Bernard Hamilton, *The Albigensian Crusade* (London: Historical Association, 1974).
43. Strayer, *The Albigensian Crusades*, 3.
44. Paterson, *The World of the Troubadours*, 4–5.
45. R. Anthony Lodge, "French and Occitan in Fourteenth-Century Auvergne," in Christopher Kleinhenz and Keith Busby, eds., *Medieval Multilingualism: The Francophone World and Its Neighbours* (Turnhout: Brepols, 2010), 285–301. According to Lodge, Latin would have been comprehensible to speakers of Romance languages such as Occitan.
46. *Sermons* 230B.6.
47. *Sermons* 230C.20.
48. *The Providence of God*, chap. 5, p. 63. He makes the same point in *On Morals*, chap. 11, pp. 211–12, where he suggests absinthe, lemons, or soot as suitably bitter tastes.

CHAPTER THREE

1. *On Morals*, chap. 11, pp. 208–9; William claims to be citing Isaiah 9, here, but he seems instead to be referencing a commentary of Jerome (209n28). *Sermons* 230B.29.
2. *The Providence of God*, chap. 5: "On the Good of Pain," p. 59.
3. M. T. Clanchy, *Looking Back from the Invention of Printing: Mothers and the Teaching of Reading in the Middle Ages* (Turnhout: Brepols, 2018).
4. David L. Wagner, ed., *The Seven Liberal Arts in the Middle Ages* (Bloomington: Indiana University Press, 1986), 23.
5. John of Salisbury, Letter 9, quoted in Elie Jalouste, "Les anciennes écoles de l'Auvergne," *Memoires de l'Académie . . . de Clermont Ferrand* 23 (1881): 69. Some sources credited the school with a chemical laboratory for experiments.
6. Third Lateran Council, c. 18: N. P. Tanner, *Decrees of the Ecumenical Councils*, 2 vols. (London: Sheed and Ward, 1990), vol. 1, p. 220; Lynn Thorn-

dike, *University Records and Life in the Middle Ages* (New York: Columbia University Press, 1944), no. 9.

7. Wagner, *The Seven Liberal Arts.*
8. Hastings Rashdall, rev. and ed. F.M. Powicke and A.B. Emden, *The Universities of Europe in the Middle Ages, Vol. 2: Italy, Spain, France, Germany, Scotland* (Oxford: Oxford University Press, 1936), 116–39; M.-Th. d'Alverny, *Alain de Lille. Textes inédits avec une introduction sur sa vie et sur ses oeuvres* (Paris: Vrin, 1965); d'Alverny, "Alain de Lille et la *Theologia*," in *L'Homme devant Dieu. Mélanges offerts au Père Henri de Lubac*, vol. 2: *Du Moyen Age au siècle des lumières* (Paris: Aubier, 1964), 111–28; G.R. Evans, *Alan of Lille: The Frontiers of Theology in the Later Twelfth Century* (Cambridge: Cambridge University Press, 1983). We do not know exactly when Alan decamped to Montpellier, but his *Dictionary of Theological Terms* was dedicated to Ermengaud, abbot of St. Gilles (near Montpellier) from 1179 to 1195.
9. *De Vitiis*, chap. 9, in *Opera omnia*, vol. 1, p. 284b.
10. John W. Baldwin, "Masters at Paris from 1179–1215: A Social Perspective," in R.L. Benson and Giles Constable, with C.D. Lanham, eds., *Renaissance and Renewal in the Twelfth Century* (Oxford: Oxford University Press, 1982), 138–72. Baldwin comes to this conclusion by a study of students' names.
11. For the scholars of the twelfth century see R.W. Southern, *Scholastic Humanism and the Unification of Europe, Vol. 1: Foundations; Vol. 2: The Heroic Age* (Oxford: Blackwell, 1995, 2001); John W. Baldwin, *Masters, Princes, and Merchants: The Social Views of Peter the Chanter and His Circle*, 2 vols. (Princeton: Princeton University Press, 1970). For highly flavored accounts of twelfth-century schooling, see John of Salisbury, *Metalogicon*, trans. J.B. Hall (Turnhout: Brepols, 2013); and Peter Abelard, "Historia calamitatum: Abelard to a Friend: *The Story of His Misfortunes*," in *The Letters of Abelard and Heloise*, trans. Betty Radice, rev. M.T. Clanchy (London: Penguin, 2003), 3–43. For the university itself: Gordon Leff, *Paris and Oxford Universities in the Thirteenth and Fourteenth Centuries: An Institutional and Intellectual History* (New York: Wiley, 1968); Stephen C. Ferruolo, *The Origins of the University: the Schools of Paris and Their Critics, 1100–1215* (Stanford: Stanford University Press, 1985); William J. Courtenay, *Teaching Careers at the University of Paris in the Thirteenth and Fourteenth Centuries* (Notre Dame, IN: University of Notre Dame Press, 1988); John van Engen, ed., *Learning Institutionalized: Teaching in the Medieval University* (Notre Dame, IN: University of Notre Dame Press, 2000). For the Masters in Theology in the thirteenth century, with short biographies and lists of their works, see Palémon Glorieux, *Repertoires des maîtres en théologie au XIIIe siècle*, 2 vols. (Paris: Vrin, 1933), especially the first pull-out table, vol. 1, between pp. 228 and 229.
12. Pearl Kibre, *Scholarly Privileges in the Middle Ages* (London: Mediaeval

Academy of America, 1961), chap. 4: "Scholarly Privileges at Paris: The Thirteenth Century"; *CUP*, no. 1. For universities more generally, see Hastings Rashdall, rev. and ed. F. M. Powicke and A. B. Emden, *The Universities of Europe in the Middle Ages, Vol. 1: Salerno, Bologna, Paris* (Oxford: Oxford University Press, 1936); Ferruolo, *The Origins of the University.*

13. Spencer E. Young, *Scholarly Community at the Early University of Paris: Theologians, Education and Society, 1215–1248* (Cambridge: Cambridge University Press, 2014); Jacques Verger and Olga Weijers, eds., *Les débuts de l'enseignement universitaire à Paris (1200–1245 environ)* (Turnhout: Brepols, 2013).
14. Quoted in Charles Homer Haskins, *Studies in Mediaeval Culture* (Oxford: Clarendon, 1929), 61: "The University of Paris in the Sermons of the Thirteenth Century." Philip and William must have worked together for a number of years, and known each other well.
15. Rashdall, *The Universities of Europe in the Middle Ages*, vol. 1, chap. 4: Bologna.
16. *CUP*, no. 32.
17. Peter the Chanter, *Verbum abbreviatum* 1.1, quoted in John W. Baldwin, *Masters, Princes, and Merchants*, vol. 1, pp. 90–91.
18. *Magistri Petri Lombardi . . . Sententiae in IV Libris Distinctae*, ed. I. C. Brady, 3 vols. (Grottaferrata: Ad Claras Aquas, 1971); trans. G. Silano, *The Sentences*, 4 vols. (Toronto: PIMS, 2007–10); Marcia Colish, *Peter Lombard*, 2 vols. (Leiden: Brill, 1994).
19. M. T. Clanchy and Lesley Smith, "Abelard's Description of the School of Laon: What Might It Tell Us about Early Scholastic Teaching?" *Nottingham Medieval Studies* 54 (2010): 1–34.
20. Clanchy and Smith, "Abelard's Description of the School of Laon"; Cédric Giraud, *"Per verba magistri": Anselme de Laon et son école au XIIe siècle* (Turnhout: Brepols, 2010); Odon Lottin, *Psychologie et morale aux XIIe et XIIIe siècles, vol. 5: L'École d'Anselme de Laon et de Guillaume de Champeaux* (Gembloux: J. Duculot, 1959).
21. Bernard C. Bazan, John F. Wippel, Gérard Fransen, and Danielle Jacquart, *Les questions disputées et les questions quodlibétiques dans les facultés de théologie, de droit et de médecine* (Turnhout: Brepols, 1985).
22. Nicole Bériou, *L'avènement des maîtres de la parole. La prédication à Paris au XIIIe siècle*, 2 vols. (Paris: Institut d'études augustiniennes, 1998); M.-M. Davy, *Les sermons universitaires parisiens de 1230–1231. Contributions à l'histoire de la prédication médiévale* (Paris: Vrin, 1931).
23. Salimbene de Adam, *Cronica*, ed. Guiseppe Scalia, 2 vols. (Bari: Laterza, 1966), vol. 1, pp. 307–8.
24. *CUP*, no. 20; Thorndike, *University Records*, no. 15. On Robert himself, see Baldwin, *Masters, Princes, and Merchants*, especially vol. 1, pp. 19–25.
25. Lateran IV, c. 11: Tanner, *Decrees of the Ecumenical Councils*, vol. 1, p. 240, and cc. 14–16 for clergy standards, pp. 242–43.

26. Valois, *Guillaume d'Auvergne*, p. 6, and *pièces justificatives*, no. 1, p. 333.
27. Teaching dates are from Glorieux, *Répertoire*; see also Baldwin, *Masters, Princes and Merchants*, vol. 1, pp. 34–36, Franco Morenzoni, *Des écoles aux paroisses. Thomas de Chobham et la promotion de la prédication au début du XIIIe siècle* (Paris: Institut d'études augustiniennes, 1995).
28. Gaines Post, "Masters' Salaries and Student-Fees in Mediaeval Universities," *Speculum* 7 (1932): 181–98.
29. Haskins, *Studies in Mediaeval Culture*, chap. 1: "The Life of Mediaeval Students as Illustrated by their Letters," 7–10.
30. Baldwin, "Masters at Paris," 151; Jean Dunbabin, "Meeting the Costs of University Education in Northern France, c. 1240–c. 1340," *History of Universities* 10 (1991): 1–27.
31. Dunbabin, "Meeting the Costs," 14–16.
32. Dunbabin, "Meeting the Costs," 14–15.
33. F. J. Pegues, "Philanthropy and the Universities in France and England in the Later Middle Ages," in A. L. Gabriel, ed., *The Economic and Material Frame of the Mediaeval University* (Notre Dame, IN: University of Notre Dame Press, 1966), 69–80, reckons it possible that only about 6.5 percent of Paris students were part of a college.
34. Rashdall, *The Universities of Europe*, vol. 1, pp. 487–539 (at 501); A. L. Gabriel, *Garlandia: Studies in the History of the Medieval University* (Frankfurt am Main, 1969). Whether the founders' motives were charitable or political—both had links to royalty—or both, is debatable.
35. The foundation document of the college is translated in Thorndike, *University Records*, no. 10.
36. Thorndike, *University Records*, no. 17.
37. *CUP* no. 60; quoted from the translation in Rashdall, *The Universities of Europe*, vol. 1, p. 503. The house had moved around the corner to the church of St. Nicholas at the Louvre, but kept the name of St. Thomas until 1284.
38. Thorndike, *University Records*, no. 42.
39. *CUP*, no. 5, translated in Thorndike, *University Records*, no. 13; Courtenay, *Teaching Careers*, 249–52.
40. For the debate about teachers' fees, see Baldwin, *Masters, Princes and Merchants*, vol. 1, pp. 125–30.
41. A. L. Gabriel, "The Ideal Master of the Mediaeval University," *Catholic Historial Review* 60 (1974): 1–40.
42. Ephesians 3:11.
43. *Sermons* 230A.234.
44. *Sermons* 230.69.
45. *De Vitiis*, in *Opera omnia*, vol. 1, chap. 9, pp. 282–85, here at 284. For a different interpretation see Young, *Scholarly Community*, 206–7, who sees it as an argument against anyone remaining as a teacher for long.
46. *On Morals*, chap. 8: "Zeal's Praises," p. 103.

47. *On Morals*, chap. 8: "Zeal's Praises," p. 96 (emphasis mine). Constant J. Mews, "Communities of Learning and the Dream of Synthesis: The Schools and Colleges of Thirteenth-Century Paris," in Mews and John N. Crossley, eds., *Communities of Learning: Networks and the Shaping of Intellectual Identity in Europe, 1000–1500* (Turnhout: Brepols, 2011), 109–35, notes some of the teachers William can be referring to (112, 112n11).
48. *Sermons* 230A.155.
49. *The Universe of Creatures*, p. 32; William expresses similar sentiments in many other places.
50. *On the Virtues*, c. 23, p. 282.

CHAPTER FOUR

1. An excellent sense of Paris at this period is to be found in the wonderful work of John W. Baldwin, on which this chapter draws heavily: see his *Paris, 1200* (Stanford: Stanford University Press, 2010), as well as his *Masters, Princes and Merchants*, especially vol. 1, pp. 63–72, and accompanying notes in vol. 2, pp. 46–50; and his *City on the Seine: Paris under Louis IX, 1226–1270* (New York: Macmillan, 1975). Simone Roux, *Paris in the Middle Ages*, trans. Jo Ann McNamara (Philadelphia, 2009), mostly deals with a later period.
2. Baldwin *Paris, 1200*, 1: the nickname was given by Rigord, the king's contemporary chronicler.
3. Elizabeth Hallam, *The Capetian Kings of France, 978–1328* (New York: Longman, 1980); Robert Fawtier, *The Capetian Kings of France: Monarchy and Nation, 987–1328*, trans. L. Butler and R. J. Adam (Basingstoke, UK: Macmillan, 1960).
4. Baldwin, *Paris, 1200*, 18 (and references therein).
5. Erwin Panofsky, *Abbot Suger on the Abbey Church of St.-Denis and Its Art Treasures*, 2d ed. (Princeton: Princeton University Press, 1979); Lindy Grant, *Abbot Suger of St.-Denis: Church and State in Early Twelfth-Century France* (New York: Routledge, 2013).
6. Baldwin, *Paris, 1200*, 25–30, describes the path of the walls, and their building, in detail.
7. Figures from Baldwin, *Paris, 1200*, 30.
8. Baldwin, *Masters, Princes and Merchants*, vol. 1, pp. 66–69, here at 68.
9. *The "Historia Occidentalis" of Jacques de Vitry: A Critical Edition*, ed. John F. Hinnebusch (Fribourg: University Press, 1972), 91.
10. Baldwin, *Paris, 1200*, 33–35; Baldwin, *Masters, Princes and Merchants*, vol. 1, pp. 133–37.
11. Baldwin, *Masters, Princes and Merchants*, vol. 2, p. 51n52: J. C. Russell gives the population of Paris, based on area enclosed, as 25,000, whereas Michel Roblin estimates it as 50,000.

12. Hastings Rashdall, rev. and ed. F. M. Powicke and A. B. Emden, *The Universities of Europe in the Middle Ages, 3: English Universities, Student Life* (Oxford: Oxford University Press, 1936), 331, says the academic population of Paris was never more than 6,000 to 7,000. Russell suggests that in 1292, when the overall population was 59,200 (from tax rolls), the clergy and academic population was 6,000.
13. William le Breton, *Gesta*, vol. 1, p. 241, in *Oeuvres de Rigord et Guillaume le Breton*, ed. Henri-François Delaborde, 2 vols. (Paris, 1882), vol. 1, pp. 168–327.
14. *Sermons* 230C.41.
15. Adrien Friedmann, *Paris, ses rues, ses paroisses du moyen âge à la révolution. Origine et évolution des circonscriptions paroissiales* (Paris: Librairie Plon, 1959).
16. Friedmann, *Paris, ses rues, ses paroisses*, details the eventual division of Saint-Germain into eight separate parishes: 71–73, 91–98, 277–78.
17. Peter Biller, *The Measure of Multitude: Population in Medieval Thought* (Oxford: Oxford University Press, 2000), 68.
18. Gregory IX, Bull of 18 December 1234, given in Valois, *Guillaume d'Auvergne, pièces justificatives*, no. 55.
19. Friedmann, *Paris, ses rues, ses paroisses*, 241, notes "la répugnance bien connue des chanoines de l'abbaye à sortir de leur cloître"; for the foundation, see 238–41, with map; also Valois, *Guillaume d'Auvergne*, 41.
20. *Sermons* 230.69.
21. Marginal scenes decorating a manuscript of the Life of St. Denis, patron saint of France, give a vivid sense of the city: Virginia Wylie Egbert, *On the Bridges of Medieval Paris: A Record of Early Fourteenth-Century Life* (Princeton: Princeton University Press, 1974).
22. *Sermons* 230B.18.
23. *Sermons* 230C.87, 230.20, 230B.1. *On the Virtues*, chap. 10, pp. 110–11; chap. 11, p. 127: two of the several places where William mentions medieval prostheses.
24. *Sermons* 230.118; *On Morals*, chap. 4, p. 49.
25. *Sermons* 230B.1, 230A.253.
26. See, for example, *Sermons* 230A.313; *On the Virtues*, c. 11, p. 139.
27. Pearl Kibre, *The Nations in the Medieval Universities* (Cambridge, MA: Harvard University Press, 1948); Rashdall, *The Universities of Europe*, vol. 1, pp. 298–320.
28. Quoted in Biller, *Measure of Multitude*, 380.
29. William Chester Jordan, *The French Monarchy and the Jews from Philip Augustus to the Last Capetians* (Philadelphia, 1989), 8–10, 113–14, 153–54, 182–84; Baldwin, *Paris, 1200*, 58–61.
30. William Chester Jordan, *The Apple of His Eye: Converts from Islam in the Reign of Louis IX* (Princeton: Princeton University Press, 2019), 122.
31. Lindy Grant, *Blanche of Castile, Queen of France* (New Haven: Yale Uni-

versity Press, 2016), 115–17. Blanche herself owned Francis of Assisi's pillow, sent to her by his companions in Assisi (208).

32. Grant, *Blanche of Castile*, 115–17.
33. Valois, *Guillaume d'Auvergne*, 145.
34. *Sermons* 230C.5.
35. *Sermons* 230A.301.
36. *De sacramentis*: "De sacramentis in generali," c. 2, in *Opera omnia*, vol. 1, pp. 407–14.
37. *Sermons* 230A.270.
38. *Parisius, paradisus*: Alexander Neckham, *De Laudibus divinae sapientiae*, ed. T. Wright, Rolls Series 34 (London, 1863), 453.

CHAPTER FIVE

1. Valois, *Guillaume d'Auvergne*, 8–16. Gregory described him to the chapter at Paris (10 April 1228) as "William . . . whom I ordained priest, then finally consecrated bishop": M. B. Hauréau, "Quelques lettres de Grégoire IX," *Notices et extraits de la bibliothèque impériale* vol. 21 (Paris, 1865), pt. 2, p. 208.
2. *Cartulaire de l'église de Notre-Dame de Paris*, ed. B. Guerard, 4 vols. (Paris, 1850), vol. 1, pp. xcix–cxv; Craig Wright, *Music and Ceremony at Notre Dame of Paris, 500–1500* (Cambridge: Cambridge University Press, 1989), 18–37; Pascal Montaubin, "Les chanoines de Notre-Dame de Paris à la mort de l'évêque Guillaume d'Auvergne (1240)," and Nathalie Gorochov, "L'évêque de Paris, le chapitre cathédral de Notre-Dame et l'université au Moyen Âge," both in *Notre-Dame de Paris 1163–2013: Actes du colloque scientifique tenu au collegè des Bernardins, à Paris, du 12 au 15 décembre 2012* (Turnhout: Brepols, 2013), 195–216, 113–24.
3. *Sermons* 230C.110.
4. Wright, *Music and Ceremony at Notre Dame*, 28.
5. *Cartulaire*, vol. 1, p. cxi.
6. Valois, *Guillaume d'Auvergne* discovered only two documents citing William as a canon of Notre-Dame. In 1224, he is named by Honorius III as part of a papal inquiry into the abbot of Saint-Symphorien in Beauvais, and in 1225 the same pope made him part of a tribunal to reform the monastery of Sainte-Colombe at Sens (Valois, *Guillaume d'Auvergne, pièces justificatives*, nos. 2, 3).
7. Baldwin, *Masters, Princes and Merchants*, 117–30.
8. Montaubin, "Les chanoines de Notre-Dame de Paris," 202, 214.
9. Gregory claimed, correctly, that canon 24 of Lateran IV gave him this power, so William could have no concerns over the legitimacy of his own appointment.
10. Valois, *Guillaume d'Auvergne*, 8–16. Gregory's letter can be found in Hauréau, "Quelques lettres de Grégoire IX," 208.

11. Spencer E. Young, *Scholarly Community at the Early University of Paris: Theologians, Education and Society, 1215–1248* (Cambridge: Cambridge University Press, 2014), 73–80.
12. Roland J. Teske, "William of Auvergne's Debt to Avicenna," in Jules Janssens and Daniel De Smet, eds., *Avicenna and His Heritage* (Leuven: Leuven University Press, 2002), 153.
13. For a comparison of the election after William, see Montaubin, "Les chanoines de Notre-Dame de Paris."
14. *Sermons* 230A.208.
15. *De Collatione beneficiorum*, in *Opera omnia*, vol. 2, *Supplementum*, pp. 248–60.
16. Bibliography for the two orders is vast and ever growing. Starting points for the history of the Dominicans: W. A. Hinnebusch, *The History of the Dominican Order: Origins and Growth to 1500*, 2 vols. (New York: Alba House, 1966, 1973); M.-H. Vicaire, *Saint Dominic and His Times*, trans. K. Pond (New York: McGraw-Hill, 1974); M. M. Mulchahey, *"First the Bow Is Bent in Study . . .": Dominican Education before 1350* (Toronto: PIMS, 1998). For the Franciscans: J. H. R. Moorman, *A History of the Franciscan Order: From Its Origins to the Year 1517* (Oxford: Clarendon Press, 1968); Kajetan Esser, *Origins of the Franciscan Order* (Chicago: Franciscan Herald Press, 1970); Şenocak Neslihan, *The Poor and the Perfect: The Rise of Learning in the Franciscan Order, 1209–1310* (Ithaca: Cornell University Press, 2012).
17. Lateran IV, c. 13: Tanner, *Decrees of the Ecumenical Councils*, vol. 1, p. 242.
18. Ephrem Longpré, "Guillaume d'Auvergne et l'École Franciscaine de Paris," in *La France Franciscaine* 5 (1922): 426–29; Caroline Bruzelius, *Preaching, Building and Burying: Friars in the Medieval City* (New Haven: Yale University Press, 2014).
19. Valois, *Guillaume d'Auvergne*, 102–3 and notes. Gregory's text can be accessed through the Brepols Ut per litteras apostolicas (LITPA) database.
20. Valois, *Guillaume d'Auvergne*, 103–4. Gregory's letter of 3 June 1233 is given in full by Valois at *pièces justificatives*, no. 38, pp. 354–56.
21. "Believing that we had found a man after our own heart and that we exulted and rejoiced in you as one rightly beloved, we poured the oil of sacred anointing on your head . . . But see—and we report this in sorrow—bearing a wound from an unexpected foe, and frustrated in the hope we had conceived, we are so confounded by your actions that we are forced to say, albeit unwillingly, 'We regret having made this man' . . . With what great shame do you think we are covered when some can mock us, saying, 'Behold the man [*Ecce homo*] you have set over the church of Paris'": translation from *The Trinity*, p. 2. The Latin text is in Valois, *Guillaume d'Auvergne, pièces justificatives*, no. 18.
22. Hastings Rashdall, ed. and rev. F. M. Powicke and A. B. Emden, *The Universities of Europe in the Middle Ages, Vol. 1: Salerno, Bologna, Paris* (Oxford: Oxford University Press, 1936), especially 334–43; Valois, *Guillaume d'Au-*

vergne, chap. 5; P. Mandonnet, "De l'incorporation des Dominicains dans l'ancienne université de Paris," *Revue Thomiste* 5 (1896): 133–70; A. Masnovo, "Guglielmo d'Auvergne e l'università di Parigi dal 1229 al 1231," in *Mélanges Mandonnet*, vol. 2 (Paris: Vrin, 1930), pp. 191–232; Pearl Kibre, *Scholarly Privileges in the Middle Ages: The Rights, Privileges, and Immunities of Scholars and Universities at Bologna, Padua, Paris, and Oxford* (London: Mediaeval Academy of America, 1961), chap. 4, especially pp. 92–97; Gordon Leff, *Paris and Oxford Universities in the Thirteenth and Fourteenth Centuries: An Institutional and Intellectual History* (New York: Wiley, 1968), part 1, chaps. 2–3; Lindy Grant, *Blanche of Castile, Queen of France* (New Haven: Yale University Press, 2016), 97–99. The contemporary source, who favored the university's side, was the English Benedictine Matthew Paris (see his *Chronica majora*, ed. H. R. Luard, Rolls Series 3 [London: Longman, 1876], 166–69).

23. *CUP*, no. 75.
24. *CUP*, no. 82; partial translation in Thorndike, *University Records*, no. 19.
25. For the legitimacy of the award of these chairs, see Mandonnet, "De l'Incorporation"; and Masnovo, "Guglielmo d'Auvergne." See also Mulchahey, *"First the Bow Is Bent in Study,"* 291.
26. Longpré, "Guillaume d'Auvergne et l'École Franciscaine de Paris," 427–28, citing Bonaventure, *Commentarius in IV Libros Sententiarum*, in *Opera omnia*, vol. 3 (Quaracchi: Ad Claras Aquas, 1885), book 3, d. 16, art. 1, qu. 1, p. 346, that William and Alexander of Hales were on the same side of a 1241 theological debate; see also book 3, d. 40, dub. 3, pp. 895–96; Roger Bacon, *Opus tertium*, ed. J. S. Brewer, Rolls Series 15 (London: Longman, 1859), chap. 23, pp. 74–75.
27. *CUP*, no. 60; *Cartulaire de l'église de Notre-Dame de Paris*, vol. 1, p. xcviii.
28. *Sermons* 230.116.
29. Lateran IV, c. 29: Tanner, *Decrees of the Ecumenical Councils*, vol. 1, pp. 248–49.
30. *CUP*, no. 108, quoting Thomas of Cantimpré, *Bonum universale de apibus*, I. c. 20.
31. Thomas B. Payne, ed., *Philip the Chancellor: Motets and Prosulas* (Middleton, WI: A-R Editions, 2011), xxv–xxvii, 161–67, 171–77; Wright, *Music and Ceremony at Notre Dame*, attributes one of these motets to William himself, but Payne's argument that it was written by Philip against William is compelling. See also Payne, "*Aurelianus civitas*: Student Unrest in Medieval France and a Conductus by Philip the Chancellor," *Speculum* 75 (2000): 589–614, which offers a musicologist's view of William's election.
32. Thomas of Cantimpré, *Bonum universale de apibus*, I. c. 19, s. 8, see Valois, *Guillaume d'Auvergne*, 34–36.
33. *De Collatione beneficiorum*, in *Opera omnia*, vol. 2, *Supplementum*, p. 252.
34. Lateran IV, c. 71: Tanner, *Decrees of the Ecumenical Councils*, vol. 1, pp. 267–71.

35. Valois, *Guillaume d'Auvergne*, 22.
36. Valois, *Guillaume d'Auvergne*, p. 113; *pièces justificatives*, nos. 36–37.
37. Valois, *Guillaume d'Auvergne*, 114–15.
38. Grant, *Blanche of Castile*, 174; in *The Universe of Creatures*, pt. II.1, chap. 31, p. 198, William refers to a word "in the vernacular Spanish."
39. Valois, *Guillaume d'Auvergne*, 150–52; and Matthew Paris, *Chronica majora*, vol. 3, p. 292.
40. *Sermons* 230A.170.
41. *Sermons*, 230C.26.

CHAPTER SIX

1. *Sermons* 230, 230A, 230B, 230C: Morenzoni's useful introduction to the edition is 230, pp. vii–xlvii. See also Morenzoni, "*Predicatio est rei predicate humanis mentibus presentatio.* Les sermons pour la Dédicace de l'église de Guillaume d'Auvergne," in *Autour*, 293–322; and Morenzoni, "Le corpus homilétique de Guillaume d'Auvergne, évêque de Paris," *Sacris Erudiri* 46 (2007): 287–369.
2. D. L. d'Avray, *The Preaching of the Friars: Sermons Diffused from Paris before 1300* (New York: Oxford University Press, 1985); Bériou, *L'avènement des maîtres de la Parole*; Beverley Maine Kienzle, ed., *The Sermon* (Turnhout: Brepols, 2000); A. Thayer, "The Medieval Sermon: Text, Performance and Insight," in J. Rosenthal, ed., *Understanding Medieval Primary Sources: Using Historical Sources to Discover Medieval Europe* (London: Routledge, 2012).
3. *Narra hystoriam/historiam* (the two forms are identical in Latin): Morenzoni calculates that William uses this formula more than 70 times, e.g., *Sermons* 230A.282. *Narra totam hystoriam Euuangelii*: e.g., *Sermons* 230.104. *Et narra de singulis*: e.g., *Sermons* 230.27 (twice). *Ad hunc modum*: e.g., *Sermons* 230.70.
4. Oliver Sacks, *The Man Who Mistook His Wife for a Hat* (London: Picador, 2011), 184–85.
5. *The Universe of Creatures*, pt. II.1, chap. 31, p. 198. In *The Soul*, chap. 2, pt. 6, William refers to Hebrew—the common word *ruah* for "spirit"—but this is undoubtedly book-learning, rather than any active linguistic knowledge.
6. *The Soul*, chap. 2, pt. 12, p. 90.
7. *Sermons* 230B.24; 230.73, 77; 230A.313; 230C.18, 25.
8. Hugh of St. Cher, *Postilla in totam bibliam*, on Ps. 18 (19):1–3. Unfortunately, there is no modern edition or facsimile of Hugh's *Postilla*, but there are many early printed editions.
9. Morenzoni, "Introduction," in *Sermons*, 230, p. vi; F. Morenzoni, "Les proverbes dans la prédication du XIIIe siècle," in H. O. Bizzarri and M. Rohde, eds., *Tradition des proverbes et des exempla dans l'Occident*

médiéval (Boston: De Gruyter, 2009), 131–49; Lesley Smith, "Slippers in Heaven: William of Auvergne Preaching to the Brethren," in L. Schumacher, ed., *The "Summa Halensis": Sources and Context* (Munich: De Gruyter, 2020), 285–97.

10. *Sermons* 230B.50.
11. Mulchahey, *"First the Bow Is Bent in Study."*
12. *Sermons* 230.35, 30; 230B.13, 34, 38. See also *On the Virtues*, chap. 9, p. 107, chap. 11, pp. 131–32, chap. 12, pp. 193–97, for curved and straight love, and for vices as something bent out of shape.
13. Augustine, *De Mendacio; Contra Mendacium*, ed. J. Zycha, Corpus Scriptorum Ecclesiasticorum Latinorum 41 (London: Tempsky, 1900); translated in *Augustine: On the Holy Trinity, Doctrinal Treatises, Moral Treatises*, ed. P. Schaff, Nicene and Post Nicene Fathers, ser. 1, vol. 3 (Edinburgh: T. and T. Clark, 1887). See also Augustine, *Enchiridion ad Laurentium*, chap. 22, ed. E. Evans, Corpus Christianorum Series Latina 46 (Turnhout: Brepols, 1969), p. 62.
14. Lesley Smith, *The Ten Commandments: Interpreting the Bible in the Medieval World* (Boston: Brill, 2014), chap. 6.
15. *Sermons* 230A.314.
16. *The Soul*, chap. 5, pt. 5, p. 196.
17. *The Trinity*, chap. 18, pp. 137–38.
18. *The Trinity*, chap. 18, p. 136.
19. *The Trinity*, chap. 18, p. 139.
20. *The Universe of Creatures*, pt. I, chap. 26, p. 91.
21. *The Universe of Creatures*, pt. I, chap. 21, p. 77.
22. *The Universe of Creatures*, pt. I, chap. 21, pp. 78–79.
23. Note by Teske, *The Trinity*, chap. 35, p. 210n2; and for grammarians see, e.g., *The Soul*, chap. 3, pt. 3, chap. 5, pt. 26.
24. *The Trinity*, chap. 29, p. 187. Nominalism, which space forces me to pass over too quickly here, stressed the particularity of all existing things, and recognized the existence of universals only in the sphere of human thought and language: see C. J. Mews, "Nominalism and Theology before Abaelard: New Light on Roscelin of Compiègne," *Vivarium* 30 (1992): 5–37.
25. *The Trinity*, chap. 29, p. 186. For other examples, see Peter Biller, *The Measure of Multitude: Population in Medieval Thought* (Oxford: Oxford University Press, 2000), 65–66.
26. Exodus 15:3; *The Trinity*, chap. 44, p. 246.
27. More than once, William discusses the problem of using prepositions to describe the relations of the Trinity: e.g., *The Trinity*, chap. 35, chap. 43, p. 239.
28. Fourth Lateran Council, canon 1, the so-called Athanasian Creed: *Decrees of the Ecumenical Councils*, ed. N. P. Tanner, 2 vols. (London: Sheed and Ward, 1990), vol. 1, pp. 230–31.
29. *The Trinity*, chap. 44, p. 246, and see also pp. 245, 247–48.

30. "It is often necessary to make up words . . .": *The Providence of God,* chap. 17, p. 108. In *The Trinity,* an earlier work than *The Providence of God,* William is working "in the mode of proofs and investigation," with the aim of his arguments being accepted by as many people as possible: see below, chapter 7, "Knowing."
31. Roland J. Teske, "William of Auvergne's Debt to Avicenna," in Jules Janssens and Daniel De Smet, eds., *Avicenna and His Heritage* (Leuven: Leuven University Press, 2002), 157–60.
32. Exodus 3:14; *De Universo,* pt. 2.2, chap. 10, p. 853a–b.
33. Étienne Gilson, "Avicenne en Occident au moyen âge," *Archives d'histoire doctrinale et littéraire du moyen âge* 44 (1969): 90–93.
34. Biller, *The Measure of Multitude,* 64–65.
35. These examples of the "I" form, and several others, can all be found, some several times, in *The Soul,* chap. 5, pt. 22; the examples of the "you" form are from one short paragraph: *The Soul,* chap. 5, pt. 24, p. 277.
36. See below, chapter 7, "Knowing." William of Auxerre: *Magistri Guillelmi Altissiodorensis. Summa Aurea,* ed. Jean Ribaillier, 7 vols. in 5 (Paris: CNRS, 1980–87).
37. *The Soul,* chap. 6, pt. 3, p. 301; chap. 5, pt. 24, p. 277.
38. See also Gilson, "Avicenne en occident," 92–93, for more examples.
39. *De Universo,* pt. 2.1, chap. 43, in *Opera omnia,* vol. 1, p. 746a.
40. *Compilatio singularis exemplorum,* quoted in Berlioz, "La Voix de l'évêque," in *Autour,* 12 (no. 10); Latin text, 33. See also A. Lecoy de la Marche, ed. J. Berlioz, *Le rire du prédicateur. Récits facétieux du Moyen Âge* (Turnhout: Brepols, 1992).
41. A. R. Hall and H. K. Kenward, "Sewers, Cesspits and Middens: A Survey of the Evidence for 2000 years of Waste Disposal in York, UK," in P. D. Mitchell, ed., *Santitation, Latrines and Intestinal Parastites in Past Populations* (Farnham, UK: Ashgate, 2015), 99–119.
42. *Sermons* 230B.1.
43. *Sermons* 230B.18, 230C.64.
44. *On the Virtues,* chap. 11, p. 144.
45. *Compilatio singularis exemplorum,* quoted in Berlioz, "La Voix de l'évêque," in *Autour,* 12 (no. 5); Latin text, 33.
46. *Sermons* 230A.229.
47. *Sermons* 230C.99, and see 230C.96; 230B.12, 47.

CHAPTER SEVEN

1. *On the Virtues,* chap. 9, p. 93, slightly adapted: the Latin here is *beatitudo,* which Teske translates as "happiness," but is more literally "blessedness"; *On Faith and the Laws,* prol., p. 74: in comparison, the Latin here is *foelicitas,* and I have retained Teske's translation.
2. *On the Virtues,* chap. 17, p. 233.

3. *On the Virtues*, chap. 17, p. 234. Both the Rule of St. Benedict and the Rules of the Franciscans forbade the brothers from laughing.
4. *On the Virtues*, chap. 17, p. 234.
5. Augustine, *Confessions*, book 13, pt. 15; trans. R. S. Pine-Coffin (Harmondsworth, UK: Penguin, 1961), 321–33.
6. *On Faith*, prol., p. 74.
7. William may be following the lead of Anselm of Canterbury (d. 1109), who also wrote a treatise *Why God Became Man*, or even Peter Abelard (d. 1142/3), who was strongly criticized for attempting to apply the rules of logic to matters of faith.
8. Josef Kramp, "Des Wilhelm von Auvergne 'Magisterium Divinale,'" *Gregorianum* 1 (1920): 538–613; 2 (1921): 42–103, 174–95. Guglielmo Corti, "Le sette parte del *Magisterium divinale et sapientiale* di Guglielmo di Auvergne," in *Studi e ricerche di scienze religiose in onore dei santi apostoli Pietro et Paolo nel XIX centenario del loro martirio* (Rome: Facultas Theologica Pontificae Universitatis Lateranensis, 1968), 289–307; R. J. Teske, "William of Auvergne on the Relation between Reason and Faith," in Teske, *Studies*, no. 10; R. J. Teske, "William of Auvergne on Philosophy as *divinalis* and *sapientialis*," in J. A. Aertsen and A. Speer, eds., *Was ist Philosophie im Mittelalter?* (Berlin: De Gruyter, 1998), 475–81.
9. For William's in-between position, see E. Gilson, *La philosophie au moyen âge*, 2d ed. (Paris: Payot, 1962), 415.
10. Smith, *The Ten Commandments*, chap. 2: "Number"; V. F. Hopper, *Medieval Number Symbolism: Its Sources, Meaning, and Influence on Thought and Expression* (New York: Columbia University Press, 1938).
11. *The Universe of Creatures*, chap. 1, pp. 31–32.
12. *The Trinity*, prol., pp. 63–64.
13. *The Trinity*, prol., p. 64.
14. *On Faith*, chap. 1, p. 84.
15. *On Faith*, chap. 1, p. 84.
16. *The Universe of Creatures*, chap. 1, p. 32.
17. *De Universo* II.iii.6, in *Opera omnia*, vol. 1, p. 1028a.
18. *On Morals*, chap. 1, p. 1.
19. *On the Virtues*, chap. 1, p. 31, slightly adapted.
20. Beryl Smalley, "Ecclesiastical Attitudes to Novelty c. 1000–c. 1250," in Derek Baker, ed., *Church, Society and Politics* (Oxford: Blackwell, 1975), 113–31.
21. Lesley Smith, *The "Glossa Ordinaria": The Making of a Medieval Bible Commentary* (Boston: Brill, 2009); Beryl Smalley, *The Study of the Bible in the Middle Ages*, 3d ed. (Oxford: Blackwell, 1983).
22. D'Alverny, "Translators and Translations," in Benson and Constable, *Renaissance and Renewal*; F. van Steenberghen, *Aristotle in the West: The Origins of Latin Aristotelianism*, trans. L. Johnston (New York: Humanities Press, 1970).

23. Valois, *Guillaume d'Auvergne*, 198–206.
24. *The Soul*, chap. 1, pt. 1, p. 43.
25. *Why God Became Man*, chap. 2, p. 22.
26. "The fool has said in his heart, 'There is no God,'" Psalm 53:1.
27. *The Trinity*, chap. 26, p. 175.
28. Beryl Smalley, "William of Auvergne, John of La Rochelle, and St. Thomas Aquinas on the Old Law," in Smalley, *Studies in Medieval Thought and Learning from Abelard to Wyclif* (London: Hambledon, 1981), 121–81, at 150–51, reprinted from *St. Thomas Aquinas 1274–1974*, 2 vols. (Toronto: PIMS, 1974), vol. 1, pp. 10–71. Smalley quotes from the text of *De Legibus* (*Opera omnia*, vol. 1, pp. 48b–49a), which she gives in an appendix, pp. 179–81.
29. 2 Samuel 11–12.
30. *De Legibus*, chap. 2, in *Opera omnia*, vol. 1, p. 29a, quoted in Smalley, "William of Auvergne," 142.
31. Smalley, "William of Auvergne," 154, referencing *De Arte praedicandi* and *De Faciebus mundi*.
32. Isaiah 34:4.
33. M.-D. Chenu, *La théologie au douzième siècle* (Paris: Vrin, 1976); Chenu, *Nature, Man and Society in the Twelfth Century: Essays on New Theological Perspective in the Latin West*, ed. and trans. J. Taylor and L. K. Little (Toronto: University of Toronto Press, 1997).
34. Hugh of St. Victor, *De tribus diebus*, ed. D. Poirel, Corpus Christianorum Continuation Mediaevalis 177 (Turnhout: Brepols, 2002), 9–10, quoted in Constant J. Mews, "The World as Text: The Bible and the Book of Nature in Twelfth-Century Theology," in T. J. Heffernan and T. E. Burman, eds., *Scripture and Pluralism: Reading the Bible in the Religiously Plural Worlds of the Middle Ages and Renaissance* (Leiden: Brill, 2005), 99.
35. R. H. Rouse and M. A. Rouse, *Manuscripts and Their Makers: Commercial Book Producers in Medieval Paris 1200–1500*, 2 vols. (Turnhout: Brepols, 2000).
36. Gilbert Ouy, *Les manuscrits de l'Abbaye de Saint-Victor. Catalogue établi sur la base du répertoire de Claude de Grandrue (1514)* (Turnhout: Brepols, 1999). Robert de Sorbon's college foundation, c. 1257, was unusual in making provision for a library: see P. Glorieux, *Aux origines de la Sorbonne*, 2 vols. (Paris: Vrin, 1965); A. L. Gabriel, *The Paris Studium: Robert of Sorbonne and His Legacy* (Notre Dame, IN: University of Notre Dame Press, 1992).
37. *Sermons* 230.15.
38. *On Faith*, chap. 1, p. 89.
39. *The Soul*, chap. 2, pt. 15, p. 98. (Readers who remember The Numskulls will find this image hard to resist.)
40. *The Universe of Creatures*, pt .I, chap. 18, p. 67.
41. *Sermons* 230.4.

42. *Sermons* 230.104.
43. *Sermons* 230B.42.
44. *Sermons* 230B.2.
45. *Sermons* 230B.29.
46. *The Providence of God*, chap. 30, pp. 173–74; *On the Virtues*, chap. 17, p. 235; *On Morals*, chap. 3, pp. 34–35. See also Brenno Boccadoro, "La musique, les passions, l'âme et le corps," in *Autour*, 77, 89–90, quoting *De Universo*.
47. *On the Virtues*, chap. 11, p. 144.
48. *The Providence of God*, chap. 30, p. 173.
49. *The Providence of God*, chap. 30, p. 174; *The Soul*, chap. 5, pt. 18, p. 256.
50. *The Soul*, chap. 5, pt. 18, p. 256.
51. *The Soul*, chap. 5, pt. 18, p. 256.
52. *De Universo*, pt. 1.2, chap. 43, in *Opera omnia*, vol. 1, p. 746a, quoted in Boccadoro, "La musique," 84–85.
53. Craig Wright, *Music and Ceremony at Notre Dame of Paris, 500–1500* (Cambridge: Cambridge University Press, 1989).
54. Boccadoro, "La musique," 75–92.

CHAPTER EIGHT

1. John Friedman, Jean Connell Hoff, and Robert Chazan, eds., *The Trial of the Talmud: Paris, 1240* (Toronto: PIMS, 2012), has English translations of the disputation and all the Hebrew and Latin sources. See also Judah M. Rosenthal, "The Talmud on Trial: The Disputation at Paris in the Year 1240," *Jewish Quarterly Review* 47 (1956–57): 58–76; Benjamin Z. Kedar, "Canon Law and the Burning of the Talmud," *Bulletin of Medieval Canon Law* 9 (1979): 79–82; Jeremy Cohen, *The Friars and the Jews: The Evolution of Medieval Anti-Judaism* (Ithaca: Cornell University Press, 1982), 51–76; Joel E. Renbaum, "The Talmud and the Popes: Reflections on the Talmud Trials of the 1240s," *Viator* 13 (1982): 203–23; Robert Chazan, "The Condemnation of the Talmud Reconsidered (1239–1248)," *Proceedings of the American Academy for Jewish Research* 55 (1988): 11–30; Gilbert Dahan, ed., *Le brûlement du Talmud à Paris, 1242–1244* (Paris: Cerf, 1999); Judah Galinsky, "The Different Hebrew Versions of the 'Talmud Trial' of 1240 in Paris," in Elisheva Carlebach and Jacob J. Schacter, eds., *New Perspectives on Jewish-Christian Relations in Honor of David Berger* (Boston: Brill, 2012), 109–40; Alexander Fidora and Görge K. Hasselhoff, eds., *The Talmud in Dispute during the High Middle Ages* (Barcelona: Universitat Autònoma de Barcelona, 2019). Despite the argument in Paul L. Rose, "When Was the Talmud Burnt at Paris? A Critical Examination of the Christian and Jewish Sources and a New Dating: June 1241," *Journal of Jewish Studies* 62 (2011): 324–39, I retain the commonly agreed date of 1242 for the book burning: Simon Schwarzfuchs, "June 13, 1242, Friday: The

Day That Talmud Was Burned in Paris," *Revue des études juives* 173 (2014): 365–69. I am grateful to Judah Galinsky for comments and suggestion for this chapter.

2. Matthew 5:17.
3. Gilbert Dahan, *The Christian Polemic against the Jews in the Middle Ages*, trans. Jody Gladding (Notre Dame, IN: University of Notre Dame Press, 1991).
4. Dahan, *The Christian Polemic against the Jews*, 7.
5. E. M. Rose, *The Murder of William of Norwich: The Origins of Blood Libel in Medieval Europe* (Oxford: Oxford University Press, 2015); Gavin Langmuir, "The Knight's Tale of Young Hugh of Lincoln," *Speculum* 47 (1972): 459–82.
6. Anna Sapir Abulafia, *Christian-Jewish Relations, 1000–1300: Jews in the Service of Medieval Christendom* (Harlow: Pearson, 2011).
7. Estimates from William Chester Jordan, *The French Monarchy and the Jews from Philip Augustus to the Last Capetians* (Philadelphia: University of Pennsylvania Press, 1989), 4–10, 50–55.
8. Jordan, *The French Monarchy and the Jews*, chap. 2; Robert Chazan, *Medieval Jewry in Northern France: A Political and Social History* (Baltimore: Johns Hopkins University Press, 1973); Norman Golb, *The Jews of Normandy. A Social and Intellectual History* (Cambridge: Cambridge University Press, 1978); Abulafia, *Christian-Jewish Relations*, 62–65.
9. The original bull does not exist; the restatement by Innocent III can be found (with translation) in Solomon Grayzel, *The Church and the Jews in the XIIIth Century*, 2 vols. (New York: Hermon, 1966), vol. 1, pp. 92–95, no. 5.
10. John Tolan, "Of Milk and Blood: Innocent III and the Jews, Revisited," in Elisheva Baumgarten and Judah D. Galinsky, eds., *Jews and Christians in Thirteenth-Century France* (New York: Palgrave Macmillan, 2015), 139–49.
11. Friedman, Hoff, and Chazan, *The Trial of the Talmud*, 33, quoting Grayzel, *The Church and the Jews*, vol. 1, pp. 200–203, no. 70.
12. Lesley Smith, "William of Auvergne and the Jews," in Diana Wood, ed., *Christianity and Judaism* (Oxford: Blackwell, 1992), 107–17.
13. Piero Capelli, "*De articulis litterarum Papae*: A Critical Edition," in Fidora and Hasselhof, *The Talmud in Dispute*, 29–56.
14. Chazan, "The Condemnation of the Talmud," 14–16, and note 21.
15. The letter is translated by Hoff in Friedman, Hoff, and Chazan, *The Trial of the Talmud*, 93; Latin text in *CUP*, no. 173. The original letter to William does not survive; Gregory's text is taken from a letter of the papal legate and former chancellor of Paris, Odo of Châteauroux, to Pope Innocent IV.
16. Allan Temko, "The Burning of the Talmud in Paris," *Commentary* 17 (1954): 446–55.
17. Grant, *Blanche of Castile*, 127–29. Joseph was also the author of a polemical treatise against Christianity: Friedman, Hoff, and Chazan, *The Trial of the Talmud*, 21, 168n382.

18. Friedman, Hoff, and Chazan, *The Trial of the Talmud*, 26–30.
19. For a discussion of the account and its "fictionalized" elements, see Galinsky, "The Different Hebrew Versions," 112.
20. Friedman, Hoff, and Chazan, *The Trial of the Talmud*, 130.
21. Lindy Grant, *Blanche of Castile, Queen of France* (New Haven: Yale University Press, 2016), 128.
22. Mary M. McLaughlin, *Intellectual Freedom and Its Limitations in the University of Paris in the Thirteenth and Fourteenth Centuries* (New York: Arno Press, 1977); J. M. M. H. Thijssen, *Censure and Heresy at the University of Paris, 1200–1400* (Philadelphia: University of Pennsylvania Press, 1998).
23. J. W. Goering, "Lateran Council IV and the *cura Judaeorum*," in G. Melville and J. Helmrath, eds., *The Fourth Lateran Council: Institutional Reform and Spiritual Renewal* (Affalterbach: Didymos-Verlag, 2017), 251–53.
24. Kedar, "Canon Law and the Burning of the Talmud," 81.
25. Yossef Schwartz, "Authority, Control, and Conflict in Thirteenth-Century Paris: Contextualizing the Talmud Trial," in Elisheva Baumgarten and Judah D. Galinsky, eds., *Jews and Christians in Thirteenth-Century France* (New York: Palgrave Macmillan, 2015), 96; and see Renbaum, "The Talmud and the Popes," 211.
26. Alexander of Hales, *Doctoris irrefragabilis Alexandri de Hales . . . Summa theologica*, 4 vols. (Quaracchi: Ad Claras Aquas, 1924–48), II.ii.3.8.1.2.1.1; vol. 1, §740.
27. *CUP*, no. 178.
28. Diana di Segni, "Early Quotations from Maimonides' *Guide of the Perplexed* in the Latin Middle Ages," in Charles H. Manekin and Daniel Davies, eds., *Interpreting Maimonides: Critical Essays* (Cambridge: Cambridge University Press, 2018), 190–207. See also Görge K. Hasselhof, "Maimonides in the Latin Middle Ages: An Introductory Survey," *Jewish Studies Quarterly* 9 (2002): 1–20; and Jacob Guttmann, "Guillaume d'Auvergne et la littérature juive," *Revue des études juives* 18 (1889): 243–55.
29. Beryl Smalley, "William of Auvergne, John of La Rochelle, and St. Thomas Aquinas on the Old Law," in Smalley, *Studies in Medieval Thought and Learning from Abelard to Wyclif* (London: Hambledon, 1981), 137–56; Lesley Smith, "William of Auvergne and the Law of the Jews and the Muslims," in T. J. Heffernan and T. E. Burman, eds., *Scripture and Pluralism: Reading the Bible in the Religiously Plural Worlds of the Middle Ages and Renaissance* (Boston: Brill, 2005), 123–42. *De Legibus* is the place in William's theological writings where Jewish ideas appear at length, but he does mention Jewish opinions in *The Universe of Creatures* (dated 1231–36) and *The Trinity* (1223), where he does appear to know the translation of the whole *Guide*, as well as critically reporting what he calls "the fables of the Jews," that is, *midrashim*, which he may have learned about from oral discussion or contacts with Jewish converts: di Segni, "Early Quotations from Maimonides," 199–203.

30. *De Legibus*, chap. 1, in *Opera omnia*, vol. 1, p. 24b; and see Guttmann, "Guillaume d'Auvergne et la littérature juive," 249.
31. *Sermons* 230.15, 16.
32. *De Legibus*, chap. 1, in *Opera omnia*, vol. 1, p. 23b.
33. Smalley, "William of Auvergne, John of La Rochelle, and St. Thomas Aquinas on the Old Law," 137–56.
34. Norman Daniel, *Islam and the West: The Making of an Image*, rev. ed. (Oxford: Oneworld, 1993), 174; Winston Black, "William of Auvergne on the Dangers of Paradise: Biblical Exegesis between Natural Philosophy and Anti-Islamic Polemic," *Traditio* 68 (2013): 233–58.
35. *De Legibus*, chap. 19, in *Opera omnia*, vol. 1, p. 54a, translated in Roland J. Teske, "William of Auvergne's Debt to Avicenna," in Jules Janssens and Daniel De Smet, eds., *Avicenna and His Heritage* (Leuven: Leuven University Press, 2002), 156.
36. See, for instance, *Sermons* 230.15, 16, 38, 227, 234 and 234A, 235; 230B.30; 230C.8.
37. *Sermons* 230A.314, 230B.14–14A.
38. *Sermons* 230.52, 53.
39. Luke 14:15–24: *Sermons* 230A.234 and 234A, 235.
40. Matthew 1:20–21: *Sermons* 230.38.
41. *Sermons* 230.15, 16.
42. *Sermons* 230A.227.

CHAPTER NINE

1. Walter Ong, "Agonistic Structure in Academia: Past to Present," *Daedalus* 103 (1974): 229–38; quoted in Monika Otter, "Dissing the Teacher: Classroom Polemics in the Early and High Middle Ages," in Almut Suerbaum, George Southcombe, and Benjamin Thompson, eds., *Polemic: Language as Violence in Medieval and Early Modern Discourse* (Farnham, UK: Ashgate, 2015), 107–24.
2. For example, Roberta Gilchrist, *Gender and Archaeology: Contesting the Past* (London: Routledge, 1999), considers the academic assumptions behind the archaeology of religious houses.
3. Richard H. Rouse and Mary A. Rouse, *Manuscripts and Their Makers: Commercial Book Producers in Medieval Paris 1200–1500*, 2 vols. (Turnhout: Brepols, 2000), chap. 9.
4. David Herlihy, *Women, Family and Society in Medieval Europe: Historical Essays 1978–1991* (Oxford: Berghahn, 1995).
5. Étienne Boileau, *Les métiers et corporations de . . . Paris, XIIIe siècle*, ed. René de Lespinasse and François Bonnardot (Paris: Imprimerie nationale, 1879); Caroline Bourlet, "The *Livre des Métiers* Attributed to Étienne Boileau and the Gradual Establishing of Written Regulations for Parisian Trades and Crafts (Late Thirteenth–Early Fourteenth Century)," *Médiéva-*

les 69 (2015): 19–47; and see Kathryn Reyerson, "Urban Economies," in Judith M. Bennett and Ruth Mazo Karras, eds., *The Oxford Handbook of Women and Gender in Medieval Europe* (Oxford: Oxford University Press, 2013), 295–310.

6. *De Sacramento matrimonii*, chap. 9, in *Opera omnia*, vol. 1, p. 525a.
7. *On Morals*, chap. 9, p. 136.
8. Genesis 3:16.
9. *The Soul*, chap. 5, pt. 10, p. 214.
10. *De Sacramento matrimonii*, chap. 8, in *Opera omnia*, vol. 1, p. 524b.
11. *Sermons* 230B.45.
12. *The Providence of God*, chap. 5, p. 63.
13. *Sermons* 230A.313.
14. *De Legibus*, chap. 28, in *Opera omnia*, vol. 1, p. 97b.
15. *Sermons* 230.61.
16. Caroline W. Bynum, *Jesus as Mother: Studies in the Spirituality of the High Middle Ages* (Berkeley: University of California Press, 1982); *The Trinity*, chap. 15, p. 131.
17. *The Trinity*, chap. 15, p. 129.
18. *The Trinity*, chap 15, p. 132.
19. *The Trinity*, chap. 14, p. 126.
20. Peter Biller, *The Measure of Multitude*, chaps. 6–8: "The Avoidance of Offspring."
21. *De Sacramento matrimonii*, chap. 8, in *Opera omnia*, vol. 1, p. 524a–b.
22. *Sermons* 230C.95, 99.
23. *Sermons* 230C.95.
24. *On Morals*, chap. 9, p. 148.
25. Conrad Rudolph, *The "Things of Greater Importance": Bernard of Clairvaux's* Apologia *and the Medieval Attitude toward Art* (Philadelphia: University of Pennsylvania Press, 1990).
26. See, for instance, *Sermons* 230.33; 230A, 287; 230B.20, 23; 230C.40, 46–47.
27. *Sermons* 230A.287 and 287A, 230C.29.
28. *Sermons* 230C.47, 230C.25, 230C.2, 230.38.
29. *Sermons* 230B.14 and 14A.
30. *Sermons* 230B.16.
31. *Sermons* 230.38.
32. *Sermons* 230A.314.
33. *Sermons* 230C.2.
34. *On the Virtues*, chap. 1, p. 45.
35. *Sermons* 230C.46.
36. *Sermons* 230C.7; *On the Virtues*, chap. 17, p. 240.
37. *Sermons* 230.33.
38. *Sermons* 230B.5.
39. *Sermons* 230.71.
40. *Sermons* 230C.28.

41. *Sermons* 230B.11.
42. *De Sacramento matrimonii*, chap. 8, chap. 6, in *Opera omnia*, vol. 1, pp. 524a, 520b.
43. *De Sacramento matrimonii*, chap. 6, in *Opera omnia*, vol. 1, p. 519b; *Sermons* 230.70. *On the Virtues*, chap. 13, p. 214.
44. *Sermons* 230C.110; *De Sacramento matrimonii*, chap. 6, in *Opera omnia*, vol. 1, p. 520a.
45. *Sermons* 230.70.
46. *De Sacramento matrimonii*, chap. 1, in *Opera omnia*, vol. 1, pp. 512b–13a: translation with slight alteration from Biller, *Measure of Multitude*, 65.
47. *De Sacramento matrimonii*, chap. 6, in *Opera omnia*, vol. 1, p. 519a.
48. *De Sacramento matrimonii*, chap. 6, in *Opera omnia*, vol. 1, pp. 520a–21a. Contracting a clandestine marriage (one that had not been announced in public for a certain time before the ceremony, to allow for objections) was forbidden in Lateran IV, c. 51: Tanner, *Decrees of the Ecumenical Councils*, vol. 1, p. 258.
49. *De Sacramento matrimonii*, chap. 6, in *Opera omnia*, vol. 1, p. 520b.
50. D. L. d'Avray, *Medieval Marriage: Symbolism and Society* (Oxford: Oxford University Press, 2005).
51. *Sermons* 230.70.
52. *De Sacramento matrimonii*, chaps. 5 and 10, in *Opera omnia*, vol. 1, pp. 518a–b, 527a–28b; *Sermons* 230.70.
53. *Sermons* 230C.30.
54. III Lateran, c. 11 and IV Lateran, c. 14: Tanner, *Decrees of the Ecumenical Councils*, vol. 1, pp. 217–18, 242.
55. *Sermons* 230B.16, 20, 230C.1.
56. *Sermons* 230C.2.
57. *Sermons* 230A.287 and 287A.
58. *On Morals*, chap. 4, p. 50.
59. *De Sacramento penitentiae*, chap. 2, in *Opera omnia*, vol. 1, p. 457b.
60. *On Morals*, chap. 9, p. 158.
61. Baldwin, *Masters, Princes and Merchants*, vol. 1, p. 133; Baldwin, *The Language of Sex: Five Voices from Northern France around 1200* (Chicago: University of Chicago Press, 1994).
62. Bronisław Geremek, *The Margins of Society in Late Medieval Paris*, trans. J. Birrell (Cambridge: Cambridge University Press, 1987), chap. 7; L. L. Otis, *Prostitution in Medieval Society: The History of an Urban Institution in Languedoc* (Chicago: University of Chicago Press, 1985); Vern L. Bullough and James Brundage, eds., *Sexual Practices and the Medieval Church* (Buffalo, NY: Prometheus Books, 1982).
63. Baldwin, *Masters, Princes and Merchants*, vol. 1, pp. 136–37.
64. Biller, *Measure of Multitude*, 75–76.
65. *On Morals*, chap. 9, p. 147.
66. *Sermons* 230B.46, and see for example 230B.20.

67. *The Providence of God*, chap. 24, pp. 137–38; chap. 27, p. 152.
68. *Sermons* 230.6.
69. *De Sacramento matrimonii*, chaps 2 and 3, in *Opera omnia*, vol. 1, pp. 513a, 515b.

CHAPTER TEN

1. Exodus 20:6. In his sermons, William often uses the analogy of a physician and a priest to discuss the difficulties of curing patients, e.g., 230B.23, 28, 36.
2. See below, chap. 12.
3. *On Faith*, chap. 1, p. 83.
4. *On Faith*, chap. 1, p. 84.
5. *On Faith*, chap. 1, p. 84.
6. *The Soul*: Teske's introduction gives a useful breakdown of this long work and *The Immortality of the Soul*. E. A. Moody, "William of Auvergne and His Treatise *De Anima*," in Moody, *Studies in Medieval Philosophy, Science, and Logic* (Berkeley: University of California Press, 1975), 1–109.
7. *De Universo*, pt. III, chap. 20, in *Opera omnia*, vol. 1, p. 1057a.
8. *The Soul*, chap. 5, pt. 22, pp. 266, 269; chap. 6, pt. 35, pp. 395–97; *Why God Became Man*, chap. 3, p. 23.
9. *The Soul*, chap. 4, pp. 154–69.
10. *The Soul*, chap. 2, pt. 13, pp. 91–94; chap. 3, pt. 11, pp. 139–44. R. J. Teske, "William of Auvergne's Debt to Avicenna," in Teske, *Studies*, no. 12.
11. *The Soul*, chap. 2, pt. 13, p. 91; chap. 3, pt. 11, p. 141.
12. *The Soul*, chap. 4, pts. 1–4, especially pp. 156–59, 165–67.
13. *The Soul*, chap. 4, pt. 1, p. 156.
14. *The Soul*, chap. 4, pt. 2, p. 156.
15. *The Soul*, chap. 4, pt. 2, p. 157.
16. Exodus 21:22.
17. *The Soul*, chap. 4, pt. 2, pp. 157–58.
18. *The Soul*, chap. 4, pt. 3, p. 159.
19. *The Soul*, chap. 4, pt. 3, p. 160.
20. *The Soul*, chap. 4, pt. 3, p. 160.
21. *The Soul*, chap. 4, pt. 4, p. 166.
22. Augustine, *De diversis quaestionibus LXXXIII*, q. 56; *Saint Augustine: Eighty-Three Different Questions*, trans. David L. Mosher (Washington, DC: Catholic University of America, 1982), q. 56, p. 98.
23. *The Soul*, chap. 4, pt. 4, p. 166.
24. *The Soul*, chap. 4, pt. 2, p. 159.
25. *The Soul*, chap. 5, pt. 5, p. 197.
26. *The Soul*, chap. 5, pt. 5, p. 197.
27. *The Soul*, chap. 5, pt. 25, p. 281.
28. *The Soul*, chap. 5, pt. 25, p. 281.

29. *The Providence of God*, chaps. 4–5.
30. *The Providence of God*, chap. 6.
31. *The Providence of God*, chap. 5, p. 63.
32. *The Providence of God*, chap. 7, p. 72.
33. *The Providence of God*, chap. 7, pp. 72–73.
34. Carole Rawcliffe, *Leprosy in Medieval England* (Woodbridge, UK: Boydell, 2006); S. N. Brody, *The Disease of the Soul: Leprosy in Medieval Literature* (Ithaca: Cornell University Press, 1974).
35. *Sermons* 230B.49.
36. *Sermons* 230C.26.
37. Thomas of Celano, *First Life of St. Francis*, chap. 7; in Marion A. Habig, *St. Francis of Assisi, Writings and Early Biographies: English Omnibus of Sources for the Life of St. Francis* (Quincy, IL: Franciscan Press, 1991), 242–43; *Legend of the Three Companions*, chap. 4, in Habig, *St. Francis of Assisi*, 900–902: all the reports of Francis mention his care for lepers. Jean de Joinville, *The Life of St. Louis*, chap. 1, in Jean de Joinville and Geoffrey of Villehardouin, *Joinville and Villehardouin, Chronicles of the Crusades*, trans. M. R. B. Shaw (Harmondsworth, UK: Penguin, 1986), 169; M. Cecilia Gaposchkin, *The Making of St. Louis: Kingship, Sanctity and Crusade in the Later Middle Ages* (Ithaca: Cornell University Press, 2008), 213–29.
38. Matthew 8:3; *Sermons* 230.75.
39. *The Soul*, chap. 5, pt. 5, p. 197.
40. *The Soul*, chap. 6, pt. 4, p. 305.
41. *On the Virtues*, chap. 10, p. 111; *The Soul*, chap. 5, pt. 23, p. 273.
42. Sophronius 3:9; *The Soul*, chap. 6, pt. 4, p. 306.
43. *The Soul*, chap. 4, pt. 2, p. 159.
44. *The Soul*, chap. 4, pt. 2, p. 159.
45. Mark 8:22–26. For William see, e.g., *The Soul*, chap. 6, pt. 31; *On the Virtues*, chaps. 6–7; *On Faith and the Laws*, chap. 2; *Sermons* 230.104, 108.
46. Luke 18:35–43. The examples in this paragraph are from *Sermons* 230.104, 108.
47. Zina Weygand, *The Blind in French Society from the Middle Ages to the Century of Louis Braille*, trans. E.-J. Cohen (Stanford: Stanford University Press, 2009), 19–21; Edward Wheatley, "Blindness, Discipline and Reward: Louis IX and the Foundation of the Hospice des Quinze-Vingts," *Disability Studies Quarterly* 22 (2002): 194–212. The date of the foundation was lost with the original statutes, sometime early in the life of the institution (which exists today as the largest ophthalmological institute in Europe).

CHAPTER ELEVEN

1. Bronisław Geremek, *The Margins of Society in Late Medieval Paris*, trans. J. Birrell (Cambridge: Cambridge University Press, 1987); Michel Mollat, *Les pauvres au Moyen âge. Étude sociale* (Paris: Hachette, 1978); English

translation: *The Poor in the Middle Ages: An Essay in Social History*, trans. Arthur Goldhammer (New Haven: Yale University Press, 1986).

2. *The Providence of God*, chap. 6, p. 68, translation slightly adjusted.
3. Lindy Grant, *Blanche of Castile, Queen of France* (New Haven: Yale University Press, 2016), 202–7; for her royal almoners, see 184–85.
4. Jean de Joinville and Geoffrey of Villehardouin, *Joinville and Villehardouin, Chronicles of the Crusades*, trans. M. R. B. Shaw (Harmondsworth, UK: Penguin, 1986), 343–44.; Grant, *Blanche of Castile*, 207; Elizabeth Hallam, *Capetian France, 987–1328* (New York: Longman, 1980), 252–53, 263–64; M. Cecilia Gaposchkin, *The Making of St. Louis: Kingship, Sanctity and Crusade in the Later Middle Ages* (Ithaca: Cornell University Press, 2008), 175–80.
5. The Rule of St Benedict, chap. 53, "The Reception of Guests": *RB 1980: The Rule of St. Benedict in English*, trans. Timothy Fry (Collegeville, MN: Liturgical Press, 1982).
6. *Sermons* 230C.19.
7. Jacques Berlioz, "La voix de l'êvèque," in *Autour*, 11, 25–26.
8. Matthew 19:16–24.
9. *The Providence of God*, chap. 6, p. 70.
10. Peter Brown, *Through the Eye of a Needle: Wealth, the Fall of Rome, and the Making of Christianity in the West, 340–550 AD* (Princeton: Princeton University Press, 2012).
11. Jean Rivière, quoted in Roland J. Teske, *William of Auvergne, Selected Spiritual Writings*, Medieval Sources in Translation 50 (Toronto, 2011), 9–10.
12. *On Morals*, chap. 9, pp. 130–31.
13. *On Morals*, chap. 9, pp. 129–31.
14. *Sermons* 230C.9, 32, 34, 50, 71, and many others.
15. *Sermons* 230C.34, 230.97.
16. *Sermons* 230A.223.
17. Matthew 19:30.
18. *Sermons* 230C.23.
19. *Sermons* 230C.22.
20. *Sermons* 230B.9.
21. *Sermons* 230C.23.
22. Quoted in Berlioz, "La voix de l'êvèque," in *Autour*, 22.
23. *Sermons* 230C.21, 32; *On Morals*, chap. 9, p. 149.
24. *Sermons* 230C.43.
25. *Sermons* 230C.50.
26. *Sermons* 230C.21, 19.
27. *Sermons* 230A.229.
28. *Sermons* 230B.5, 230C.22.
29. *Sermons* 230B.24, quoting Bernard of Clairvaux. All these orders had houses in the diocese, but they are also represented in the sermons about particular saints that William preached.

30. *Sermons* 230C.28, 31.
31. *Sermons* 230C.19, 40.
32. *On Morals*, chap. 9, p. 148.
33. *Sermons* 230C.113.
34. *On Morals*, chap. 9, pp. 148–49.
35. *Sermons* 230C.59, 58.
36. *Sermons* 230B.24.
37. *Sermons* 230C.19.
38. *Sermons* 230B.24.
39. *Sermons* 230C.36.
40. *On Morals*, chap. 9, p. 143.
41. *Sermons* 230B.24.
42. *On Morals*, chap. 9, p. 150; for the arguments against common property, see pp. 143–50.
43. For 1241, see Ephrem Longpré, "Guillaume d'Auvergne et l'École Franciscaine de Paris," *La France Franciscaine* 5 (1922): 427–28, citing Bonaventure, *Commentarius in IV Libros Sententiarum*, in *Opera omnia*, vol. 3 (Quaracchi: Ad Claras Aquas, 1885), book III, d. 16, art. 1, q. 1, p. 346. For the causality debate: Bonaventure, *Commentarius in IV Libros Sententiarum*, in *Opera omnia*, vol. 3, book III, d. 40, dub. 3, pp. 895–96.
44. *Sermons* 230C.113.
45. Penn Szittya, *The Antifraternal Tradition in Medieval Literature* (Princeton: Princeton University Press, 1986); David Burr, *The Spiritual Franciscans: From Protest to Persecution in the Century after Saint Francis* (University Park: Pennsylvania State University Press, 2001); Guy Geltner, *The Making of Medieval Antifraternalism: Polemic, Violence, Deviance and Remembrance* (Oxford: Oxford University Press, 2012).
46. *On Morals*, chap. 9, pp. 143–50.
47. *On Morals*, chap. 9, p. 133. *The Mirror of Perfection*, chaps. 3, 5: in M. A. Habig, *St. Francis of Assisi, Writings and Early Biographies: English Omnibus of Sources for the Life of St. Francis* (Quincy, IL: Franciscan Press, 1991), 1128–29, 1131–32.
48. *Sermons* 230C.69–71.
49. *Sermons* 230.97.
50. *Sermons* 230B.5.
51. *Sermons* 230C.43.

CHAPTER TWELVE

1. This claim comes from the *Compilacio singularis exemplorum*, compiled by a Dominican from Angers, by about 1285; quoted in Jacques Berlioz, "La voix de l'èvêque: Guillaume d'Auvergne dans les exempla (XIIIe–XIVe siècle)," in *Autour*, 15 and 32 (Latin text).
2. Among other examples, Lindy Grant, *Blanche of Castile, Queen of France*

(New Haven: Yale University Press, 2016), notes that William was among the churchmen, all "personally close to the royal family, and in particular to Blanche herself," in attendance in 1241, when Louis IX made his wife Margaret swear obedience to him on the Gospels (123): see Valois, *Guillaume d'Auvergne*, 145. For the Spanish circle, see Grant, *Blanche of Castile*, 174, 185–86.

3. See note 1, above. Grant, *Blanche of Castile*, 210, notes that Blanche and Louis IX were honored by the Dominicans with a special mass, an honor only otherwise accorded to the pope, Gregory IX, suggesting that the friars recognized her support and generosity.
4. Grant, *Blanche of Castile*, 193.
5. Berlioz, "La voix de l'èvêque," in *Autour*, 16 and 32 (Latin text); and see Valois, *Guillaume d'Auvergne*, 149–50. The story takes place in 1240.
6. Jean de Joinville, *The Life of St. Louis*, chap. 1, in Jean de Joinville and Geoffrey of Villehardouin, *Joinville and Villehardouin: Chronicles of the Crusades*, trans. M. R. B. Shaw (Harmondsworth, UK: Penguin, 1986), 173–74. In a similar vein, in *The Soul*, chap. 5, pt. 20, p. 261, William argues that a soldier who has to fight often is a better soldier than one who lacks the practice.
7. Grant, *Blanche of Castile*, 186–87.
8. Grant, *Blanche of Castile*, chaps. 7, 10.
9. *Sermons* 230.60; *On Morals*, chap. 9, pp. 143–60.
10. *The Providence of God*, chap. 14, p. 98. William uses a similar image to describe the well-ordered soul: *The Soul*, chap. 2, pt. 14, pp. 98–99; cf. *On the Virtues*, chap. 3, p. 60.
11. *The Providence of God*, chap. 14, p. 95.
12. *Sermons* 230A.314, 230.97.
13. *Sermons* 230C.64.
14. *On Morals*, chap. 9, p. 158, translation slightly adapted.
15. *On Morals*, chap. 9, p. 158.
16. *The Providence of God*, chap. 12, pp. 91–92.
17. *Sermons* 230.61.
18. *Sermons* 230C.43.
19. William notes that God recognizes the intention of those who wish to give alms, even though they are too poor to do so: *Sermons* 230C.43.
20. Berlioz, "La voix de l'èvêque," in *Autour*, 22–23, with Latin text from MS Paris, Bibliothèque nationale française, lat. 15971, fols. 124a–25c.
21. *Sermons* 230C.43.
22. Thomas of Celano, *Second Life of Francis*, chaps. 35–38, in Marion A. Habig, *St. Francis of Assisi, Writings and Early Biographies: English Omnibus of Sources for the Life of St. Francis* (Quincy, IL: Franciscan Press, 1991), 417–21.
23. *On the Virtues*, chap. 11, pp. 166–67, citing Hab. 2:6; Ecclus. 13:1; Ps. 138:13; Phil. 3:8; Lk 8:7; Mt 13:22.

24. *On the Virtues*, chap. 11, p. 167.
25. *On the Virtues*, chap. 11, pp. 167–68.
26. *On the Virtues*, chap. 11, p. 168.
27. *Sermons* 230B.5; *On the Virtues*, chap. 11, p. 169.
28. *Sermons* 230B.5.
29. *Sermons* 230C.43; unless noted, the rest of this and the subsequent paragraph references this sermon.
30. *Sermons* 230C.18.
31. *Sermons* 230C.19, 22, 43.
32. *Sermons* 230B.5.
33. *Sermons* 230C.30.
34. *Sermons* 230C.19–21.
35. *Sermons* 230C.50.
36. See, for instance, John W. Baldwin, *Masters, Princes, and Merchants: The Social Views of Peter the Chanter and His Circle*, 2 vols. (Princeton: Princeton University Press, 1970), chap. 14; John T. Noonan, *The Scholastic Analysis of Usury* (Cambridge, MA: Harvard University Press, 1957); Robert Chazan, *Medieval Jewry in Northern France* (Baltimore: Johns Hopkins University Press, 1973), 80–93; Joseph Shatzmiller, *Shylock Reconsidered: Jews, Moneylending and Medieval Society* (Berkeley: University of California Press, 1990).
37. Deuteronomy 23:19–20.
38. *Sermons* 230A.314.
39. William as reported in the *Compilacio singularis exemplum*, no. 14, in Berlioz, '"La voix de l'évêque," in *Autour*, 12, 17, 34 (Latin).
40. *Sermons* 230B.14 and 14A.
41. *Sermons* 230C.18.
42. *On the Virtues* chap. 11, p. 142.
43. *Sermons* 230A.270.
44. *Sermons* 230C.100: the reference to thieves would remind a medieval congregation of the two thieves crucified with Christ.
45. *Sermons* 230B.14.
46. B. H. Rosenwein and Lester K. Little, "Social Meaning in the Monastic and Mendicant Spiritualities," *Past and Present* 63 (1974): 4–32; Lester K. Little, *Religious Poverty and the Profit Economy in Medieval Europe* (London: Paul Elek, 1978); D. L. d'Avray, *The Preaching of the Friars: Sermons Diffused from Paris before 1300* (New York: Oxford University Press, 1985); J. Hanska, *"And the rich man also died: and he was buried in hell": The Social Ethos in Mendicant Sermons* (Helsinki: Suomen Historiallinen Seura, 1997).
47. Morenzoni, Introduction, *Sermons* 230, pp. vi, xxxv.
48. F. N. M. Diekstra, "The Language of the Marketplace in the Sermons of Robert de Sorbon (1201–1274)," *Recherches de Théologie et philosophie médiévales* 75 (2008): 337–94; Diekstra does not make the link with Wil-

liam. For the manuscripts of William's sermons, see Morenzoni's Introduction to *Sermons*.

49. *Sermons* 230B.13.
50. *Sermons* 230C.43.
51. *Sermons* 230C.43.

CHAPTER THIRTEEN

1. Boethius, *The Consolation of Philosophy*, trans. S. J. Tester (Cambridge, MA: Loeb Classical Library, 1918), IV.iii, p. 335.
2. *Sermons* 230B.18.
3. *Sermons* 230A.249.
4. *Sermons* 230A.245.
5. Brigitte Resl, ed., *A Cultural History of Animals in the Medieval Age* (New York: Berg, 2007). See especially the introduction (Resl, "Introduction: Animals in Culture ca. 1000–ca. 1400"), and chapter 1 by Sophie Page, "Good Creation and Demon Illusions: The Medieval Universe of Creatures," 27–57.
6. Willene B. Clark, *A Medieval Book of Beasts: The Second-Family Bestiary: Commentary, Art, Text and Translation* (Woodbridge, UK: Boydell, 2006).
7. Sophie Delmas, "La réception des encyclopédies naturelles dans les sermons au XIIIe siècle. Quelques examples," *Rursus: poétique, réception et réécriture des textes antiques* 11 (2017): online only at www.journals .openedition.org/rursuspicae/268. Two other important works of the same type were Alexander Neckam (d. 1217), *On the Nature of Things* (*De Naturis rerum*), and Bartolomeus Anglicus (d. 1240), *On the Properties of Things* (*De Proprietatibus rerum*). Thomas of Cantimpré also wrote a moralizing book about bees, the *Bonum universale de apibus*.
8. Aristotle, *Parts of Animals, Movement of Animals, Progression of Animals*, trans. A. L. Peck and E. S. Forster (Cambridge, MA: Harvard University Press, 1945); M. Th. d'Alverny, "Translators and Translations," in R. L. Benson and G. Constable with C. D. Lanham, eds., *Renaissance and Renewal in the Twelfth Century* (Oxford: Oxford University Press, 1982), 421–62; Lynn Thorndike, *Michael Scot* (Edinburgh: Nelson, 1965), chap. 2.
9. Albertus Magnus, *On Animals: A Medieval Summa Zoologica*, trans. K. E. Kitchell Jr. and I. M. Resnick, 2 vols. (Baltimore: Johns Hopkins University Press, 1999); Simon Tugwell, ed. and trans., *Albert and Thomas: Selected Writings* (New York: Paulist, 1988); Pieter Beullens, "Like a Book Written by God's Finger: Animals Showing the Path Towards God," in Resl, ed., *A Cultural History of Animals*, 147–50.
10. *Sermons* 230B.29, 230C.64.
11. Esther Pascua, "From Forest to Farm and Town: Domestic Animals from ca. 1000 to ca. 1450," in Resl, ed., *A Cultural History of Animals*, 81.
12. Job 12:7, quoted by William in *The Soul*, chap. 5, pt. 20, p. 262.

13. *Sermons* 230B.38; *On Faith*, chap. 4, p. 114.
14. *The Soul*, chap. 5, pt. 20, p. 262, slightly adapted. William is quoting or paraphrasing Augustine, *Confessions* 10.6.9.
15. *Sermons* 230.58.
16. *Sermons* 230B.48.
17. Luke 2:22–24.
18. Lesley Smith, *The Ten Commandments: Interpreting the Bible in the Medieval World* (Boston: Brill, 2014).
19. *On Faith; De Legibus*, in *Opera omnia*, vol. 1, pp. 18a–102b; Winston Black, "William of Auvergne on the Dangers of Paradise: Biblical Exegesis between Natural Philosophy and Anti-Islamic Polemic," *Traditio* 68 (2013): 233–58.
20. *On Faith*, chap. 4, p. 106.
21. *The Universe of Creatures*, I.2, p. 34.
22. *On the Virtues*, chap. 11, p. 141.
23. David Burr, *Olivi and Franciscan Poverty: The Origins of the* Usus Pauper *Controversy* (Philadelphia: University of Pennsylvania Press, 1989), 4.
24. Thomas of Celano, *First Life of St Francis*, cc. 21, 29; Francis, *Legend of Perugia*, no. 43 (Canticle of the Sun); Francis, *The Canticle of Brother Sun*; all in M. A. Habig, *St. Francis of Assisi, Writings and Early Biographies: English Omnibus of Sources for the Life of St. Francis* (Quincy, IL: Franciscan Press, 1991), 277–80, 295–99; 1020–24; and 127–31.
25. Bonaventure, *Major Life of St. Francis*, ch. 12, no. 3, in Habig, *St. Francis of Assisi, Writings and Early Biographies*, 722–23.
26. Luke 12:6.
27. *The Providence of God*, chap. 2, pp. 39, 40.
28. *The Providence of God*, chap. 10, p. 85.
29. *The Providence of God*, chap.10, p. 87.
30. *The Providence of God*, chap.11, p. 89.
31. *De Universo* I.ii, chap. 39, in *Opera omnia*, vol. 1, p. 741b.
32. *The Providence of God*, chap. 2, p. 40.
33. *On the Virtues*, chap. 11, p. 140.
34. *The Soul*, chap. 5, p. 205; *Sermons* 230C.113.
35. *The Providence of God*, chap. 11, p. 90; *Sermons* 230A.270; *The Universe of Creatures*, pt. I, chap. 22, p. 79; *Why God Became Man*, chap. 4, pp. 26–27.
36. *On the Virtues*, chap. 9, pp. 76–77.
37. *Sermons* 230.23.
38. *On Morals*, chap. 4, p. 61.
39. *On Morals*, chap. 5, p. 78; *The Soul*, chap. 5, pt. 14, p. 237; *Sermons* 230C.25.
40. *Sermons* 230A.163.
41. *On the Virtues*, chap. 11, p. 140.
42. *Sermons* 230C.22.
43. *Sermons* 230B.16, 230B.18.
44. *Sermons* 230B.1, 230A.162.
45. *Sermons* 230B.28; *On the Soul*, chap. 5, pt. 5, p. 196.

46. *Sermons* 230C.29, 230C.46.
47. *Compilacio singulorum exemplorum*, no. 6, in Berlioz, "La voix de l'évêque," in *Autour*, 12, 18–20, 33 (Latin); and see Resl, ed., *A Cultural History of Animals*, 102 for this (to us) odd behavior.
48. *Sermons* 230.68.
49. *The Providence of God*, chap. 3, p. 45.
50. *The Soul*, chap. 5, pt. 14, p. 237.
51. *Sermons* 230.12.
52. *Sermons* 230C.64; *The Universe of Creatures*, pt. II, chap. 32, p. 199.
53. *The Soul*, chap.2, pt. 9, p. 81; chap. 6, pt. 36, p. 399.
54. *On Morals*, chap. 3, p. 32.
55. *The Soul*, chap. 5, pt. 7, p. 203.
56. *The Soul*, chap. 5, pt. 7, p. 203.
57. *The Soul*, chap. 2, pt. 9, p. 81; *The Providence of God*, chap. 14, p. 94.
58. *The Providence of God*, chap. 14, pp. 94–95.
59. *The Soul*, chap. 5, pt. 10, p. 211.
60. *The Providence of God*, chap. 11, p. 90.
61. Teske, in *The Soul*, chap. 5, note 69; John Magee, *Calcidius on Plato's "Timaeus"* (Cambridge, MA: Harvard University Press, 2016), § 220.
62. *The Soul*, chap. 6, pt. 37, pp. 400–401.
63. Resl, "Animals in Culture," 25, calculates that the forty or so biblical passages referring to dogs are "consistently unfavorable." J.-C. Schmitt, *The Holy Greyhound* (Cambridge: Cambridge University Press, 1983).
64. *Sermons* 230.69, 230B.48.
65. *The Providence of God*, chap. 3, pp. 42–43.
66. *Sermons* 230.11.
67. *On Morals*, chap. 9, p. 147.
68. *On Morals*, chap. 1, p. 7.
69. *Sermons* 230C.64; *On Morals*, chap. 11, p. 199.
70. *Sermons* 230C.17, 230A.233.
71. *Sermons* 230B.5, 230C.25.
72. *On Morals*, chap. 11, pp. 200, 227.
73. *Sermons* 230C.28.
74. *The Soul*, chap. 5, pt. 5, p. 196.
75. *The Providence of God*, chap. 3, p. 43.
76. *Sermons* 230A.233, 230A.313; *On the Virtues*, chap. 11, p. 139.
77. *The Providence of God*, chap. 11, p. 90.
78. *The Soul*, chap. 4, pt. 3, p. 162.

CHAPTER FOURTEEN

1. *Sermons* 230C.5.
2. Quoted from the *Compilatio singularis exemplorum* by Berlioz, "La voix de l'évêque. Guillaume d'Auvergne dans les exempla (XIIIe–XIVe siècle),"

in *Autour*, 12, 17, 32 (Latin text). A. Lecoy de la Marche, *Le rire du prédicateur. Récits facétieux du Moyen Âge*, ed. J Berlioz (Turnhout: Brepols, 1992), no. 5, p. 22, quotes the embellished version by Valois, *Guillaume d'Auvergne*, 147–48.

3. *The Soul*, chap. 2, pt. 12, p. 93.
4. *On Morals*, chap. 6, p. 81.
5. *On Morals*, chap. 7, p. 93, slightly adapted.
6. *On Morals*, chap. 8, p. 102; chap. 11, p. 202.
7. *On Morals*, chap. 7, p. 197.
8. *De Faciebus mundi*, book 1: MS Oxford, Bodleian Library, Bodl. 281, fol. 150v.
9. *Sermons* 230C.49.
10. *On Morals*, chap. 11, p. 201.
11. *Sermons* 230A.213.
12. *Sermons* 230.20.
13. *Sermons* 230B.42, 230.55.
14. *On the Virtues*, chap. 11, p. 156.
15. *Sermons* 2320.2; *The Universe of Creatures*, chap. 9, pp. 54–55; *Sermons* 230.18.
16. *Sermons* 230.15.
17. *The Soul*, chap. 7, pt. 8, p. 453; *The Providence of God*, chap. 5, p. 64.
18. *Sermons* 230.5.
19. *De Vitiis*, chap. 4, in *Opera omnia*, vol. 1, p. 266b.
20. *The Soul*, chap. 7, pt. 8, p. 453.
21. *The Soul*, chap. 3, pt. 10, p. 137.
22. *The Providence of God*, chap. 8, pp. 75–76.
23. *On Morals*, chap. 11, p. 211.
24. *Sermons* 230C.44.
25. Matthew 5:13; Leviticus 2:13.
26. *Sermons* 230B.42, on 2 Kings 6:25.
27. *Sermons* 230A.313/313A.
28. *On Morals*, chap. 11, pp. 205–6.
29. *Sermons* 230B.41, on 2 Kings 2:20.
30. *Sermons* 230B.42.
31. *Sermons* 230.42.
32. *Sermons* 230B.42.
33. *Sermons* 230A.245 and 246.
34. *On Morals*, chap. 6, p. 81.
35. *The Providence of God*, chap. 10, pp. 86–87.
36. Fiona Whelan, *The Making of Manners and Morals in Twelfth-Century England: The Book of the Civilised Man* (New York: Routledge, 2017), has an overview of this *facetus* literature, and especially Daniel of Beccles's *Urbanus magnus*.
37. *Sermons* 230.42.

38. *On Morals*, chap. 11, p. 214.
39. *On Morals*, chap. 9, p. 134.
40. *Sermons* 230B.45.
41. *Sermons* 230A.229.
42. *On Morals*, chap. 10, p. 166.
43. *Sermons* 230A.229.
44. *Sermons* 230A.155, 99; 230C.40.
45. *On the Virtues*, chap. 11, pp. 170–71, slightly adapted.
46. *On the Virtues*, chap. 13, p. 217.
47. *On Morals*, chap. 11, p. 202.
48. *De sacramento penitentie*, chap. 12, in *Opera omnia*, vol. 1, p. 487a–b.
49. *On the Virtues*, chap. 17, p. 236.
50. The developing theology of the Eucharist in the twelfth and thirteenth centuries is beyond the scope of this chapter, but see Gary Macy, *The Theologies of the Eucharist in the Early Scholastic Period: A Study of the Salvific Function of the Sacrament according to the Theologians, c. 1080–c. 1220* (Oxford: Clarendon Press, 1984); Miri Rubin, *Corpus Christi: The Eucharist in Late Medieval Culture* (Cambridge: Cambridge University Press, 1991). The feast of Corpus Christi, championed by the canoness Juliana of Liège, was recognized by the Church in 1264.
51. Luke 14:15–24.
52. *Sermons* 230A.234–36.
53. IV Lateran, c. 63: Tanner, *Decrees of the Ecumenical Councils*, vol. 1, p. 264.
54. Revelation 19:17–18; Ezekiel 39:17; Hosea 4:8.
55. John Edwards, *The Roman Cookery of Apicius* (London: Century, 1988); Constance B. Hieatt and Sharon Butler, *Curye on Inglysch: English Culinary Manuscripts of the Fourteenth Century (including the Form of Cury)* (London: EETS, 1985); Constance B. Hieatt, Brenda Hosington, and Sharon Butler, *Pleyn Delit: Medieval Cookery for Modern Cooks*, 2d ed. (Toronto: University of Toronto Press, 1996).

CHAPTER FIFTEEN

1. Valois, *Guillaume d'Auvergne*, 152n1, lays out all the possibilities.
2. John W. Baldwin, *Paris, 1200* (Stanford: Stanford University Press, 2010), 140. A number of previous bishops had been buried at St. Victor, including Maurice of Sully.
3. Valois, *Guillaume d'Auvergne*, 153, gives both inscriptions in full.
4. *Cartulaire de l'église Notre-Dame de Paris*, ed. B. E. C. Guérard, 4 vols. (Paris, 1850), vol. 2, p. 87 (no. 93); vol. 4, pp. 38–39 (no. 91).
5. Valois, *Guillaume d'Auvergne*, 151–52, 134–36; *CUP*, vol. 1, no. 178.
6. For example, *On Morals*, chap. 4, pp. 49–50, chap. 10, p. 181; *Sermons* 230B.5.
7. *The Soul*, chap. 5, pt. 13, pp. 226–27.

8. *Sermons* 230.1, 13, 46; 230B.23.
9. *The Providence of God*, chap. 5, p. 60.
10. *On Morals*, chap. 11, pp. 208–10.
11. *On Morals*, chap. 11, p. 211.
12. *Sermons* 230C.7.
13. *On Morals*, chap. 11, p. 212, quoting Seneca, *Ad Lucilium* 1.4.2, ed. A. Beltrami, 2 vols. (Rome: Typis publicae officinae polygraphicae, 1949), vol. 1, p. 9.
14. *The Soul*, chap. 6, pt. 6, pp. 313–14.
15. *The Soul*, chap. 7, pt. 15, p. 472.
16. *On the Virtues*, chap. 23, pp. 278–79.
17. *Why God Became Man*, chap. 3, p. 25.
18. *The Universe of Creatures*, pt. 2.1, chap. 23, p. 184.
19. Exodus 33:18–23; *On the Virtues*, chap. 11, pp. 112–13.
20. *Sermons* 230C.29.
21. *The Soul*, chap. 6, pt. 14, p. 331.
22. *The Soul*, chap. 6, pt. 5, pp. 309–10.
23. *The Soul*, chap. 6, pt. 13, p. 330.
24. *The Soul*, chap. 6, pt. 33, p. 390.
25. *The Soul*, chap. 6, pt. 30, p. 380; pt. 33, pp. 390–91. Note that this is not the "rapture" described by St. Paul (2 Corinthians 12:1–4), which William describes separately.
26. *On the Providence of God*, chap. 6, p. 70.
27. *The Soul*, chap. 6, pt. 13, p. 328.
28. *The Providence of God*, chap. 6, p. 70.
29. *Sermons* 230C.50.
30. *On the Virtues*, chap. 11, p. 126 and note 192; chap. 21, p. 269: the heretics he has in mind seem to be those described in Augustine of Hippo, *On Heresies*, rather than any contemporary sects.
31. *Sermons* 230A.236.
32. Teske's *The Universe of Creatures* translates only part of the work; the complete treatise is in *Opera omnia*, vol. 1, pp. 592–1074.
33. *The Universe of Creatures*, pt. 2, chap. 1, p. 140.
34. *De Vitiis*, chap. 7, in *Opera omnia*, vol. 1, p. 278a.
35. *De Universo*, pt. 1, c. 60, in *Opera omnia*, vol. 1, p. 676b.
36. Jacques Le Goff, *The Birth of Purgatory*, trans. Arthur Goldhammer (London: Scolar, 1984); A. E. Bernstein, "Esoteric Theology: William of Auvergne on the Fires of Hell and Purgatory," *Speculum* 57 (1982): 509–31. Le Goff and Bernstein differ on the soul and the "real" world; my position here is closer to Le Goff's.
37. *De Universo*, pt. 1, c. 62, in *Opera omnia*, vol. 1, p. 679a–b; also quoted in Bernstein, "William of Auvergne," 511.
38. *De Universo*, pt. 1, c. 61, in *Opera omnia*, vol. 1, p. 679a.

39. *De Universo*, pt. 1, c. 61, in *Opera omnia*, vol. 1, p. 678a–b; and see chap. 63, p. 680a.
40. *De Universo*, pt. 1, c. 62, in *Opera omnia*, vol. 1, p. 679b.
41. Genesis 19; Isaiah 6.
42. *De Universo*, pt. 1, c. 63, in *Opera omnia*, vol. 1, p. 680a.
43. *De Universo*, pt. 1, c. 63, in *Opera omnia*, vol. 1, p. 680a.
44. *De Universo*, pt. 1, c. 65, in *Opera omnia*, vol. 1, p. 681b.
45. *De Universo*, pt. 1, c. 65, in *Opera omnia*, vol. 1, p. 682a.
46. Bernstein, "Esoteric Theology."
47. *De Universo*, pt. 1, c. 65, in *Opera omnia*, vol. 1, p. 682b.
48. A.E. Bernstein, "Theology between Heresy and Folklore: William of Auvergne on Punishment after Death," *Studies in Medieval and Renaissance History* 5 (1982): 1–44. In 1241, William endorsed a list of ten errors of belief compiled by the chancellor of Paris, Odo of Châteauroux, which affirmed that souls in heaven would see the divine essence, as well as the placement of heaven, and the correct formulation of the Trinity, among other points: *CUP*, vol. 1, no. 128.
49. G.W. Butterworth, *Origen on First Principles* (New York: Harper and Row, 1966), book 2, chap. 10, fragment 25, p. 146; Henry Chadwick, *The Early Church* (Harmondsworth, UK: Penguin, 1967), 100–113, especially 104–6.
50. *De Legibus*, chap. 21, in *Opera omnia*, vol. 1, p. 57a; Biller, *The Measure of Multitude*, 86; Bernstein, "Between Heresy and Folklore," 20–30.
51. *On Morals*, chap. 2, p. 11.
52. *Sermons* 230.11, 18, 50, 84; 230A.213, 229, 259, 287, 287A, 299.
53. *Sermons* 230C.35.
54. *The Trinity*, chap. 2, p. 71.
55. *The Trinity*, chap. 7, p. 90.
56. *The Trinity*, chap. 7, pp. 90–91.
57. *The Trinity*, chap. 7, p. 91.

CHAPTER SIXTEEN

1. *On the Virtues*, chap. 15, p. 227.
2. *On Morals*, chap. 9, p. 135.
3. *The Soul*, chap. 6, pt. 2, p. 300, corrected.
4. *The Soul*, chap. 6, pt. 2, p. 300.
5. A. Beckers, R. van Buggenhout, E. Vrieze, "Klinische zoantropie; een vrouw met de zeldzame waan een dier te zijn," *Tijdschrift voor Psychiatrie* 62 (2020): 582–86.
6. *De Universo*, pt. II.3, chap. 19, in *Opera omnia*, vol. 1, p. 1056a–b.
7. *On the Virtues*, chap. 17, p. 233.
8. *On the Virtues*, chap. 2, pp. 51, 57.
9. *The Soul*, prol., p. 41.

10. *The Soul*, chap. 1, pt. 6, pp. 59, 60.
11. *The Soul*, chap. 3, pt. 1, p. 104.
12. *The Soul*, chap. 3, pt. 2, p. 105; chap. 3, pt. 5, p. 113; chap. 3, pt. 7, p. 120.
13. *The Soul*, p. 39, note 13.
14. Alexander III (d. 1181), Lucius III (d. 1185), Urban III (d. 1187), Gregory VIII (d. 1187), Clement III (d. 1191), Celestine III (d. 1198), Innocent III (d. 1216), Honorius III (d. 1227), Gregory IX (d. 1241), Celestine IV (d. 1241), Innocent IV (d. 1254).
15. *On Morals*, chap. 6, p. 83.
16. *On Faith*, chap. 3, pp. 104–5.
17. *On Faith*, chap. 3, pp. 100, 102, 104 (slightly adapted).
18. *The Providence of God*, chap. 6, p. 71.
19. *On the Virtues*, chap. 9, p. 99.
20. *On Faith*, chap. 3, p. 104.
21. *On the Virtues*, chap. 21, p. 269.

BIBLIOGRAPHY

See also the list of abbreviations preceding the notes.

Abelard, Peter. "Historia calamitatum: Abelard to a Friend: *The Story of His Misfortunes*." In *The Letters of Abelard and Heloise*, translated by Betty Radice, rev. M. T. Clanchy, 3–43. London: Penguin, 2003.

Abulafia, Anna Sapir. *Christian-Jewish Relations, 1000–1300: Jews in the Service of Medieval Christendom*. Harlow: Pearson, 2011.

Albertus Magnus. *On Animals: A Medieval Summa Zoologica*. Translated by K. E. Kitchell Jr. and I. M. Resnick. 2 vols. Baltimore: Johns Hopkins University Press, 1999.

Alexander Neckham. *De Laudibus divinae sapientiae*. Edited by T. Wright. Rolls Series 34. London: Longman, 1863.

Alexander of Hales. *Doctoris irrefragabilis Alexandri de Hales . . . Summa theologica*. 4 vols. Quaracchi: Ad Claras Aquas, 1924–48.

Aristotle. *Parts of Animals, Movement of Animals, Progression of Animals*. Translated by A. L. Peck and E. S. Forster. Cambridge, MA: Harvard University Press, 1945.

Audisio, Gabriel. *The Waldensian Dissent: Persecution and Survival, c. 1170–c. 1570*. Cambridge: Cambridge University Press, 1999.

Augustine. *Confessions*. Translated by R. S. Pine-Coffin. Harmondsworth, UK: Penguin, 1961.

Augustine. *De Mendacio; Contra Mendacium*. Edited by J. Zycha. Corpus Scriptorum Ecclesiasticorum Latinorum 41. London: Tempsky, 1900. Translated in *Augustine: On the Holy Trinity, Doctrinal Treatises, Moral Treatises*, edited by Philip Schaff. Nicene and Post Nicene Fathers, ser. 1, vol. 3. Edinburgh: T. and T. Clark, 1887.

Augustine. *Enchiridion ad Laurentium*. Edited by E. Evans. Corpus Christianorum Series Latina 46. Turnhout: Brepols, 1969.

Augustine. *Saint Augustine: Eighty-Three Different Questions*. Translated by David L. Mosher. Fathers of the Church: A New Translation 70. Washington, DC: Catholic University of America Press, 1982.

Augustine. *Treatises on Marriage and Other Subjects*. Edited and translated by Roy J. Deferrari and Charles T. Wilcox. Washington, DC: Catholic University of America Press, 1999.

Bacon, Roger. *Opus tertium*. Edited by J. S. Brewer. Rolls Series 15. London: Longman, 1859.

Baldwin, John W. *City on the Seine: Paris under Louis IX, 1226–1270*. New York: Macmillan, 1975.

Baldwin, John W. *The Language of Sex: Five Voices from Northern France around 1200*. Chicago: University of Chicago Press, 1994.

Baldwin, John W. "Masters at Paris from 1179 to 1215: A Social Perspective." In Robert L. Benson and Giles Constable, with Carole D. Lanham, eds., *Renaissance and Renewal in the Twelfth Century*, 138–72. Oxford: Oxford University Press, 1982.

Baldwin, John W. *Masters, Princes, and Merchants: The Social Views of Peter the Chanter and His Circle*. 2 vols. Princeton: Princeton University Press, 1970.

Baldwin, John W. *Paris, 1200*. Stanford: Stanford University Press, 2010.

Barber, Malcolm. *The Cathars: Dualist Heretics in Languedoc in the High Middle Ages*. Harlow: Longman, 2000.

Barber, Richard. *Bestiary*. Woodbridge, UK: Boydell, 1999.

Bazan, Bernard C., John F. Wippel, Gérard Fransen, and Danielle Jacquart. *Les questions disputées et les questions quodlibétiques dans les facultés de théologie, de droit et de médecine*. Turnhout: Brepols, 1985.

Beckers, A., R. van Buggenhout, and E. Vrieze. "Klinische zoantropie; een vrouw met de zeldzame waan een dier te zijn." *Tijdschrift voor Psychiatrie* 62 (2020): 582–86.

Benedict of Nursia. *RB 1980: The Rule of St. Benedict in English*. Translated by Timothy Fry. Collegeville, MN: Liturgical Press, 1982.

Benson, Robert L., and Giles Constable, with Carol D. Lanham, eds. *Renaissance and Renewal in the Twelfth Century*. Oxford: Oxford University Press, 1982.

Benton, John F. *Self and Society in Medieval France: The Memoirs of Abbot Guibert of Nogent*. Toronto: University of Toronto Press, 1984.

Bériou, Nicole. *L'avènement des maîtres de la parole: La prédication à Paris au XIIIe siècle*. 2 vols. Paris: Institut d'études augustiniennes, 1998.

Berlioz, Jacques. "La voix de l'évêque. Guillaume d'Auvergne dans les exempla (XIIIe–XIVe siècle)." In *Autour*, 9–34. (See list of abbreviations.)

Bernstein, Alan E. "Esoteric Theology: William of Auvergne on the Fires of Hell and Purgatory." *Speculum* 57 (1982): 509–31.

Bernstein, Alan E. "Theology between Heresy and Folklore: William of Auvergne on Punishment after Death." *Studies in Medieval and Renaissance History* 5 (1982): 1–44.

Beullens, Pieter. "Like a Book Written by God's Finger: Animals Showing the Path Towards God." In Brigitte Resl, ed., *A Cultural History of Animals in the Medieval Age*, 127–51. New York: Berg, 2007.

Biller, Peter. *The Measure of Multitude: Population in Medieval Thought*. Oxford: Oxford University Press, 2000.

Biller, Peter. *The Waldenses, 1170—1530: Between a Religious Order and a Church*. Aldershot, UK: Ashgate, 2001.

Black, Winston. "William of Auvergne on the Dangers of Paradise: Biblical Exegesis between Natural Philosophy and Anti-Islamic Polemic." *Traditio* 68 (2013): 233–58.

Boccadoro, Brenno. "La musique, les passions, l'âme et le corps." in *Autour*, 75–92. (See list of abbreviations.)

Boethius, Anicius Manlius Severinus. *The Consolation of Philosophy*. Translated by S. J. Tester. Loeb Library. Cambridge, MA: Harvard University Press, 1918.

Boileau, Étienne. *Les métiers et corporations de . . . Paris, XIIIe siècle*. Edited by René de Lespinasse and François Bonnardot. Paris: Imprimerie nationale, 1879.

Bonaventure. *Commentarius in IV Libros Sententiarum, Book 3. Opera omnia*, vol. 3. Quaracchi: Ad Claras Aquas, 1885.

Bossuat, André. "L'Auvergne." In F. Lot and R. Fawtier, *Histoire des institutions françaises au Moyen Age*, vol. 1, 102–22. Paris: Presses universitaires de France, 1957.

Bourlet, Caroline. "The *Livre des Métiers* Attributed to Étienne Boileau and the Gradual Establishing of Written Regulations for Parisian Trades and Crafts (Late Thirteenth–Early Fourteenth Century)." *Médiévales* 69 (2015): 19–47.

Brody, Saul N. *The Disease of the Soul: Leprosy in Medieval Literature*. Ithaca: Cornell University Press, 1974.

Brooke, Christopher N. L. *The Medieval Idea of Marriage*. Oxford: Oxford University Press, 1994.

Brown, Peter. *Through the Eye of a Needle: Wealth, the Fall of Rome, and the Making of Christianity in the West, 340–550 AD*. Princeton: Princeton University Press, 2012.

Bruzelius, Caroline. *Preaching, Building, and Burying: Friars in the Medieval City*. New Haven: Yale University Press, 2014.

Bullough, Vern L., and James Brundage, eds. *Sexual Practices and the Medieval Church*. Buffalo, NY: Prometheus Books, 1982.

Burr, David. *Olivi and Franciscan Poverty: The Origins of the* Usus Pauper *Controversy*. Philadelphia: University of Pennsylvania Press, 1989.

Burr, David. *The Spiritual Franciscans: From Protest to Persecution in the Century after Saint Francis*. University Park: Pennsylvania State University Press, 2001.

Butterworth, G.W. *Origen on First Principles*. New York: Harper and Row, 1966.

Bynum, Caroline W. "Did the Twelfth Century Discover the Individual?" In Bynum, *Jesus as Mother: Studies in the Spirituality of the High Middle Ages*, 82–109. Berkeley: University of California Press, 1982.

Bynum, Caroline W. *Fragmentation and Redemption: Essays on Gender and the Human Body in Medieval Religion*. New York: Zone Books, 2012.

Capelli, Piero. "*De articulis litterarum Papae*: A Critical Edition." In Alexander Fidora and Görge K. Hasselhoff, eds., *The Talmud in Dispute during the High Middle Ages*, 29–56. Barcelona: Universitat Autònoma de Barcelona, 2019.

Cartulaire de l'église Notre-Dame de Paris. Edited by Benjamin E.C. Guérard. 4 vols. Paris: Crapelet, 1850.

Chadwick, Henry. *The Early Church*. Harmondsworth, UK: Penguin, 1967.

Chazan, Robert. "The Condemnation of the Talmud Reconsidered (1239–1248)." *Proceedings of the American Academy for Jewish Research* 55 (1988): 11–30.

Chazan, Robert. *Medieval Jewry in Northern France*. Baltimore: Johns Hopkins University Press, 1973.

Chenu, Marie-Dominique. *Nature, Man and Society in the Twelfth Century: Essays on New Theological Perspective in the Latin West*. Edited and translated by Jerome Taylor and Lester K. Little. Toronto: University of Toronto Press, 1997.

Chenu, Marie-Dominique. *La théologie au douzième siècle*. Paris: Vrin, 1976.

Clanchy, Michael T. *Abelard: A Medieval Life*. Oxford: Blackwell, 1997.

Clanchy, Michael T. *From Memory to Written Record: England 1066–1307*. 3d ed. Malden, MA: Wiley-Blackwell, 2013.

Clanchy, Michael T. *Looking Back from the Invention of Printing: Mothers and the Teaching of Reading in the Middle Ages*. Turnhout: Brepols, 2018.

Clanchy, Michael T., and Lesley Smith. "Abelard's Description of the School of Laon: What Might It Tell Us about Early Scholastic Teaching?" *Nottingham Medieval Studies* 54 (2010): 1–34.

Clark, Willene B. *A Medieval Book of Beasts: The Second-Family Bestiary: Commentary, Art, Text and Translation*. Woodbridge, UK: Boydell, 2006.

Cohen, Jeremy. *The Friars and the Jews: The Evolution of Medieval Anti-Judaism*. Ithaca: Cornell University Press, 1982.

Cohn, Norman. *The Pursuit of the Millennium*. Rev. ed. New York: Secker and Warburg, 1961.

Colish, Marcia. *Peter Lombard*. 2 vols. Leiden: Brill, 1994.

Corti, Guglielmo. "Le sette parte del *Magisterium divinale et sapientiale* di Guglielmo di Auvergne." In *Studi e ricerche di scienze religiose in onore dei santi apostoli Pietro et Paolo nel XIX centenario del loro martirio*, 289–307. Rome: Facultas Theologica Pontificiae Universitatis Lateranensis, 1968.

Courtenay, William J. *Teaching Careers at the University of Paris in the Thirteenth and Fourteenth Centuries*. Notre Dame, IN: University of Notre Dame Press, 1988.

Craplet, Bernard, Gérard Franceschi, and Pierre Belzeaux. *Auvergne romane.* 3d ed. La-Pierre-Qui-Vire: Zodiaque, 1962.

Dahan, Gilbert, ed. *Le brûlement du Talmud à Paris, 1242–1244.* Paris: Cerf, 1999.

Dahan, Gilbert. *The Christian Polemic against the Jews in the Middle Ages.* Translated by Jody Gladding. Notre Dame, IN: University of Notre Dame Press, 1991.

Dahan, Gilbert. "L'exégèse de la Bible chez Guillaume d'Auvergne." In *Autour,* 237–70. (See list of abbreviations.)

D'Alverny, Marie-Thérèse. *Alain de Lille: Textes inédits avec une introduction sur sa vie et sur ses oeuvres.* Paris: Vrin, 1965.

D'Alverny, Marie-Thérèse. "Alain de Lille et la *Theologia.*" In *L'Homme devant Dieu. Mélanges offerts au Père Henri de Lubac,* vol. 2: *Du Moyen Age au siècle des lumières,* 111–28. Paris: Aubier, 1964.

D'Alverny, Marie-Thérèse. "Translations and Translators." In Robert L. Benson and Giles Constable with Carole D. Lanham, eds., *Renaissance and Renewal in the Twelfth Century,* 421–62. Oxford: Oxford University Press, 1982.

Daniel, Norman. *Islam and the West: The Making of an Image.* Rev. ed. Oxford: Oneworld, 1993.

D'Avray, David L. *Medieval Marriage: Symbolism and Society.* Oxford: Oxford University Press, 2005.

D'Avray, David L. *The Preaching of the Friars: Sermons Diffused from Paris before 1300.* New York: Oxford University Press, 1985.

Davy, Marie-Madeleine. *Les sermons universitaires parisiens de 1230–1231. Contributions à l'histoire de la prédication médiévale.* Paris: Vrin, 1931.

Decrees of the Ecumenical Councils. Edited by Norman P. Tanner. 2 vols. London: Sheed and Ward, 1990.

Delaborde, Henri-François, ed. *Oeuvres de Rigord et Guillaume le Breton.* 2 vols. Paris: H. Loones, 1882.

Delmas, Sophie. "La réception des encyclopédies naturelles dans les sermons au XIIIe siècle. Quelques examples." *Rursus: poétique, réception et réécriture des textes antiques* 11 (2017). Online journal. www.journals.openedition.org/rursuspicae/268.

Déribier du Chatelet, J.-B. *Dictionnaire statistique du Département du Cantal.* Vol. 1. Aurillac, 1824.

Diekstra, F. N. M. "The Language of the Marketplace in the Sermons of Robert de Sorbon (1201–1274)." *Recherches de théologie et philosophie médiévales* 75 (2008): 337–94.

Di Segni, Diana. "Early Quotations from Maimonides' *Guide of the Perplexed* in the Latin Middle Ages." In Charles H. Manekin and Daniel Davies, eds., *Interpreting Maimonides: Critical Essays,* 190–207. Cambridge: Cambridge University Press, 2018.

Duby, Georges. *Medieval Marriage: Two Models from Twelfth-century France.*

Translated by Elborg Forster. Baltimore: Johns Hopkins University Press, 1991.

Dunbabin, Jean. "Meeting the Costs of University Education in Northern France, c. 1240–c. 1340." *History of Universities* 10 (1991): 1–27.

Edwards, John. *The Roman Cookery of Apicius*. London: Century, 1988.

Egbert, Virginia Wylie. *On the Bridges of Medieval Paris: A Record of Early Fourteenth-century Life*. Princeton: Princeton University Press, 1974.

Esser, Kajetan. *Origins of the Franciscan Order*. Chicago: Franciscan Herald Press, 1970.

Evans, G. R. *Alan of Lille: The Frontiers of Theology in the Later Twelfth Century*. Cambridge: Cambridge University Press, 1983.

Fawtier, Robert. "L'Auvergne." In J. Favier, ed., *Dictionnaire de la France médiévale*. Paris: Fayard, 1993.

Fawtier, Robert. *The Capetian Kings of France: Monarchy and Nation, 987–1328*. Translated by Lionel Butler and R. J. Adam. Basingstoke, UK: Macmillan, 1960.

Ferruolo, Stephen C. *The Origins of the University: The Schools of Paris and Their Critics, 1100–1215*. Stanford: Stanford University Press, 1985.

Fidora, Alexander, and Görge K. Hasselhoff, eds. *The Talmud in Dispute during the High Middle Ages*. Barcelona: Universitat Autònoma de Barcelona, 2019.

Fournier, Gabriel. *Le peuplement rural en basse Auvergne durant le haut moyen âge*. Clermont-Ferrand: Presses universitaires de France, 1962.

Frassetto, Michael, ed. *The Year 1000: Religious and Social Response to the Turning of the First Millennium*. New York: Palgrave Macmillan, 2002.

Friedman, John, Jean Connell Hoff, and Robert Chazan, eds. *The Trial of the Talmud: Paris, 1240*. Toronto: PIMS, 2012.

Friedmann, Adrien. *Paris, ses rues, ses paroisses du moyen âge à la révolution. Origine et évolution des circonscriptions paroissiales*. Paris: Librairie Plon, 1959.

Gabriel, Astrik L. *Garlandia: Studies in the History of the Medieval University*. Frankfurt am Main: Knecht, 1969.

Gabriel, Astrik L. "The Ideal Master of the Mediaeval University." *Catholic Historical Review* 60 (1974): 1–40.

Gabriel, Astrik L. *The Paris Studium: Robert of Sorbonne and His Legacy*. Notre Dame, IN: University of Notre Dame Press, 1992.

Galinsky, Judah. "The Different Hebrew Versions of the 'Talmud Trial' of 1240 in Paris." In Elisheva Carlebach and Jacob J. Schacter, eds., *New Perspectives on Jewish-Christian Relations in Honor of David Berger*, 109–40. Boston: Brill, 2012.

Gaposchkin, M. Cecilia. *The Making of St. Louis: Kingship, Sanctity and Crusade in the Later Middle Ages*. Ithaca: Cornell University Press, 2008.

Geltner, Guy. *The Making of Medieval Antifraternalism: Polemic, Violence, Deviance and Remembrance*. Oxford: Oxford University Press, 2012.

Geremek, Bronisław. *The Margins of Society in Late Medieval Paris*. Translated by J. Birrell. Cambridge: Cambridge University Press, 1987.

Gilchrist, Roberta. *Gender and Archaeology: Contesting the Past*. London: Routledge, 1999.

Gilson, Étienne. "Avicenne en Occident au moyen âge." *Archives d'histoire doctrinale et littéraire du moyen âge* 44 (1969): 89–121.

Gilson, Étienne. *La philosophie au moyen âge*. 2d ed. Paris: Payot, 1962.

Giraud, Cédric. *"Per verba magistri": Anselme de Laon et son école au XIIe siècle*. Turnhout: Brepols, 2010.

Glorieux, Palémon. *Aux origines de la Sorbonne*. 2 vols. Paris: Vrin, 1965.

Glorieux, Palémon. *Répertoires des maîtres en théologie au XIIIe siècle*. 2 vols. Paris: Vrin, 1933.

Goering, Joseph W. "Lateran Council IV and the *cura Judaeorum*." In Gert Melville and Johannes Helmrath, eds., *The Fourth Lateran Council: Institutional Reform and Spiritual Renewal*, 243–54. Affalterbach: Didymos-Verlag, 2017.

Golb, Norman. *The Jews of Normandy. A Social and Intellectual History*. Cambridge: Cambridge University Press, 1978.

Gorochov, Nathalie. "L'évêque de Paris, le chapitre cathédral de Notre-Dame et l'université au Moyen Âge." In Cédric Giraud, ed., *Notre-Dame de Paris 1163–2013: Actes du colloque scientifique tenu au collège des Bernardins, à Paris, du 12 au 15 décembre 2012*, 113–24. Turnhout: Brepols, 2013.

Grant, Lindy. *Abbot Suger of St.-Denis: Church and State in Early Twelfth-Century France*. New York: Routledge, 2013.

Grant, Lindy. *Blanche of Castile, Queen of France*. New Haven: Yale University Press, 2016.

Grayzel, Solomon. *The Church and the Jews in the XIIIth Century*. 2 vols. New York: Hermon, 1966.

Guttmann, Jacob. "Guillaume d'Auvergne et la littérature juive." *Revue des études juives* 18 (1889): 243–55.

Habig, Marion A. *St. Francis of Assisi, Writings and Early Biographies: English Omnibus of Sources for the Life of St. Francis*. Quincy, IL: Franciscan Press, 1991.

Hall, Allan R., and Harry K. Kenward. "Sewers, Cesspits and Middens: A Survey of the Evidence for 2000 Years of Waste Disposal in York, UK." In Piers D. Mitchell, ed., *Santitation, Latrines and Intestinal Parasites in Past Populations*, 99–119. Farnham, UK: Ashgate, 2015.

Hallam, Elizabeth. *The Capetian Kings of France, 978–1328*. New York: Longman, 1980.

Hamilton, Bernard. *The Albigensian Crusade*. London: Historical Association, 1974.

Hanska, Jussi. *"And the rich man also died: and he was buried in hell": The Social Ethos in Mendicant Sermons*. Helsinki: Suomen Historiallinen Seura, 1997.

Haskins, Charles Homer. *The Renaissance of the Twelfth Century*. Cambridge, MA: Harvard University Press, 1939.

Haskins, Charles Homer. *Studies in Mediaeval Culture*. Oxford: Clarendon Press, 1929.

Hasselhof, Görge K. "Maimonides in the Latin Middle Ages: An Introductory Survey." *Jewish Studies Quarterly* 9 (2002): 1–20.

Hauréau, M. B. "Quelques lettres de Grégoire IX." *Notices et extraits de la bibliothèque impériale*. Vol. 21 (Paris, 1865), pt. 2, pp. 203–47.

Herlihy, David. *Women, Family and Society in Medieval Europe: Historical Essays 1978–1991*. Oxford: Berghahn, 1995.

Hieatt, Constance B., and Sharon Butler. *Curye on Inglysch: English Culinary Manuscripts of the Fourteenth Century (including the Form of Cury)*. London: Early English Texts Society, 1985.

Hieatt, Constance B., Brenda Hosington, and Sharon Butler. *Pleyn Delit: Medieval Cookery for Modern Cooks*. 2d ed. Toronto: University of Toronto Press, 1996.

Hinnebusch, W. A. *The History of the Dominican Order*. 2 vols. New York: Alba House, 1966, 1973.

Hopper, V. F. *Medieval Number Symbolism: Its Sources, Meaning, and Influence on Thought and Expression*. New York: Columbia University Press, 1938.

Hugh of St. Victor. *De tribus diebus*. Edited by D. Poirel. Corpus Christianorum Continuatio Mediaevalis 177. Turnhout: Brepols, 2002.

Jaeger, C. Stephen. *The Envy of Angels: Cathedral Schools and Social Ideals in Medieval Europe, 950–1200*. Philadelphia: University of Pennsylvania Press, 1994.

Jalouste, Elie. "Les anciennes écoles de l'Auvergne." *Mémoires de l'Academie . . . de Clermont-Ferrand* 23 (1881): 33–560.

James, M. R. *The Bestiary*. Oxford: Roxburghe Club, 1928.

Jean de Joinville and Geoffrey of Villehardouin. *Joinville and Villehardouin, Chronicles of the Crusades*. Translated by M. R. B. Shaw. Harmondsworth, UK: Penguin, 1986.

John of Salisbury. *Metalogicon*. Translated by J. B. Hall. Turnhout: Brepols, 2013.

Jordan, William Chester. *The Apple of His Eye: Converts from Islam in the Reign of Louis IX*. Princeton: Princeton University Press, 2019.

Jordan, William Chester. *The French Monarchy and the Jews from Philip Augustus to the Last Capetians*. Philadelphia: University of Pennsylvania Press, 1989.

Kedar, Benjamin Z. "Canon Law and the Burning of the Talmud." *Bulletin of Medieval Canon Law* 9 (1979): 79–82.

Kibre, Pearl. *The Nations in the Medieval Universities*. Cambridge, MA: Harvard University Press, 1948.

Kibre, Pearl. *Scholarly Privileges in the Middle Ages*. London: Mediaeval Academy of America, 1961.

Kienzle, Beverley Mayne, ed. *The Sermon*. Turnhout: Brepols, 2000.

Kramp, Josef. "Des Wilhelm von Auvergne 'Magisterium Divinale.'" *Gregorianum* 1 (1920): 538–613; 2 (1921): 42–103, 174–95.

Lambert, Malcolm. *The Cathars*. Oxford: Blackwell, 1998.

Langmuir, Gavin I. "L'absence d'accusation de meurtre rituel à l'ouest du Rhône." *Cahiers de Fanjeaux* 12 (1977): 235–50.

Langmuir, Gavin. "The Knight's Tale of Young Hugh of Lincoln." *Speculum* 47 (1972): 459–82.

Leader, Zachary, ed. *On Life-Writing*. Oxford: Oxford University Press, 2015.

Lecoy de la Marche, Albert. *Le rire du prédicateur: Récits facétieux du Moyen Âge*. Edited by Jacques Berlioz. Turnhout: Brepols, 1992.

Lecoy de la Marche, Albert. "Saint Louis, sa famille et sa cour d'après les anecdotes contemporaires." *Revue des questions historiques* 22 (1877): 465–84.

Leff, Gordon. *Paris and Oxford Universities in the Thirteenth and Fourteenth Centuries: An Institutional and Intellectual History* (New York: Wiley, 1968).

Le Goff, Jacques. *The Birth of Purgatory*. Translated by Arthur Goldhammer. London: Scolar, 1984.

Le Roy Ladurie, Emmanuel. *Montaillou: Cathars and Catholics in a French Village, 1294–1324*. Translated by Barbara Bray. London: George Braziller, 1978.

Lesnick, Daniel R. *Preaching in Medieval Florence: The Social World of Franciscan and Dominican Spirituality*. Athens: University of Georgia Press, 1989.

Little, Lester K. *Religious Poverty and the Profit Economy in Medieval Europe*. London: Paul Elek, 1978.

Lodge, R. Anthony. "French and Occitan in Fourteenth-Century Auvergne." In Christopher Kleinhenz and Keith Busby, eds., *Medieval Multilingualism: The Francophone World and Its Neighbours*, 285–301. Turnhout: Brepols, 2010.

Longpré, Ephrem. "Guillaume d'Auvergne et l'École Franciscaine de Paris." *La France Franciscaine* 5 (1922): 426–29.

Lottin, Odon. *Psychologie et morale aux XIIe et XIIIe siècles*, vol. 5: *L'École d'Anselme de Laon et de Guillaume de Champeaux*. Gembloux: J. Duculot, 1959.

Macy, Gary. *The Theologies of the Eucharist in the Early Scholastic Period: A Study of the Salvific Function of the Sacrament according to the Theologians, c. 1080–c. 1220*. Oxford: Clarendon Press, 1984.

Magee, John. *Calcidius On Plato's "Timaeus."* Cambridge, MA: Harvard University Press, 2016.

Mandonnet, Pierre. "De l'incorporation des Dominicains dans l'ancienne université de Paris." *Revue Thomiste* 5 (1896): 133–70.

Manry, André-Georges, ed. *Histoire de l'Auvergne*. Toulouse: Privat, 1979.

Masnovo, Amato. "Guglielmo d'Auvergne e l'università di Parigi dal 1229 al 1231." In *Mélanges Mandonnet*, 2:191–232. Paris: Vrin, 1930.

Matthew Paris. *Chronica majora*. Edited by H. R. Luard. Rolls Series 3. London: Longman, 1876.

McLaughlin, Mary M. *Intellectual Freedom and Its Limitations in the University of Paris in the Thirteenth and Fourteenth Centuries*. New York: Arno Press, 1977.

Mews, Constant J. "Communities of Learning and the Dream of Synthesis: The Schools and Colleges of Thirteenth-Century Paris." In C. J. Mews and John N. Crossley, eds., *Communities of Learning: Networks and the Shaping of Intellectual Identity in Europe, 1000–1500*, 109–35. Turnhout: Brepols, 2011.

Mews, Constant J. "Nominalism and Theology before Abaelard: New Light on Roscelin of Compiègne." *Vivarium* 30 (1992): 5–37.

Mews, Constant J. "The World as Text: The Bible and the Book of Nature in Twelfth-Century Theology." In Thomas J. Heffernan and Thomas E. Burman, eds., *Scripture and Pluralism: Reading the Bible in the Religiously Plural Worlds of the Middle Ages and Renaissance*, 95–122. Leiden: Brill, 2005.

Mollat, Michel. *Les pauvres au Moyen âge: Étude sociale*. Paris: Hachette, 1978. English translation: *The Poor in the Middle Ages: An Essay in Social History*. Translated by Arthur Goldhammer. New Haven: Yale University Press, 1986.

Montaubin, Pascal. "Les chanoines de Notre-Dame de Paris à la mort de l'évêque Guillaume d'Auvergne (1240)." In Cédric Giraud, ed., *Notre-Dame de Paris 1163–2013: Actes du colloque scientifique tenu au collège des Bernardins, à Paris, du 12 au 15 décembre 2012*, 195–216. Turnhout: Brepols, 2013.

Moody, Ernest A. "William of Auvergne and His Treatise *De Anima*." In Moody, *Studies in Medieval Philosophy, Science, and Logic*, 1–109. Berkeley: University of California Press, 1975.

Moorman, J. H. R. *A History of the Franciscan Order: From Its Origins to the Year 1517*. Oxford: Clarendon Press, 1968.

Morenzoni, Franco. "Le corpus homilétique de Guillaume d'Auvergne, évêque de Paris." *Sacris Erudiri* 46 (2007): 287–369.

Morenzoni, Franco. *Des écoles aux paroisses. Thomas de Chobham et la promotion de la prédication au début du XIIIe siècle*. Paris: Institut d'études augustiniennes, 1995.

Morenzoni, Franco. "*Predicatio est rei predicate humanis mentibus presentatio*: Les sermons pour la Dédicace de l'église de Guillaume d'Auvergne." In *Autour*, 293–322. (See list of abbreviations.)

Morenzoni, Franco. "Les proverbes dans la prédication du XIIIe siècle." In Hugo O. Bizzarri and Martin Rohde, eds., *Tradition des proverbes et des exempla dans l'Occident médiéval*, 131–49. Boston: De Gruyter, 2009.

Morris, Colin. *The Discovery of the Individual, 1050–1200*. Toronto: University of Toronto Press, 1987.

Mulchahey, M. Michèle. *"First the bow is bent in study. . ." Dominican Education before 1350*. Toronto: PIMS, 1998.

Neslihan, Şenocak. *The Poor and the Perfect: The Rise of Learning in the Franciscan Order, 1209–1310*. Ithaca: Cornell University Press, 2012.

Noonan, John T. *The Scholastic Analysis of Usury*. Cambridge, MA: Harvard University Press, 1957.

Ong, Walter. "Agonistic Structure in Academia: Past to Present." *Daedalus* 103 (1974): 229–38.

Otis, L. L. *Prostitution in Medieval Society: The History of an Urban Institution in Languedoc.* Chicago: University of Chicago Press, 1985.

Otter, Monika. "Dissing the Teacher: Classroom Polemics in the Early and High Middle Ages." In Almut Suerbaum, George Southcombe, and Benjamin Thompson, eds., *Polemic: Language as Violence in Medieval and Early Modern Discourse*, 107–24. Farnham, UK: Ashgate, 2015.

Ouy, Gilbert. *Les manuscrits de l'Abbaye de Saint-Victor. Catalogue établi sur la base du répertoire de Claude de Grandrue (1514).* Turnhout: Brepols, 1999.

Page, Sophie. "Good Creation and Demon Illusions: The Medieval Universe of Creatures." In Brigitte Resl, ed., *A Cultural History of Animals in the Medieval Age*, 27–57. New York: Berg, 2007.

Panofsky, Erwin. *Abbot Suger: On the Abbey Church of St.-Denis and Its Art Treasures.* 2d ed. Princeton: Princeton University Press, 1979.

Partner, Nancy. "The Hidden Self: Psychoanalysis and the Textual Unconscious." In Partner, ed., *Writing Medieval History*, 42–64. London: Hodder Arnold, 2005.

Pascua, Esther. "From Forest to Farm and Town: Domestic Animals from ca. 1000 to ca. 1450." In Brigitte Resl, ed., *A Cultural History of Animals in the Medieval Age*, 81–102. New York: Berg, 2007.

Paterson, Linda M. *The World of the Troubadours: Medieval Occitan Society, c. 1100–c. 1300* Cambridge: Cambridge University Press, 1993.

Payne, Thomas B. "*Aurelianus civitas*: Student Unrest in Medieval France and a Conductus by Philip the Chancellor." *Speculum* 75 (2000): 589–614.

Payne, Thomas B., ed. *Philip the Chancellor: Motets and Prosulas.* Middleton, WI: A-R Editions, 2011.

Pegues, Franklin J. "Philanthropy and the Universities in France and England in the Later Middle Ages." In A. L. Gabriel, ed., *The Economic and Material Frame of the Mediaeval University*, 69–80. Texts and Studies in the History of Mediaeval Education 15. Notre Dame, IN: University of Notre Dame Press, 1966.

Peter of Les-Vaux-de-Cernay. *History of the Albigensian Crusade.* Translated by W. A. Sibly and M. D. Sibly. Woodbridge, UK: Boydell, 1998.

Peter Lombard. *Magistri Petri Lombardi . . . Sententiae in IV libris distinctae.* Edited by I. C. Brady. 3 vols. Grottaferrata: Ad Claras Aquas, 1971. English translation: *The Sentences.* Translated by Giulio Silano. 4 vols. Toronto: PIMS, 2007–10.

Post, Gaines. "Masters' Salaries and Student-Fees in Mediaeval Universities." *Speculum* 7 (1932): 181–98.

Rashdall, Hastings. *The Universities of Europe in the Middle Ages. Vol. 1: Salerno, Bologna, Paris.* Revised and edited by F. M. Powicke and A. B. Emden. Oxford: Oxford University Press, 1936.

Rashdall, Hastings, *The Universities of Europe in the Middle Ages. Vol. 2: Italy, Spain, France, Germany, Scotland.* Revised and edited by F. M. Powicke and A. B. Emden. Oxford: Oxford University Press, 1936.

Rashdall, Hastings, *The Universities of Europe in the Middle Ages. Vol. 3: English Universities, Student Life*. Revised and edited by F. M. Powicke and A. B. Emden. Oxford: Oxford University Press, 1936.

Rawcliffe, Carole. *Leprosy in Medieval England*. Woodbridge, UK: Boydell, 2006.

Renbaum, Joel E. "The Talmud and the Popes: Reflections on the Talmud Trials of the 1240s." *Viator* 13 (1982): 203–23.

Resl, Brigitte. *A Cultural History of Animals in the Medieval Age*. New York: Berg, 2007.

Reyerson, Kathryn. "Urban Economies." In Judith M. Bennett and Ruth Mazo Karras, eds., *The Oxford Handbook of Women and Gender in Medieval Europe*, 295–310. Oxford: Oxford University Press, 2013.

Rose, E. M. *The Murder of William of Norwich: The Origins of Blood Libel in Medieval Europe*. Oxford: Oxford University Press, 2015.

Rose, Paul L. "When Was the Talmud Burnt at Paris? A Critical Examination of the Christian and Jewish Sources and a New Dating: June 1241." *Journal of Jewish Studies* 62 (2011): 324–39.

Rosenthal, Judah M. "The Talmud on Trial: The Disputation at Paris in the Year 1240." *Jewish Quarterly Review* 47 (1956–57): 58–76.

Rosenwein, Barbara H., and Lester K. Little. "Social Meaning in the Monastic and Mendicant Spiritualities." *Past and Present* 63 (1974): 4–32.

Rouse, Richard H., and Mary A. Rouse. *Manuscripts and Their Makers: Commercial Book Producers in Medieval Paris 1200–1500*. 2 vols. Turnhout: Brepols, 2000.

Roux, Simone. *Paris in the Middle Ages*. Translated by Jo Ann McNamara. Philadelphia: University of Pennsylvania Press, 2009.

Rubenstein, Jay. *Guibert of Nogent: Portrait of a Medieval Mind*. New York: Routledge, 2002.

Rubin, Miri. *Corpus Christi: The Eucharist in Late Medieval Culture*. Cambridge: Cambridge University Press, 1991.

Rudolph, Conrad. *The "Things of Greater Importance": Bernard of Clairvaux's* Apologia *and the Medieval Attitude toward Art*. Philadelphia: University of Pennsylvania Press, 1990.

Sacks, Oliver. *The Man Who Mistook His Wife for a Hat*. London: Picador, 2011.

Salimbene de Adam. *Cronica*. Edited by Guiseppe Scalia. 2 vols. Bari: Laterza, 1966.

Schmitt, Jean-Claude. *The Holy Greyhound*. Cambridge: Cambridge University Press, 1983.

Schwartz, Yossef. "Authority, Control, and Conflict in Thirteenth-Century Paris: Contextualizing the Talmud Trial." In Elisheva Baumgarten and Judah D. Galinsky, eds., *Jews and Christians in Thirteenth-Century France*, 93–110. New York: Palgrave Macmillan, 2015.

Schwarzfuchs, Simon. "June 13, 1242, Friday: The Day That Talmud Was Burned in Paris." *Revue des études juives* 173 (2014): 365–69.

Seneca, *Ad Lucilium*. Edited by A. Beltrami. 2 vols. Rome: Typis publicae officinae polygraphicae, 1949.

Shatzmiller, Joseph. *Shylock Reconsidered: Jews, Moneylending and Medieval Society*. Berkeley: University of California Press, 1990.

Shinners, John, and William J. Dohar. *Pastors and the Cure of Souls in Medieval England*. Notre Dame, IN: University of Notre Dame Press, 1998.

Smalley, Beryl. "Ecclesiastical Attitudes to Novelty c. 1000–c. 1250." In Derek Baker, ed., *Church, Society and Politics*, 113–31. Studies in Church History 12. Oxford: Blackwell, 1975.

Smalley, Beryl. *English Friars and Antiquity in the Early Fourteenth Century*. Oxford: Blackwell, 1960.

Smalley, Beryl. *The Study of the Bible in the Middle Ages*. 3d rev. ed. Oxford: Blackwell, 1983.

Smalley, Beryl. "William of Auvergne, John of La Rochelle, and St. Thomas Aquinas on the Old Law." In Smalley, *Studies in Medieval Thought and Learning from Abelard to Wyclif*, 121–81. London: Hambledon, 1981. Reprinted from *St. Thomas Aquinas 1274–1974*, 1:10–71. 2 vols. Toronto: PIMS, 1974.

Smith, Lesley. *The "Glossa Ordinaria": The Making of a Medieval Bible Commentary*. Boston: Brill, 2009.

Smith, Lesley. "Slippers in Heaven: William of Auvergne Preaching to the Brethren." In Lydia Schumacher, ed., *The "Summa Halensis": Sources and Context*, 285–97. Munich: De Gruyter, 2020.

Smith, Lesley. *The Ten Commandments: Interpreting the Bible in the Medieval World*. Boston: Brill, 2014.

Smith, Lesley. "William of Auvergne and the Jews." In Diana Wood, ed., *Christianity and Judaism*, 107–17. Studies in Church History 29. Oxford: Blackwell, 1992.

Smith, Lesley. "William of Auvergne and the Law of the Jews and the Muslims." In Thomas J. Heffernan and Thomas E. Burman, eds., *Scripture and Pluralism: Reading the Bible in the Religiously Plural Worlds of the Middle Ages and Renaissance*, 123–42. Boston: Brill, 2005.

Southern, R. W. "The Place of England in the Twelfth Century Renaissance." In Southern, *Medieval Humanism and Other Studies*, 158–80. Oxford: Blackwell, 1970.

Southern, R. W. *Saint Anselm: A Portrait in a Landscape*. Cambridge: Cambridge University Press, 1990.

Southern, R. W. *St Anselm and His Biographer: A Study of Monastic Life and Thought, 1059–c. 1130*. Cambridge: Cambridge University Press, 1963.

Southern, R. W. *Scholastic Humanism and the Unification of Europe. Vol. 1: Foundations*. Oxford: Blackwell, 1995.

Southern, R. W. *Scholastic Humanism and the Unification of Europe. Vol. 2: The Heroic Age*. Oxford: Blackwell, 2001.

Strayer, Joseph. *The Albigensian Crusades.* Ann Arbor: University of Michigan Press, 1992.

Swanson, Robert N. *The Twelfth-Century Renaissance.* Manchester, UK: Manchester University Press, 1999.

Szittya, Penn. *The Antifraternal Tradition in Medieval Literature.* Princeton: Princeton University Press, 1986.

Tanner, Norman P. *Decrees of the Ecumenical Councils.* 2 vols. London: Sheed and Ward, 1990.

Temko, Allan. "The Burning of the Talmud in Paris." *Commentary* 17 (1954): 446–55.

Teske, Roland J. "William of Auvergne." In Jorge J. E. Garcia and Timothy B. Noone, eds., *A Companion to Philosophy in the Middle Ages,* no. 131. Oxford: Blackwell, 2003.

Teske, Roland J. "William of Auvergne on Philosophy as *divinalis* and *sapientialis*." In Jan A. Aertsen and Andreas Speer, eds., *Was ist Philosophie im Mittelalter?* 475–81. Berlin: De Gruyter, 1998.

Teske, Roland J. "William of Auvergne on the Relation between Reason and Faith." *Modern Schoolman* 75 (1998): 279–91. Reprinted in Teske, *Studies,* no. 10. (See list of abbreviations.)

Teske, Roland J. "William of Auvergne's Debt to Avicenna." In Jules Janssens and Daniel De Smet, eds., *Avicenna and His Heritage,* 153–70. Leuven: Leuven University Press, 2002. Reprinted in Teske, *Studies,* no. 12. (See list of abbreviations.)

Thayer, Anne. 'The Medieval Sermon: Text, Performance and Insight." In Joel Rosenthal, ed., *Understanding Medieval Primary Sources: Using Historical Sources to Discover Medieval Europe.* London: Routledge, 2012.

Thijssen, J. M. M. H. *Censure and Heresy at the University of Paris, 1200–1400.* Philadelphia: University of Pennsylvania Press, 1998.

Thorndike, Lynn. *Michael Scot.* Edinburgh: Nelson, 1965.

Thorndike, Lynn. *University Records and Life in the Middle Ages.* New York: Columbia University Press, 1944.

Tolan, John. "Of Milk and Blood: Innocent III and the Jews, Revisited." In Elisheva Baumgarten and Judah D. Galinsky, eds., *Jews and Christians in Thirteenth-Century France,* 139–49. New York: Palgrave Macmillan, 2015.

Tugwell, Simon, ed. and trans. *Albert and Thomas: Selected Writings.* New York: Paulist Press, 1988.

Valois, Noël. *Guillaume d'Auvergne, évêque de Paris (1228–1249). Sa vie et ses ouvrages.* Paris: Librairie d'Alphonse Picard, 1880.

Van Engen, John, ed. *Learning Institutionalized: Teaching in the Medieval University.* Notre Dame, IN: University of Notre Dame Press, 2000.

Van Steenberghen, Fernand. *Aristotle in the West: The Origins of Latin Aristotelianism.* Translated by L. Johnston. New York: Humanities Press, 1970.

Verger, Jacques, and Olga Weijers, eds. *Les débuts de l'enseignement universitaire à Paris (1200–1245 environ).* Turnhout: Brepols, 2013.

Vicaire, M.-H. *Saint Dominic and His Times*. Translated by Kathleen Pond. New York: McGraw-Hill, 1974.

Wagner, David L., ed. *The Seven Liberal Arts in the Middle Ages*. Bloomington: Indiana University Press, 1986.

Weygand, Zina. *The Blind in French Society from the Middle Ages to the Century of Louis Braille*. Translated by Emily-Jane Cohen. Stanford: Stanford University Press, 2009.

Wheatley, Edward. "Blindness, Discipline and Reward: Louis IX and the Foundation of the Hospice des Quinze-Vingts." *Disability Studies Quarterly* 22 (2002): 194–212.

Whelan, Fiona. *The Making of Manners and Morals in Twelfth-Century England: The Book of the Civilised Man*. New York: Routledge, 2017.

William of Auxerre. *Magistri Guillelmi Altissiodorensis. Summa Aurea*. Edited by Jean Ribaillier. 7 vols in 5. Spicilegium Bonaventurianum 16–20. Paris: CNRS, 1980–87.

William of St. Thierry. *The First Life of Bernard of Clairvaux by William of St. Thierry*. Translated by Hilary Costello. Collegeville, MN: Liturgical Press, 2015.

Wright, Craig. *Music and Ceremony at Notre Dame of Paris, 500–1500*. Cambridge: Cambridge University Press, 1989.

Young, Spencer E. *Scholarly Community at the Early University of Paris: Theologians, Education and Society, 1215–1248*. Cambridge: Cambridge University Press, 2014.

INDEX